59.95

Chronic
Depression

Chronic Depression

INTERPERSONAL SOURCES, THERAPEUTIC SOLUTIONS

Jeremy W. Pettit

Thomas E. Joiner

AMERICAN PSYCHOLOGICAL ASSOCIATION

WASHINGTON, DC

Published by
American Psychological Association
750 First Street, NE
Washington, DC 20002
www.apa.org

To order
APA Order Department
P.O. Box 92984
Washington, DC 20090-2984
Tel: (800) 374-2721; Direct: (202) 336-5510
Fax: (202) 336-5502; TDD/TTY: (202) 336-6123
Online: www.apa.org/books/
E-mail: order@apa.org

In the U.K., Europe, Africa, and the Middle East, copies may be ordered from
American Psychological Association
3 Henrietta Street
Covent Garden, London
WC2E 8LU England

Typeset in Goudy by Stephen D. McDougal, Mechanicsville, MD

Printer: Sheridan Books, Ann Arbor, MI
Cover Designer: Berg Design, Albany, NY
Technical/Production Editor: Devon Bourexis

The opinions and statements published are the responsibility of the authors, and such opinions and statements do not necessarily represent the policies of the American Psychological Association.

Library of Congress Cataloging-in-Publication Data

Pettit, Jeremy W.
    Chronic depression: interpersonal sources, therapeutic solutions / Jeremy W. Pettit and Thomas E. Joiner.—1st ed.
        p. cm.
    Includes bibliographical references and index.
    ISBN 1-59147-306-3
    1. Depression, Mental. 2. Interpersonal psychotherapy. I. Title.

    RC537.P438 2006
    616.85'27—dc22   2005008956

British Library Cataloguing-in-Publication Data
A CIP record is available from the British Library.

Printed in the United States of America
First Edition

To Dolores, for encouraging me to pursue those things of importance.
Jeremy W. Pettit

To Ezekiel, Malachi, and Graciela, con amor.
Thomas E. Joiner

CONTENTS

ACKNOWLEDGMENTS

Many factors contribute to the development of books like this one: education and academic interests, research pursuits, and clinical and personal experiences, just to name a few. While recognizing the influence of each of those, we specifically highlight the importance of our interactions with chronically depressed persons. These interactions fully embody the two components at the heart of this book—chronic depression and interpersonal relationships. We are grateful to our patients for teaching us much about depression, for reminding us that we still have much to learn, and for repeatedly showing us the joy of growth and change. Our primary goal in undertaking the writing of this book is to further contribute to the body of ongoing work aimed at ameliorating and ending the painful, chronic scourge of depression.

In addition, I, Thomas E. Joiner, owe my development as a scientist, scholar, psychologist, and writer to a group of colleagues, friends, and students who, taken together, represent a true cornucopia of inspiration, talent, knowledge, and support. What a bounty! They include Lyn Abramson, Lauren Alloy, Steve Beach, Tim Beck, Jan Blalock, Jim Coyne, Anders Ericsson, Connie Hammen, Todd Heatherton, Jenny Katz, Al Lang, Chris Lonigan, David Rudd, Bill Sacco, Natalie Sachs-Ericsson, Brad Schmidt, Kristen Schmidt, Bill Swann, Katie Vohs, and Karen Wagner. My graduate students Marisol Perez, Jeremy W. Pettit, Zach Voelz, and Rheeda Walker see to my continued development.

I want to single out Jerry Metalsky, who, through long and patient SPSS sessions on the mainframe in Austin (and many, many other exchanges), somehow forged links in my mind interconnecting the minutiae of data analysis with the grandeur of theory and philosophy, and with everything in between.

Works like this are hounded by distractions: I am thankful to Rob Contreras, Janet Kistner, and Karen Wagner, who, in various ways and at various stages, kept these hounds at bay.

I am also grateful to Margaret Sullivan and APA Books for their initial belief in the project and ongoing support of it.

My family, Graciela, Malachi, and Ezekiel, to whom this book is lovingly dedicated, not only tolerate my professional excesses but also seem to encourage and enjoy them, and definitely inspire them.

Chronic
Depression

1

DEPRESSION CHRONICITY: PERSPECTIVES ON FORMS AND REASONS

This book develops a new explanatory framework for chronic depression that is based, where possible, on psychological science. The framework rests on the premise that depression appears to include self-sustaining processes, that these processes may be, at least in part, interpersonal, and that understanding of these processes from an interpersonal standpoint may be useful in applied settings. The book thus builds on this framework to develop clinical implications.

The audience for the book should, therefore, include anyone who is concerned with depression; as we argue in chapter 2, most everyone should be concerned with depression because it cuts such a wide societal swath. The writing style is thus intended for as wide as possible an audience; the content, however, is intended to be of direct use to people on depression's "front line" (e.g., psychological and other scientists, psychologists, psychiatrists, social workers, nurses, licensed professional counselors, marriage and family counselors) and mental health trainees (i.e., psychology graduate students, psychiatric residents, and others in training). In writing this book, we draw from a large base of empirical research on interpersonal processes in depression, much of which has focused on depressed women, and much of which has not examined potential ethnic and cultural differences. The research emphasis on ethnic majority women is due in part to the higher rates of depression among women (discussed in chap. 2) and in part to practical issues of obtaining research participants, but it also reflects the need for more investigation of depression in men and members of ethnic minority groups. Evidence thus far suggests that the processes outlined in this book may work similarly among women and men from different ethnic backgrounds, although we emphasize the importance of further study in these areas.

In addition to the book's foundation on research, there are also speculations included herein; we believe they are reasonable ones, and we label them as speculations in the book, but ultimately, the judgment as to whether they are reasonable and useful is left to subsequent psychological and clinical science.

We begin with a discussion of the chronic nature of depression, including the forms depression chronicity can take and current explanations for why depression is often a chronic problem. We present this discussion first because depression chronicity represents the heart of this book. In chapter 2, we examine depression in broader terms to address questions like what is depression, what is its typical course, and how prevalent is it?

FORMS OF CHRONIC DEPRESSION

There is good reason to emphasize the chronic nature of depression. First, some forms of depression, such as *dysthymia*, are chronic by definition (at least 2 years' persistence in the case of dysthymia). Second, depression appears to be persistent within an episode, and, once it finally lets up, it tends to come back. Depression is both persistent within episodes and recurrent across episodes.

In general, three forms of depression chronicity can be distinguished. The first has to do with the fact that depression lasts so long (i.e., it is persistent within a particular episode). This dimension of depression chronicity is of obvious importance in that long episodes involve prolonged experience of the most acute, painful, and debilitating aspects of depression. As we explain in chapter 2, the average episode length of major depression is around 8 months in adults, and is similar or even longer in youth.

It is worth dwelling on this point. The most severe, acute, impairing, and painful aspect of major depression lasts months. There are other acutely painful conditions (e.g., stomach flu), but there are few that are acutely painful for such an extended period of time (e.g., the stomach flu remits in 72 hours or so). Of course, several months is the average episode length; those who experience above-average episode lengths may face years of suffering and impairment.

The story with dysthymia is equally astounding. What dysthymia lacks in acute pain (it is a low-grade depression) it makes up for in sheer length of episodes. The average length of dysthymic episodes is around a decade, and it is relatively common for people in their 40s and older to report decades-long dysthymias (e.g., a woman in her 50s who had experienced persistent, low-grade depressive symptoms since her teens; a 40-year episode!).

Therefore, episode length or duration is an important form of depression chronicity. As noted earlier, once depression finally does go away, it tends to return. The two other important forms of depression chronicity have to do with depression's return.

Recurrence is defined as the reestablishment of clinical depression following a diagnosis-free period. Someone who recovers fully from a past depression, but then experiences a future depression, can be said to have experienced a recurrence. Recurrence, too, is of considerable importance, in that it can affect substantial portions of people's lives (Lee & Murray, 1988).

There are times when people get somewhat better from a past depression, but some depressive symptoms remain nonetheless. Someone who partially recovers from a past depression but then experiences a subsequent depression is said to have experienced a *relapse*. Relapse is the resumption of symptoms in the vulnerable timeframe just following remission of a depressive episode. Here, as with recurrence and with *episode duration*, depression relapse is an important concept in that it conveys the very chronic nature of depression.

There is an important distinction among these three forms of depression chronicity. In a scenario in which someone is experiencing a long-lasting episode, depressive symptoms are an obvious part of the clinical picture. So, too, with relapse: The person has partially recovered, but depressive symptoms remain. In both of these cases, depressive symptoms are part of the picture. Depression recurrence, however, is different. By definition, recurrence includes a period of time when symptoms were not present (i.e., the person has fully recovered).

Why is this an important distinction? Several theorists have argued that depressive symptoms have a way of sustaining themselves. In this view, it is as if depression "feeds off itself," "maintains its own momentum," and "self-amplifies." A key argument of this book is that these self-sustaining processes in depression may be interpersonal in nature. But for something to sustain itself, it has to be there in the first place. Most of the interpersonal explanations provided here thus apply to episode duration and to relapse (when some depressive symptoms are present), but they may not apply equally well to recurrence (when depressive symptoms have been absent for a period of time). For each of the interpersonal factors described in the following chapters, application to episode duration versus relapse versus recurrence is noted.

Although not specifically a form of depression chronicity, one other fact about depression deserves mention. As pernicious and chronic as it can be, it can also spontaneously disappear (i.e., *spontaneous remission*). A powerful view of depression chronicity will have at least something to say about spontaneous remission; this too is addressed in later chapters on the interpersonal factors.

SOME CURRENT EXPLANATIONS
FOR DEPRESSION CHRONICITY

Three forms of depression chronicity (i.e., episode duration, relapse, and recurrence) have been defined, but an explanation as to why depression is chronic has not been. The remainder of this book turns to an interpersonal explanation of depression chronicity, but first, other explanations are summarized.

Scarring and Erosion

A very intriguing explanation for why depression lasts so long is that a past episode of depression leaves a type of permanent "scar" that represents a vulnerability for future depression. Stated another way, past depression erodes protections against future depression. The central idea of this perspective is that a depressive episode erodes personal and psychological resources such that episodes may be lengthened and, on recovery, the formerly depressed individual is left with fewer buffers to protect against future depression. This is an intuitively appealing view because health problems often operate in just this manner, as anyone who has injured a joint and then reinjured the same joint, can tell you.

Consider, for example, a generally optimistic man who experiences a string of negative life events, including job loss and divorce, and subsequently experiences his first depressive episode. His depression is replete with pessimism and hopelessness (common symptoms of depression) as well as the tendency to blame himself for all of the stress he is experiencing. His extreme focus on all things negative drives others away from him and prevents him from pursuing opportunities that might reduce his depression. For instance, he skips job interviews because he believes he that no employer will hire "a loser like me." Consequently, he remains inactive, alone, and depressed, mired in a slough of pessimism.

Eventually, his depression begins to lift (as most do), and he resumes a degree of normal functioning. Nevertheless, he remains relatively pessimistic about life, about his worth as a person, and about his future job and relationship prospects. On the occurrence of further setbacks and negative life events, his pessimism is reaggravated to the point that he rapidly falls back into depression. In this sense, the experience of depression left him with a scar of pessimism that both prolonged his depressive episode and increased the likelihood of experiencing future episodes.

Do scenarios like the one just described actually occur? Despite the intuitive appeal of the scarring model, there are questions about whether scar and erosive explanations stand up to empirical scrutiny. This view has been applied primarily to the domains of personality, cognitive style, and neurobiology, with varying degrees of empirical attention and support.

The possibility that depression changes personality has received the most empirical attention, and findings are mostly unsupportive of the erosive perspective. In a compelling test of the prediction that a depressive episode would change personality, Shea, Leon, Mueller, and Solomon (1996) conducted a 6-year study of a group of people who, at the outset of the study, were nondepressed and had no past history of depression. At the study's conclusion, those who experienced their first-episode of depression during the 6-year study were compared with those who remained well. No support for the erosive perspective was obtained: The amount of personality change—for the better or for the worse—was not different between the groups. The Shea et al. study replicates earlier findings by Rohde, Lewinsohn, and Seeley (1990) and Zeiss and Lewinsohn (1988). It is interesting to note that few studies on this question have been conducted among children and adolescents, perhaps because of the complexities of conceptualization and measurement of personality among youth. As exceptions to this, Ge and Conger (1999) found that psychological distress and emotional problems in early adolescence predicted personality levels of positive and negative emotionality in late adolescence, and Rohde et al. found that self-rated social skills remained lower after recovery from a depressive episode. Drawing from those studies, one can make an interesting speculation that depression may erode personality resources in youth but not adults, because personality may be more malleable in youth than in adults. In adults at least, depression apparently does not erode personality strengths; depression does not appear to leave a personality scar.

It may, however, erode cognitive and attributional resources, such as the ability to maintain optimism or to explain the causes of life events in optimistic ways. This appears to be particularly the case among children but may not apply to adults (e.g., Hamilton & Abramson, 1983), perhaps because children's cognitive style is more malleable than that of adults (Turner & Cole, 1994). In the most comprehensive studies on this issue, Nolen-Hoeksema, Girgus, and Seligman (1986, 1992) found that the attributional styles of depressed children deteriorated and did not later ameliorate, even on remission of symptoms. These results are consistent with the model of Segal, Williams, Teasdale, and Gemar (1996), who theorized that negative cognitive patterns, once used and practiced, become more and more easily activated. With regard to cognitive style, then, depression may be erosive. We elaborate on this point in our chapter on the interplay of propagatory and erosive processes (chap. 10).

Beck (1996) hypothesized that a key depression-related phenomenon, suicidality, may operate similarly. Briefly, Beck theorized that previous suicidal experience sensitizes suicide-related thoughts and behaviors such that they later become more accessible and active. The more accessible and active the schemas and modes become the more easily they are triggered (even in the absence of negative events), and the more severe are the subsequent suicidal episodes. In recent research, we and our colleagues have found that as past suicide attempts accumulate, subsequent episodes of suicidality take on distinct qualities, including stress-independence and a particularly unpredictable course (Joiner & Rudd, 2000; Rudd, Joiner, & Rajab, 1996).

Similar to the cognitive models of Segal et al. (1996) and Beck (1996), Post (1994) has theorized that the experience of acute stress or of a depressive episode may leave behind "memory" traces at the level of gene expression that heighten subsequent vulnerability. The model thus proposes a neurobiological sensitization process in which the underlying biological mechanisms responsible for depression-free functioning are permanently eroded, thus sensitizing the individual to stress. As the individual becomes more sensitized, less stress is required to trigger a depressive reaction.

The erosive perspective, with regard to cognitive style and neurobiology (but probably not to personality), holds promise with regard to explaining depression chronicity and guiding clinical interventions (e.g., rehabilitating eroded domains of functioning). The perspective is limited, however, by a small empirical base. An additional difficulty is that there are features of depressive chronicity that the perspective does not adequately explain. For example, why is it that interpersonal factors, arguably above all others (e.g., Hooley & Teasdale, 1989), comprise very strong predictors of depression chronicity? Once erosion has occurred, the resulting sensitivities should be similarly impinged on by an array of stressors, interpersonal and noninterpersonal alike.

Yet, interpersonal factors are among the strongest predictors of depression chronicity. Hooley and Teasdale (1989) reported that perceived criticism was a powerful predictor of relapse. People with more interpersonal problems experience longer duration of depressive episodes (Hale, Jansen, Bouhuys, Jenner, & van den Hoffdakker, 1997). Lara, Leader, and Klein (1997) found that social support was predictive of recovery from depressive episodes, even controlling for common clinical variables, such as episode severity and the presence of "double depression." Impaired relationships predict long-lasting episodes of several disorders, including depression (Miller, Ingham, Kreitman, & Surtees, 1987). Interpersonal problems have also been implicated in chronicity of a depression-related disorder, bulimia nervosa (e.g., Steiger, Leung, & Thibaudeau, 1993), discussed in detail in chapter 11.

The erosion–scarring perspective does not fully explain why interpersonal factors, as opposed to other forms of life stress, appear to be closely related to depression chronicity. Moreover, there are features of depression's aftermath that are not best described as mere diminutions of resources but, rather, appear to be active, motivated processes that propagate life problems and depression (depression feeding off itself). These latter processes, described in chapters 3 through 8, are, in the main, actively performed by the depression-prone person, whereas erosion happens to the person—a passive process. Depression not only may erode existing resources but also may "build up" processes that maintain depression vulnerability. These latter processes—the building of depression-maintaining patterns—as well as the suggestion that they are interpersonal in nature, compose the heart of this book.

As a prelude to following chapters, reflect back on the man whose optimism was eroded by a depressive episode. This was a passive process in that it happened as a result of depression. As we briefly have alluded to, and expand on in chapter 3, his pessimism then drove others away from him, creating the risk factor of decreased social support. How did this happen? It was an active interpersonal process of communicating his hopeless outlook to others. As others grew weary of hearing his negative views on life and himself, they distanced themselves from him. In this sense, the interpersonal expression of his pessimism built up problems in his social network, which likely lengthened his current depressive episode and increased his risk for future episodes.

Stable Vulnerabilities

Another important perspective on depression chronicity is that people are persistently depressed because they possess persistent vulnerability factors. Chapter 9 expands on this perspective in more detail, but as a preface, there are several genetic–neurobiological as well as psychological vulnerability factors postulated to be stable risks for depression.

Regarding genetic–neurobiological factors, it appears that unspecified genetic factors contribute to—but do not fully account for—the development of depression. Adoption and twin studies show that genetic factors make up approximately 40% of the risk for becoming depressed (Kendler, Neale, Kessler, & Heath 1992). The nature of this risk (i.e., its location on the genome; its mechanism of action) is not well understood.

Dysregulations of serotonin neurotransmitter systems, as well as of the hypothalamic-pituitary-adrenal axis (which regulates cortisol levels), have also been proposed as a stable depression risk. There is little question that serotonin and cortisol levels are altered during depressive episodes (and related phenomena such as suicide). It is interesting to note that animals defeated in social skirmishes display behavioral and neurochemical similarities to depressed people (e.g., Mehlman et al., 1995; cf. Price & Gardner, 1999, social competition view of depression). However, there is little persuasive evidence that dysregulation of these systems provides a full account of depression's causes.

Regarding psychological explanations (covered more fully in chap. 9), these theories can be grouped into those emphasizing cognitive vulnerability factors (e.g., pessimism), those emphasizing interpersonal vulnerability factors (e.g., excessive dependency), and those emphasizing personality-based vulnerability factors (e.g., high neuroticism, low extroversion). As with genetic–neurobiological explanations, psychological approaches have made some progress but cannot claim to provide a complete account of depression's causes.

As with erosion–scarring, the stable vulnerability perspective does not easily explain depression's chronicity, including its apparent tendency to prolong itself. If people are persistently vulnerable, why do they have depression-free periods? One answer to this question is that stable vulnerabilities only eventuate in depression when activated, for example, by the occurrence of negative life events. Consider a person who has been shy "since birth." As we discuss in chapter 6, shyness represents a stable vulnerability for depression. However, this person is not always depressed; rather, shyness only appears to promote depression when the person also feels lonely (Joiner, 1997), perhaps after the termination of a romantic relationship. In this case, the stable vulnerability (shyness) must be activated by some stressor (romantic breakup) to produce depression. Although the notion that stable vulnerabilities like shyness only lead to depression in the context of some stressor is a reasonable view, it does not account for the finding that some shy (or otherwise vulnerable) people experience depression independent of negative life events.

Partly in response to this quandary, a main purpose of this book is to explore interpersonal mechanisms whereby depression prolongs itself, even in the absence of external causes like negative life events. Other theorists, too, have focused on the self-propagating nature of depression (although not from an interpersonal perspective). For example, Lyubomirsky, Caldwell, and Nolen-Hoeksema (1998) have shown that the tendency to ruminate about negative things in response to a negative mood prolongs the mood and may serve as an entryway to full-blown episodes of depression (which themselves may be prolonged because of rumination). These researchers have shown, for example, that people who experience negative moods and who ruminate during negative moods recall more painful autobiographical memories. These, in turn, may only exacerbate negative mood, encourage further rumination, and prolong dysphoria and possibly depression.

Somewhat similarly, Pyszczynski and Greenberg (1987) have maintained that potentially depressed people become caught in a cycle of excessive self focus, which leads to an increase in negative affect, self-blame, self-criticism, and the like. As a result, self-image may become more negative, and this new, negative self-image is sustained by the "depressive self-focusing style." Both of these models of depression chronicity are examined further in chapter 9.

SUMMARY

There are three forms of depression chronicity: episode duration, relapse (i.e., when one becomes depressed again after incomplete symptom remission), and recurrence (i.e., when one becomes depressed again after complete symptom remission). There are several current explanations of depression chronicity, including scarring–erosion and stable vulnerabilities. Although the perspective offered in this book is different from current explanations, there is potential compatibility among the various perspectives, and chapter 10 is devoted to exploring this topic.

Chapter 2, presented next, describes depression in depth, addressing the nature, course, and prevalence of the disorder. We view this as an essential background that is necessary to understand prior to an exploration of interpersonal processes in depression. In chapters 3 through 8, six processes are described, each of which may represent a contributory factor as to why depression may, in a sense, sustain itself. It is noted that the six processes differ from one another with regard to the empirical attention paid to each; nonetheless, each at least holds promise in explaining the pernicious phenomenon of depression chronicity. The first, *stress generation* (defined as contributing to the occurrence of one's own negative life events, especially negative interpersonal events), is viewed as a broad, higher order concept that is inclusive of several of the other five processes, and thus is described first, in chapter 3.

2

DEPRESSION AS A PERSISTENT AND RECURRENT SCOURGE

The nature, definition, epidemiology, consequences, and comorbidity of depression deserve a book unto themselves (and have several). The goal of this chapter is not to exhaustively review each of these voluminous literatures. Rather, this chapter touches on several important facts about depression, exploring some in more depth than others, so that subsequent chapters on an interpersonal view of depression chronicity are set in a broader context, and so that chapters 12 and 13 on assessment and treatment are foreshadowed. The chapter's perspective is thus selective and is not intended as comprehensive.

MOOD DISORDER NOSOLOGY: WHAT IS DEPRESSION?

The *Diagnostic and Statistical Manual of Mental Disorders* (3rd ed.; 3rd ed., rev.; 4th ed.; *DSM–III; DSM–III–R; DSM–IV;* American Psychiatric Association, 1980, 1987, 1994) defined major depression as a condition that (a) is relatively persistent (e.g., symptoms occur more days than not for at least 2 weeks), (b) is associated with significant distress and impairment, and

(c) includes a majority of the following symptoms: loss of capacity for plea-sure (anhedonia), sadness, low energy, suicidal thoughts or behaviors, sleep disturbance, appetite disturbance, psychomotor disturbance (slowing or agi-tation), concentration difficulty, and feelings of guilt or worthlessness. As we point out in the chapters that follow, major depression is a chronic condi-tion, but less so than dysthymia, that can be viewed as a low-grade, more chronic version of major depression. The *DSM* definition for dysthymia is that depressed mood has persisted (most of the day, more days than not) for at least 2 years, accompanied by at least two of the following: low energy, sleep disturbance, appetite disturbance, concentration difficulty, low self-esteem, and feelings of hopelessness.

Major depression can be superimposed on dysthymia. For example, con-sider a patient who has had depressed mood more days than not for about 4 years, accompanied by energy and concentration problems (i.e., has dys-thymia). This patient's symptoms become precipitously much more severe and expand to include sleep and appetite disturbance, suicidal thoughts, and psychomotor retardation. A major depression has developed in addition to the dysthymia, a phenomenon termed *double depression*. Double depression is not a formal term in the *DSM–IV* but is worth noting because patients who experience double depression may respond to treatment more slowly than patients with major depression or dysthymia alone.

This book presents an interpersonal view of major depression, dysthymia, and related chronic mood problems. The *DSM*s present useful definitions of these phenomena. It is important to note, however, that the *DSM* defini-tions are works in progress and are defined by committed consensus. Al-though things like major depression and dysthymia seem to exist in nature, precise, scientifically supported definitions have been difficult to come by.

Can it seriously be questioned that major depression, as defined in cur-rent classificatory systems such as the *DSM–IV* (American Psychiatric Asso-ciation, 1994), represents a true and valid construct? From diverse perspec-tives ranging from the genetic (Kendler et al., 1996) to the interpersonal (Coyne, 1976a), the construct enjoys considerable support. To take just one example, Kendler et al. (1996) have shown that "typical depression," similar in composition to major depression, can be discerned as a syndromal class, distinct from nondepression as well as from "atypical depression" (character-ized by increased eating and sleep), among a large sample of women from a population-based twin registry. These and other results, when added to the actuarial, historical, grantmaking, industrial, and conventional momentum enjoyed by the concept of major depression, combine to make it a formidable concept indeed.

Yet, despite all this, there are disquieting strands of evidence and thought. For example, is depression a category, an all-or-none, "either-you-have-it-or-you-don't" phenomenon, similar to heart attack, or, a clearer ex-ample, biological gender? Or is depression a continuum distributed along a graded dimension, similar to temperature or mass, where a thing can have very little of it, or a little more of it, and so on up to having very much of it?

On the categorical view, there is a gap in nature between those who have depression and those who do not. Those who have it are categorically different from those who do not. By contrast, on the continuum view, we are all in the same boat, just at different places along the boat. That is, depression applies to all of us, just in varying degrees.

Those who assert that depression is categorical (and they are legion)—and, for that matter, those who assert that it is a dimensional continuum—all display a lack of awareness that this is, at bottom, a *taxometric* question. The whole point of taxometrics, developed by Waller and Meehl (1998), is to discern categories (i.e., taxa) from dimensional continua and to establish the true indicators and base rates of established taxa. The technique capitalizes on the brilliant insight that any reasonably valid indicators of a potential taxon behave in a certain way—they intercorrelate in samples in which taxon members and nonmembers are mixed, and they do not correlate in pure samples of taxon members or in pure samples of taxon nonmembers.

What, then, is the verdict of the taxometric jury? If ever a jury were still out, it is this jury. A handful of early studies that used taxometric methods to examine depression had important methodological limitations and did not assess major depressive disorder (MDD) per se (e.g., Franklin, Strong, & Greene, 2002; Grove, Andreasen, Young, & Endicott, 1987; Haslam & Beck, 1994; Whisman & Pinto, 1997). As such, they had little conclusive to say about the taxonicity of clinical depression. Two additional taxometric studies on depression stand out in terms of their quality but have reached different conclusions (Beach & Amir, 2003; Ruscio & Ruscio, 2000,). Ruscio and Ruscio found some evidence of depression taxonicity using self-reported depressive symptoms but concluded that the majority of their findings supported a dimensional view (see also Hankin, Fraley, Lahey, & Waldman, 2005, for similar results among depressed youth). Beach and Amir (2003) examined MDD and reached different conclusions. Crucially, they distinguished between symptoms of mere distress and hallmark symptoms of MDD (e.g., depressed mood, anhedonia) and found evidence for taxonicity of hallmark symptoms but not of general distress symptoms (see also Ambrosini, Bennett, Cleland, & Haslam, 2002, for a similar finding in adolescents). This raises the possibility that depression is taxonic but that most studies to date have not used rigorous enough indicators to detect depression taxa. Researchers who are interested in whether depression represents a continuum or a discrete category would do well to learn and apply taxometrics; in this as in all areas, mere assertion is not good enough and may even retard progress. It is disquieting that this basic question is currently unresolved (and has hardly even been broached regarding dysthymia).

As another disquieting example, it is well-known that depression is a very heterogeneous thing—well over 200 different possible combinations of symptoms all satisfy the current definition of just one form of depression—a bewildering array of manifestations for a supposedly singular entity (whether continuous or dichotomous). Buchwald and Rudick-Davis (1993) found that of the 227 possible combinations of symptom presentations for *DSM–III–R* major depression, 42 were represented among their sample of depressed people, and 26 of these 42 were single occurrences (i.e., a combination of symptoms that occurred in only one person in the sample).

Resolution of fundamental definitional issues is a virtual prerequisite of real progress in science. A lurking but neglected issue in depression research, then, is the very definition of the syndrome in the population at large, not to mention the possibility that the properties of the syndrome may vary in different subpopulations (e.g., older people). And there is some reason to suspect that depression's properties may differ in certain subsets of people. Regarding late-life populations—for example, depressions that first occur in later life, as compared with those that first occur in early adulthood—occurrences may be about equally common in men and women (whereas "early" depressions are more common in women; Krishnan, Hays, Tupler, & George, 1995). In addition, late-life first occurrences are less associated with first-degree relatives' depression risk (Bland, Newman, & Orn, 1986); more related to neurological or medical disease (Alexopoulos, Young, Meyers, Abrams, & Shamoian, 1988); less severe (Burvill, Hall, Stampfer, & Emmerson, 1989); less associated with suicidal and anxious symptoms (Cassano et al., 1993); and less related to personality problems, such as excessive dependency and avoidance (Abrams, Rosendahl, Card, & Alexopoulos, 1994).

Definitional problems plague depression research. As the search for true and deep definitions evolves (using, one would hope, taxometrics), how should we proceed in the meantime? A workable approach is to fall back on *DSM*-like working definitions of major depression and dysthymia but, at the same time, to avoid the trap of viewing these as the final word in depression nosology. Throughout this book, then, research on and therapeutics for major depression and dysthymia is emphasized but so too is research on subsyndromal depressive symptoms as they occur in unselected populations (e.g., community participants, college undergraduates).

THE COURSE OF DEPRESSION

Course—the way that a disorder "behaves" over time—is informative for a number of reasons. Clinically, it can aid in differential diagnosis. Imagine, for example, that a mother brings her son to a pediatrician's office and says, "He's irritable, down on himself, fidgety, and his teachers say he's not paying attention in class." From this description alone, depression is a diagnostic possibility—depressed kids are irritable, have self-esteem problems, can be agitated, thus, fidgety, and have concentration problems. But another good possibility is attention-deficit/hyperactivity disorder (ADHD)—children with ADHD also can be moody, fidgety, and inattentive. How does one discern between these possibilities? The following question may do the trick: "Is he always like this, or do these problems come and go?"

Mothers of ADHD boys will often reply "he's been like this since he was a baby," whereas mothers of depressed boys may reply "the problems are really bad at times but disappear at other times." (Children can both be depressed and have ADHD, a complicated diagnostic picture.) The reply of the mother of the ADHD boy conveys a constant and persistent course, with little variation in symptom picture; the reply of the mother of the depressed boy conveys an episodic, recurrent course, in which symptoms come and go in episodic and recurrent fashion. Knowing symptoms' course can aid in differential diagnosis, even in situations in which the current symptom picture is consistent with more than one diagnosis.

Major depression's course is episodic and recurrent. The disorder comes and goes; at times it is in full swing, with numerous and severe symptoms; at other times, it is mild or moderate, with symptoms present but less noticeable; and at still other times, it is absent, with symptoms in full remission. Dysthymia, by contrast, has a less episodic, more chronic course. The symptoms of dysthymia tend to remain at relatively constant levels, with little variation over time.

The implications of depression's course for an interpersonal explanation of depression chronicity are discussed in chapter 1. There, we present a main argument of this book, that depressive symptoms have a way of sustaining themselves. Depression appears to "feed off itself," a process that we argue may be interpersonal in nature.

DEPRESSION AND ANXIETY CO-OCCUR

Although depression can co-occur with an array of other conditions (e.g., substance use disorders, personality disorders), there is reason to single out its relation to anxiety and its disorders. First, the co-occurrence of depression and anxiety is very common. As many as 50% of people with major depression also experience an anxiety disorder (Regier, Rae, Narrow, Kaelber, & Schatzberg, 1998). Second, it is possible that this co-occurrence relates to the same underlying cause for depressive and anxiety disorders (Kendler, Neale, Kessler, & Heath, 1992). For example, Kendler et al. found that the same genetic factors are implicated in the development of MDD and generalized anxiety disorder, although environmental factors differed between the two disorders. Third, comorbid depression and anxiety are more clinically complicated than depression or anxiety alone (e.g., the prognosis can be worse, and suicidality and general impairment greater, for those who are comorbid vs. those who are not). We return to this point in chapter 13 on therapeutics. Fourth, depressive and anxious symptoms are phenomenologically similar, to the point that it can be difficult to discern one from the other. In this regard, a useful heuristic is Clark and Watson's (1991; Mineka, Watson, & Clark, 1998) tripartite model of depression and anxiety. The model posits that both depression and anxiety disorders are characterized by a shared, non-specific factor of general negative affect and that each disorder includes a specific, nonshared component. In particular, depression is distinguished by anhedonia (low positive affect), and each anxiety disorder is characterized by its own unique component (e.g., physiological hyperarousal is specific to panic disorder). Empirical support for the model is promising (Clark, Steer, & Beck, 1994; Joiner, Catanzaro, & Laurent, 1996; Steer, Clark, Beck, & Ranieri, 1995; Watson, Clark, et al., 1995; Watson, Weber, et al., 1995). We return to the tripartite model in chapter 12 on clinical assessment, because the measures associated with the model can be very useful in making the often difficult distinction between depressive symptoms alone, anxious symptoms alone, and their co-occurrence.

THE (INCREASING) PREVALENCE OF DEPRESSION

At any given time, somewhere between 4% and 10% of the population experience major depression or dysthymia, with lifetime prevalence rates somewhere around 20%. With regard to depression prevalence, an enormously important age-related phenomenon may be occurring (Seligman, 1998). If, in the late 1990s, you are about 70 years old, the chance that you have experienced depression in your lifetime is about 2%. If, in the late 1990s, you are in your 50s, your lifetime chance of depression is approximately 5%. Despite fewer years in which to get depressed, this younger group is nonetheless about twice as likely to have experienced depression. This is remarkable enough, but the same pattern continues as younger and younger groups are examined. Those in their 30s in the late 1990s experience approximately an 8% risk of lifetime depression; teenagers in the late 1990s, despite approximately four times fewer years than their 70 year-old counterparts, experience approximately six times more risk for lifetime depression. If this trend continues, imagine the rates when these teenagers reach late life!

More remarkable still, this pattern is not limited to a country or two. The trend is similar across all industrialized countries examined to date (Cross-National Collaborative Group, 1992). As nonindustrialized countries are better studied, the same trend may emerge there as well.

Apparently, depression is on the rise across much of the world. Why? One possibility is that the trend is artificial and not really representative of a true increase in depression across time. For example, perhaps the older one gets, the more prone one is to forget having experienced a prior depression! Or perhaps depressed people die earlier and thus are not around to report on past depressions when older cohorts are assessed. (In fact, there is some evidence that mortality rates are elevated among depressed people, even accounting for higher suicide rates among depressed people.) Or perhaps health care professionals are doing an increasingly better job of detecting depression; if so, what has changed is the behavior of health professionals, not the rates of depression. Or perhaps it is increasingly acceptable to report depression. If so, what has changed is the perceived stigma of depression, rather than the actual rates of depression.

All of these alternative explanations should be considered, but for an array of reasons, they are not completely convincing. For one thing, if increased prevalence were merely due to forgetting, why would 30-year-olds differ so much from 18-year-olds? Also, we could only wish that depression were stigma-free or that health care professionals detect it carefully! Although there has been progress on both these fronts, there has not been so much progress as to account for the large cohort difference in depression prevalence rates. Finally, researchers who conduct this work make efforts to control for various confounds like these, and even when they use stringent controls, the effect emerges nonetheless.

The increase in prevalence rates thus may be a real phenomenon. Why might depression be on the increase? Many possible explanations exist, including (among other things) changes in environmental toxins, increased drug abuse, increased divorce rate, changes in parenting practices, and changes in communication methods (i.e., more electronic, less face-to-face), but none yet has good scientific backing.

Regardless of why (and assuming the trend is real), the upshot of all this is a looming (if not current) epidemic of depression. In the middle of the 21st century, when those in their teens at the turn of the century are in their 70s, their lifetime prevalence of depression may be astonishingly high. And, as we discuss, depression is rarely a once-in-a-lifetime event—someone with a lifetime history of depression is far more likely than others to experience current depression. A cohort with a very high lifetime rate of depression is thus quite likely to have a high rate of current depression. Accordingly, as younger and more vulnerable cohorts age, depression looms as an even more urgent international health problem than it already is.

GENDER, ETHNICITY, AND DEPRESSION

If the prevalence of depression is on the rise, as appears to be the case, who is most likely to be affected? In this section, we briefly review what is currently known about gender and ethnic variations in the rate of depression.

Gender

We have just seen that age may represent an important factor regarding depression prevalence. There is little question that gender is as well. The incidence of clinical depression and depressive symptoms is two to three times higher among women than men. In their review of large epidemiologic and family studies, Klerman and Weissman (1989) noted that women show a higher lifetime prevalence of major depression across all birth cohorts. A recent report on epidemiologic surveys conducted in a number of industrialized countries, including the United States, showed higher rates of depression in women across all sites (Weissman et al., 1993). The effect seems resilient: It tends to persist when demographic variables such as race, income level, education, and occupation are controlled (McGrath, Keita, Strickland, & Russo, 1990; Radloff, 1977). It is interesting to note that the gender difference emerges at adolescence because there is no gender difference in depression for preadolescent children (e.g., Hankin et al., 1998).

Although the gender differential in depression is consistent and well documented, little is known about the processes that underlie these differences. The *artifact* hypothesis suggests that gender differences in depression result from women's greater reporting of stress and symptoms (Weissman & Klerman, 1977), and the *masked depression* hypothesis posits that depression in men remains undetected, or is masked by their higher rates of alcohol and substance use (e.g., Egeland & Hostetter, 1983). Biological hypotheses suggest that greater vulnerability among women is due to genetically transmitted factors and that women are at greater risk because of mood changes associated with their reproductive cycles (Nolen-Hoeksema, 1987; Weissman & Klerman, 1977, 1985). Psychosocial explanations include the social status hypothesis, which suggests that the disproportionate rate of exposure to stressors resulting from women's lower social status is responsible for their higher rates of depression (Weissman & Klerman, 1977, 1985). Social role hypotheses focus on aspects of the traditional female role, such as concern with relationships and dependence, which may increase women's vulnerability (see also Nolen-Hoeksema, 1987; Weissman & Klerman, 1977, for review). Evidence for each of these hypotheses has been largely inconclusive (Nolen-Hoeksema, 1987; Weissman & Klerman, 1977, 1985). Although researchers continue their search for clues that might explain the gender difference in depression, this consistent finding goes largely unexplained.

A promising explanation was provided by Nolen-Hoeksema and Girgus (1994). These authors focused on the intriguing fact that the gender difference in depression does not exist in young children but emerges in adolescence and persists throughout adulthood. They suggested that the combination of preexisting risk factors for depression and the social and biological challenges faced by adolescents lead to gender differences in depression. According to this view, girls have more childhood risk factors for depression and are confronted with more biological and social challenges in early adolescence than boys. Nolen-Hoeksema and Girgus cite lower instrumentality, lower aggression and dominance in interpersonal interactions, and greater ruminative coping in girls than boys as specific risk factors for depression.

In addition to being depressotypic, ruminative coping is also anxiotypic (i.e., involves worry and fear). Because ruminative coping is more common among girls, a comorbid depressive and anxious presentation may also be more common among girls, consistent with our findings. Anxiety may be a preexisting risk factor for the development of depressive symptoms in adolescent girls. For example, Reinherz et al. (1993) found that early onset (by age 9) of anxious symptoms in girls was significantly related to the development of depression in adolescence. Anxiety was not found to be a significant childhood risk factor for male adolescent depression.

In addition, the contribution of parental psychopathology to gender differences in adolescent depression requires further exploration. Children of parents with affective disorders are more than twice as likely to develop major depression than children whose parents have no disorder (Beardslee, Keller, Lavori, Staley, & Sacks, 1993). Furthermore, daughters of parents with recurrent major depression have three times the risk of major depression compared with sons of recurrently depressed parents (Warner, Mufson, & Weissman, 1995). Radke-Yarrow, Nottelman, Belmont, and Welsh (1993) provided interesting observations about the affective interactions between depressed mothers and their children as they relate to gender. Depressed mothers exhibited more negative affect (e.g., irritability, anxiety, fear) toward their daughters than mothers without depression. However, this finding did not apply to depressed mothers and their sons. In addition, depressed mother's episodes of negative affect corresponded to episodes of negative affect in their daughters.

Ethnicity

In contrast to the consistent finding regarding depression gender differences, there are few well-documented ethnic differences in depression. Although some studies find ethnic differences, these differences tend to disappear when variables such as socioeconomic status are accounted for.

Mexican American adolescents represent one possible exception to this rule. In perhaps the most compelling study on this issue, Roberts, Roberts, and Chen (1997) assessed major depression in several thousand 10- through 17-year-olds from diverse ethnic backgrounds (e.g., African American, Anglo American, Asian American, and Native American). Only Mexican American youths displayed elevated rates of major depression, and this was true even when socioeconomic status, gender, and age were statistically controlled. In a study of over 2,000 African American, Anglo American, and Mexican American 12- through 17-year-olds, Roberts and Sobhan (1992) reported the same finding regarding self-reported depressive symptoms, now controlling for age, gender, perceived health, and occupation level of the family's primary wage earner.

As with so many group differences in depression (e.g., age cohorts, gender), there is persuasive evidence that Mexican American adolescents, as compared with other adolescents, experience higher rates of depressive symptoms, but there is little understanding as to why Mexican American adolescents, among all others, experience heightened depression (again, previous work suggests that this effect is not due to lower socioeconomic status; e.g., Roberts et al., 1997).

Acculturative stress (i.e., the strain of leaving behind a first culture and adapting to another) has been suggested as a reason that Mexican American adolescents experience heightened depression. Although there does appear to be a positive relationship between acculturative stress and depressive symptoms among Mexican American adolescents (Hovey & King, 1996), there are at least two reasons why it may not provide a complete explanation. First, many of the ethnic groups in Roberts et al.'s (1997) study experienced acculturative challenges, yet some of these (e.g., Chinese Americans) had very low rates of depression. Second, the research base regarding acculturation in Mexican American adolescents is very small, and research on acculturation in Mexican American adults is contradictory: Some studies find that high assimilation into a new culture is related to more depression (Golding, Karno, & Rutter, 1990), whereas others find that high assimilation relates to less depression (e.g., Garcia & Marks, 1989). Although more research on the question is needed, acculturation, in itself, appears unlikely to explain elevated depression levels among Mexican American adolescents.

Another potential explanation is genetic: People of Mexican descent may have a higher genetic risk for depression than those of other ethnicities. Two lines of evidence contradict this possibility. First, among adults, depression rates vary within people of Mexican descent depending on country of birth, with depressive symptoms among U.S.-born Mexicans higher than for those born in Mexico (Golding et al., 1990). If U.S.-born Mexicans and those born in Mexico have similar genetic makeups, depression differences within this group are difficult to explain from a genetic perspective. Second, in contrast to the finding that Mexican American adolescents have higher depression rates than their Anglo American counterparts (e.g., Roberts et al., 1997), when Mexican adolescents living in Mexico were compared with non-Hispanic Whites, depression rates were, if anything, lower among Mexican adolescents (Swanson, Linskey, Quintero-Salinas, & Pumariega, 1992). A purely genetic explanation thus does not seem particularly plausible.

Therefore, genetics—or any stable predisposition—is unlikely to fully explain elevated Mexican American adolescent depression, because Mexican people with the same predispositions, but who do not face acculturative challenges, have relatively low depression rates. Yet, acculturation alone cannot explain the effect either, because other ethnic groups who confront acculturative stress do not have elevated depression rates. A possible resolution to this quandary is the following hypothesis: On average, Mexican people (wherever born) possess a depression risk that (a) many other ethnic groups do not possess to the same degree and (b) is activated by the experience of acculturative stress.

What is the nature of this hypothesized depression risk? There is preliminary evidence that a negative cognitive style (e.g., pessimism) is culturally favored among Mexican people (Domino, Fragoso, & Moreno, 1991; cf. Fehrenbach's, 1995, statement that "The people of the United States like to believe that political will and good intentions can solve most human dilemmas. They often find it hard to understand Mexicans, who know better"). This style may represent a depression risk factor, but only among those who are faced with serious stress (including acculturative stress). Joiner, Perez, Wagner, Berenson, and Marquina (2001) obtained evidence in favor of this view among Mexican American adolescents; namely, that higher rates of pessimism accounted in part for the higher rates of depression among these adolescents. The role of negative cognitive style in depression in general is returned to in chapter 9 on stable vulnerabilities.

CONSEQUENCES OF A DEPRESSION EPIDEMIC

Depression has been termed *the common cold* of mental disorders. With regard to prevalence, this analogy may be apt: Depression is becoming more and more common. But otherwise, the analogy may be unfortunate because it belies the pernicious quality of a depressive episode.

Depression is among the most debilitating and costly of any health problem. In a recent large-scale study of medical outcomes, only heart disease was associated with more bed days, physical symptoms, and social and role impairment than depression. Depression was associated with worse outcomes than all other conditions studied, including chronic lung disease, diabetes, arthritis, gastrointestinal problems, back problems, and hypertension (Stewart et al., 1989; Wells, 1991). Furthermore, depression is associated with the ultimate health index: In a study of nursing home residents, depressed people died at higher rates than nondepressed people (O'Connor & Vallerand, 1998), and this was true even controlling for general health status. Numerous other studies likewise support the association between depression and increased early mortality rates (e.g., Cuijpers & Smit, 2002).

In a 2-year follow-up of over a thousand participants in the medical outcomes study, Hays, Wells, Sherbourne, Rogers, and Spritzer (1995) reported that depressed patients were similar to or worse off than all patients with other medical problems, including congestive heart failure and myocardial infarction. It is interesting to note that this result applied to many types of depression, including an acute episode of clinically severe depression (i.e., major depression), subclinical but disruptive depressive symptoms, and persistent but less acute and severe forms (e.g., dysthymia). Thus, as Hays et al. stated, "depressed patients have substantial and long-lasting decrements in multiple domains of functioning and well-being that equal or exceed those of patients with chronic medical illnesses" (p. 11). When depression goes untreated, the impairment in functioning and well-being is worse still (Coryell et al., 1995).

In addition to its impact on individual suffering and impairment, depression burdens the health care system. Simon, Ormel, VonKorff, and Barlow (1995) found that among primary care patients, those with clinical depression were twice as costly to treat than other patients. This finding was not due to increased medical problems among the depressed, although it appears true that depression may exacerbate some physical symptoms, and there is no question that depression prevalence is extremely high in most general medical samples (e.g., Wells, Rogers, Burnam, & Greenfield, 1991). Rather, the increased cost derived from increased utilization of health care services. Even when improvement in depression had occurred 1 year later, the costs associated with the care of formerly depressed patients had not decreased substantially.

The burden of depression on those who have it and on society is clear. It is disturbing that the amount of money spent on depression research pales compared with that spent for conditions that cause similar or lower levels of distress and impairment. Depending on how computations are done, depression can be viewed as the most debilitating of the major conditions, as well as the least well funded (Gross, Anderson, & Powe, 1999; World Health Organization, 2002). This disparity must be repaired, one would hope, by increasing health research spending overall instead of by "robbing Peter to pay Paul" (e.g., diverting funds for cancer research to depression research).

Depression can be fatal. One of its primary features is suicidal thoughts or actions. Of all the people who commit suicide, a majority experienced some form of diagnosable depression at the time of their death (Hawton, 1992). In a recent study, approximately 70% of young adults who had recently attempted suicide had a diagnosable mood disorder (Rudd et al., 1996). Compared with the general population, depressed people's risk of death by suicide is around 30 times higher (Hawton, 1992). Suicide affects all age ranges. Among adolescents, suicide is the third leading cause of death, accounting for 14% of total deaths in this age group, and the overall suicide rate among this age group has increased 312% from 1957 to 1987 (Berman & Jobes, 1991). Suicide also affects older people. Indeed, suicide rates for people over the age of 65 are at least as high, if not higher than those for other age groups. This is particularly true for Anglo American men, whose suicide rate among those 65 and older is at least double that of any other group (U. S. Bureau of the Census, 1993).

All of this would be bad enough, even if depression were an isolated event in the lives of people who have experienced it. But depression is remarkably persistent and recurrent (Wells, Burnam, Rogers, Hays, & Camp, 1992). The average length of major depressive episodes is approximately 8 months in adults (Shapiro & Keller, 1981), and 9 months in children (Kovacs, Obrosky, Gatsonis, & Richards, 1997). And the mean length of dysthymic episodes may be as much as 30 years in some adult samples (Shelton, Davidson, Yonkers, & Koran, 1997); the corresponding figure for children is 4 years (Kovacs et al., 1997). Emslie, Rush, Weinberg, and Guillon (1997) found that 61% of depressed children experienced recurrence of depression within 2 years; similar 2-year relapse rates have been reported among adults (Bothwell & Scott, 1997). Tsuang and Coryell (1993) found that 56% of people with psychotic depression at intake remained ill 8 years later. In studies with follow-ups of 10 years or more, Coryell and Winokur (1992) found that 70% of people with one depressive episode subsequently experienced at least one more. Lee and Murray (1988) reported that 18 years after an initial depressive episode, approximately 20% of patients remained incapacitated by depression. Depression is thus persistent within acute episodes, and recurrent across substantial portions of people's lives.

SUMMARY

This chapter summarized (a) definitions and related problems regarding the concept of depression; (b) the course of depression; (c) the comorbidity of depression and anxiety; (d) the possibility that depression prevalence is increasing; (e) the relation of depression to gender and ethnicity; and (f) the pernicious quality of depression, including its chronicity. The next chapter describes the phenomenon of stress generation as a potential propagating factor in depression.

3

STRESS GENERATION

.

The link between life stress and depression is well-known—in general, the occurrence of life stressors appears to contribute to the development of depression (e.g., Lewinsohn, Hoberman, & Rosenbaum, 1988; Monroe & Simmons, 1991), although life stress is by no means a full explanation of who does and who does not become depressed. A prominent example comes from the work of Brown and Harris (1978), who argued that the occurrence of particular stressors (e.g., the loss of a loved one) causally contributes to the development of depression. In this and related work (e.g., Lewinsohn et al., 1988), the direction of theorizing has always been from stress to depression. Stress is construed as essentially unsystematic—it is foisted on people in basically random fashion, much as an accident suddenly occurs in the life of an unsuspecting victim. And in stress' wake comes depression.

But some people seem more accident-prone than others. Is stress a mere accident in the lives of unlucky people or, rather, might the occurrence of stress be systematically tied to the actions of those experiencing the stress? Just as some people are accident-prone, might some people be stress-prone?

One might hypothesize that a stress-prone person might, for example, engage in a pattern of decision making that routinely causes problems in close relationships or at work. Or a stress-prone person might gravitate toward the relationship partners who are unsupportive or even hurtful.

Hammen (1991) theorized that depressed people are particularly stress-prone, in the sense that they actively generate negative life events. (It is important to distinguish *active* from *intentional* here—we do not believe that depressed people intentionally create problems for themselves, but that some of their behaviors have the unintended consequence of making life more stressful). If so, a self-sustaining process would be implicated in which formerly depressed people actively generate future life events that, in turn, sow the seeds of future depression. This would explain, at least in part, why depression persists and recurs.

In a series of empirical studies, Hammen, Davila, Brown, Ellicott, and Gitlin, (1992) have documented the phenomenon of "stress generation." Most of these studies have focused on depressed women to the exclusion of depressed men, although limited evidence suggests that the processes may work similarly in both genders (e.g., Hammen et al., 1992; Potthoff, Holahan, & Joiner, 1995). In a 1-year study of women with depression, bipolar disorder, medical illness, or no disorder, Hammen (1991) showed that depressed women experienced more interpersonal stress to which the women themselves contributed (e.g., disputes with teachers or bosses; conflicts with children or partners), even compared with the women with bipolar disorder and medical illness. The finding was specific to interpersonal events—depressed women did not differ from others with regard to "fateful" events (i.e., those that really are randomly foisted on people). This result highlights the importance of interpersonal events, as well as the idea that nonrandom, self-produced negative events are characteristic of depressed people. Notably, the depressed women in Hammen's (1991) study all experienced chronic forms of depression. This finding has been replicated in samples of men and women (Hammen et al., 1992), marital couples (Davila, Bradbury, Cohan, & Tochluk, 1997), adolescent women (Daley, Hammen, Burge, & Davila, 1997; Davila, Hammen, Burge, & Paley, 1995), children (Adrian & Hammen, 1993), as well as by other research groups (Potthoff et al., 1995; Simons, Angell, Monroe, & Thase, 1993). This line of research implicates the important possibility that, although depression may occur in the wake of stress, so may stress occur in depression's wake.

A series of studies of adolescent girls attending an obstetric-gynecology clinic provides a potential example of a stress generation process (Wagner, Berenson, Harding, & Joiner, 1998). Wagner et al. had suspected that the combination of a pessimistic attitude style and the experience of teenage pregnancy might produce depression, consistent with cognitive theories of depression (e.g., Abramson, Metalsky, & Alloy, 1989). However, in the first of these studies, they found that pessimistic, pregnant girls were less depressed than optimistic, pregnant girls and nonpregnant girls.

This result was the opposite of the prediction, and Wagner et al. (1998) speculated that depression-prone (e.g., pessimistic) girls may attempt to "solve" problems such as loneliness, lack of identity, lack of status, and so on, by becoming pregnant. If so, they reasoned that this "solution" would backfire postpartum, when illusions were shattered by the travail of teenage motherhood.

In the second study of the series, Wagner et al. (1998) replicated the original surprising result—again, pessimistic, pregnant girls were less depressed than other girls. However, as many parents know, that which applies during pregnancy need not apply after delivery. In the third study of the series, they found that postpartum, pessimistic teenage mothers were far more depressed than optimistic teenage mothers.

Wagner et al. (1998) interpreted the pattern of findings as follows: The depression-prone girls—along with their partners—generated the stressor of teenage pregnancy and motherhood, and the generated stress eventually caused the pessimistic girls, but not the optimistic girls, to experience depression. As we discuss in chapter 9, self-sustaining processes (like stress generation) may interact with persistent vulnerabilities (like pessimism) to encourage depression chronicity (cf. Hankin & Abramson, 2001). A possible example occurred in the study, in which a sample of girls generates a stressor (i.e., pregnancy), but only a vulnerable subsample (i.e., pessimistic girls) reacts to the generated stress with depression.

Hammen (1999) made a very interesting point with regard to the stress generation phenomenon in her studies: Women tended to generate stress (e.g., initiate interpersonal conflicts) at times when they were not in a depressive episode. This finding leads to an important speculation about recovery from depression; namely, depression—because it is generally incapacitating—may shut down many processes, including stress generation processes. While things are shut down, stress may recede, and recovery may be facilitated. Once depression lets up, however, stress generation may reactivate, inducing stress and sowing the seeds for future depression. In this way, the stress generation perspective may accomplish something that other models do not, in that it provides at least a tenable explanation of why depression lets up (cf. Jack, 1991). We caution, however, that some stress-generating behaviors likely continue to occur during active depression, and speculate that perhaps they simply slow down at times of greatest incapacitation.

The stress generation model appears to provide prima facie evidence of an interpersonally sustaining process. Indeed, in the stress generation studies, it seems that recurrently depressed people are actively doing something to produce stress. Moreover, it has been shown that generated stress, in turn, exacerbates or reinstills depression (Davila et al., 1995; Potthoff et al., 1995; Simons et al., 1993). But what are depression-prone people doing to produce stress and thus perpetuate depression?

On the surface, this question is not difficult. According to the stress generation literature, depression-prone people are initiating interpersonal conflicts and disagreements, a form of interpersonal stress. But the deeper question—why certain people initiate interpersonal problems—is not quite as easily answered.

DYSFUNCTIONAL MATE SELECTION

Like not only finds like; it can't even escape from being found by its
like. . . .

—William Faulkner

One important way that depression-prone people may contribute to
the occurrence of stress in their lives is to choose "stressful" relationship
partners. As a prelude to psychotherapy for depressed people, I (Joiner) often
ask patients to list the most important people in their lives, both positive and
negative, and for each, to describe what they got out of the relationship (cf.
McCullough et al., 1997; see also chap. 12 on clinical assessment). As patients describe their relationships, I make notes. After this exercise is completed, I often show patients my notes, and it is not uncommon for them to
exclaim something like, "no wonder I'm depressed; look at the people I get
into romantic relationships with!" Relationships are rarely foisted on people;
rather, by and large, people seek out or drift toward certain types of partners
(a phenomenon called *assortative mating*)—which is why patterns emerge in
the exercise I do with my patients. In this exercise, I emphasize that there is
no reason for self-blame about these patterns—the pattern is what it is, and
the question merely is whether it is something the person would like to alter.

Consider, for example, a woman who, for whatever reasons, tends to
"choose wrong" when it comes to romantic partners. More specifically, she
tends to gravitate toward men who are unsupportive, preoccupied with themselves, and at times verbally abusive. It is no mystery that this woman is in for
some stressful experiences, partly because of her choice; her relationship choice
can be seen as an instance of stress generation. (It is discussed in chap. 4 on
self-verification theory that poor choices such as this probably have very
little do with masochism, the enjoyment of pain. Indeed, it is clear that people
in these situations do not enjoy them at all. But this is a separate question
from whether they gravitate toward them, even despite not enjoying them).
Thus, relationship choice can be viewed as one way that people generate
stress.

Do depression-prone people choose badly? There is preliminary evidence that they may. As one example, Hammen (1999) reported that in
her series of studies on stress generation in depressed and other women,
depressed women tended to gravitate toward men who themselves are prone
to psychopathology.

For two reasons, it appeared that the women were attracted to the men,
in part, on the basis of the men's preexisting psychopathology (as opposed to
the alternative explanation that living with a depressed woman may instill
psychopathology in the men—which, as discussed in chap. 5, may happen as
well). First, the type of psychopathology displayed by the men was usually
substance use disorders or antisocial personality disorder, both of which rep-

resent long-standing problems. In this context, it is interesting to note that, at odds with the Faulkner (1932) quote, "like is not finding like" here. Rather, women and men with one form of psychopathology appear to gravitate toward partners with a distinct form of psychopathology. Second, the men appeared to have high rates of past psychopathology (before they met the women). The end result is both people with elevated chances of experiencing their own as well as each other's psychopathology—a stressful scenario indeed. If both experience depression (which men with substance use disorders often do), and both generate stress as a result of depression, stress and depression will abound for this couple. Dysfunctional mate selection thus may represent one way that a depressed person contributes to the phenomenon of stress generation.

Consider the case of Carla, a depressed woman in her mid-40s who had experienced a string of relationships with neglectful, at times abusive, and often heavy-drinking men. After completing the previously described exercise of listing the most important people in her life, Carla noted that she had given a lot—but received little—in her relationships. This served as a launching point for addressing several important issues in therapy, such as qualities to look for (and to avoid) when forming new relationships, developing assertiveness skills to even the balance of her giving and receiving in relationships, and examining the role of loneliness in her becoming involved with men who might mistreat her.

IMPAIRED INTERPERSONAL PROBLEM SOLVING

In addition to dysfunctional mate selection, Davila et al. (1995) proposed that poor interpersonal problem solving is a way that depression-prone people generate stress. Evidence suggests that people who are depressed demonstrate average problem-solving skills in impersonal settings (e.g., solving a puzzle), yet display specific problem-solving deficits in interpersonal settings (Gotlib & Asarnow, 1979). Examples of lapses in interpersonal problem solving may include the misperception of an offhand, trivial comment as an insulting attack; persistently avoiding someone who represents a key source of social support because of a minor misunderstanding; and angry, accusing confrontation of someone who was sincerely trying to help. Indeed, dysfunctional mate selection can also be viewed as an instance of poor interpersonal problem solving. Davila et al. showed that poor interpersonal problem solving led to increased stress, that in turn led to increased depressive symptoms.

The explanation of why some people appear to possess good problem-solving skills, whereas others do not, is complex. Hammen et al. (1992) theorized that the effects of early depression and dysfunctional family experiences were implicated in stress generation. Other work has shown that both early age of depression onset (e.g., Lewinsohn et al., 1994) and family dysfunction are associated with impaired problem solving (Ebata & Moos, 1994; Holahan & Moos, 1987). Thus, early depression and family dysfunction may prevent the development of good problem solving; impaired problem solving, in turn, may generate stress and perpetuate depression. As we see in chapter 13 on clinical intervention, treatments focused on improving problem solving appear to work, even if the ultimate source of impaired problem solving remains somewhat unclear.

For example, consider a depressed man who reacts negatively when his wife (sincerely) suggests that his productivity in sales might increase if he updated his wardrobe. He views her comment as a veiled criticism of his appearance, and he responds by "shutting down" and withholding affection from her but does not directly express his feelings. His wife picks up on his aloofness and hostility, and responds in turn (i.e., she also shuts down). After a day in this cold environment, the man explodes with an outburst of anger toward his wife over a trivial, unrelated matter. He feels both angry with his wife and disappointed about his own behavior and appearance. Although the developmental roots of his poor interpersonal problem-solving skills are uncertain, it is likely that strategic coaching in problem solving and assertion would help him manage his negative feelings more appropriately and avoid the ensuing generation of interpersonal conflict.

THE PERNICIOUS INTERPERSONAL EFFECTS OF HOPELESSNESS

In a recent series of studies, Joiner, Wingate, Gencoz, and Gencoz (2005) examined a somewhat different explanation for why depression is associated with stress generation. Many stress generation studies examine the links between self-reported depression and self-reported negative life stress. Because self-report is the source for assessment of both depression and stress, it is possible that increases in reported negative life events may merely reflect an increasingly hopeless outlook, rather than actual stress increases. A depressed person may thus perceive and report stress, even when stress is not actually present. Although Hammen et al. (1992) used careful assessment approaches to negative life events (approaches that should be relatively immune to this artifact; e.g., Hammen, 1991), the possible influence of increasing hopelessness in stress generation deserves attention nonetheless, especially insofar as hopelessness is a hallmark of major descriptive and etiological accounts of depression (Abramson et al., 1989; American Psychiatric Association, 1994; Beck, Rush, Shaw, & Emery, 1979). Moreover, hopelessness, because of its embittering and stultifying effects on other people, may be particularly likely to disaffect others (i.e., to generate the stress of interpersonal rejection).

If it were found that increased hopelessness accounted for stress generation in depression, two interpretations would be possible. First, of course, it may be that depression induces a hopeless outlook, rather than inducing actual negative events; or second, depression may generate actual stress, and hopelessness may be depression's "active ingredient" in the generation of actual stress increases.

A main purpose of Joiner et al.'s (2005) studies was to evaluate these two possibilities. Does depression merely induce a hopeless outlook that, in turn, generates the perception but not the occurrence of stress? Might depression generate actual stress—for example, interpersonal rejection—through the generation of a hopeless outlook (which others may find aversive)? Joiner et al. suggested that answers to these questions bear on the very existence of a true stress generation effect, as well as on how the effect happens (i.e., its mechanism).

Joiner et al. (2005) conducted three studies among undergraduate men and women, all longitudinal using a relatively short time frame, and all examining self-reported depressive symptoms (not clinical diagnoses of depression). In each study, they tested the hypothesis that depressive symptoms would be predictive of prospective increases in reported negative life events—that depression would generate stress.

The first study represented a straightforward replication of the stress generation effect. Students who reported depression at Time 1 were more likely than other students to experience increases over time in self-reported negative life events.

The second study, too, provided a replication of the stress generation effect—here again, depressed students, as compared with their nondepressed counterparts, experienced more increases in self-reported negative events. But this second study also addressed the important possibility that a hopeless outlook on the part of the depressed person may account for the stress generation effect. In fact, it was the case that depressed students tended to experience increases in hopelessness (in addition to increases in self-reported negative events) over the course of the study. Furthermore, it appeared that depressed students' perception of life stress occurred as a function of increased hopelessness. As the students became more hopeless, they reported more negative events in their lives.

But was there actually more stress in their lives (perhaps encouraged by evolving hopelessness), or were the students merely perceiving more stress (because they were becoming more hopeless)? The third study in the series provided at least a partial answer to this question. In this study, instead of assessing respondents' own perceptions of life stress, an instance of actual life stress—roommate rejection—was directly assessed by including respondents' roommates in the study. Joiner et al. (2005) reasoned that if depression was leading to actual stress (here, roommate rejection), and that if increased roommate rejection occurred as a function of increased hopelessness, then hopelessness may be a main "carrier" of the generation of actual stress (not merely perceived stress). In fact, results showed just this: Students who reported depression experienced increased roommate rejection, and this appeared to occur as a function of respondents' increased hopelessness.

How might hopelessness operate as an actual stress generator? Future work may benefit from exploration of several related speculations (it is emphasized that these are speculations in need of future research).

First, depression chronicity itself may be involved in stress generation. As depression persists, those who experience it may become more and more hopeless, and their significant others may become more and more burdened and disaffected. Consistent with this speculation, Sacco, Milana, and Dunn (1988) provided participants with transcripts of depressed people whose episodes were long lasting, and transcripts of depressed people who experienced short episodes. Compared with short-episode transcripts, long-duration "depressives" elicited more anger and more interpersonal rejection. It is worth remembering that Hammen's (1991) study on stress generation in depression focused on people with chronic forms of depression.

A second possibility is that hopelessness, because it has embittering and stultifying effects, may lead to cognitive representations of depressed people in the minds of significant others that are negative and change resistant. Sacco (1999) argued that once these representations are developed, they selectively guide attention and expectancies to confirm the representation. These social-cognitive processes may occur spontaneously and outside of awareness (Lewicki, Hill, & Czyzewska, 1992). Such processes may be particularly attention grabbing with regard to negative as opposed to positive behaviors. There is evidence that, as compared with positive behaviors, negative behaviors are more likely to draw attention (Pratto & John, 1991). Furthermore, when negative behaviors are attributed to the person (as opposed to the situation), they are more likely to be remembered (Ybarra & Stephan, 1996). Once crystallized, cognitive representations of negative behaviors are more change resistant than representations of positive behaviors (Rothbart & Park, 1986). Moreover, such representations gain momentum with use, in that they come to disproportionately influence social cognition relative to actual subsequent behaviors of the represented person (Sherman & Klein, 1994). These processes are emphasized again in chapter 8 on blame maintenance.

Hopelessness, then, may generate stress by producing in others a person-schema that negatively biases subsequent perceptions of the hopeless person and is difficult to change. Others' negative views may, in turn, encourage critical communications from others to the hopeless person, and these communications have been shown to be strong predictors of depression chronicity (Hooley & Teasdale, 1989). With regard to others' perceptions, the hopeless and potentially depressed person may face a very difficult problem: Continued hopelessness may only serve to maintain others' negative views and thus generate stress in the form of criticism; positive changes, because they do not match others' schemata, may be unnoticed or misattributed, leaving others' negative representations unchanged.

To summarize the three studies, each replicated the stress generation effect. The second study of the series showed that as hopelessness increases, so does generated stress. The third study demonstrated that this process applied to the generation of actual stress (at least as reflected by roommate rejection), instead of merely applying to the perception that stress is increasing. It is important to note that the findings from this series of studies suggest that similar processes are at work in both depressed women and men (in contrast to earlier studies that focused exclusively on depressed women).

One other aspect of these three studies deserves mention, in that they compared the specificity of the stress generation effect with depressive versus anxious symptoms. It is conceivable that many mental disorders and numerous types of emotional distress may be associated with generated stress. Is there something special about depression in terms of generating stress? Hammen (1991) reported that people with depression, as compared with those with bipolar disorder and those with nonpsychiatric medical illness, experienced higher rates of generated stress, in line with the specificity of stress generation to depression. My studies extended this finding to anxious symptoms—depression generated actual (not merely perceived) stress through increased hopelessness, whereas anxious symptoms did not operate in this fashion. Because anxious symptoms overlap considerably with depressive symptoms (Clark & Watson, 1991), a finding that generated stress stemmed from depressive but not anxious symptoms lends strong support for the specificity of stress generation to depression. An important reason that stress generation processes may be specific to depression is that depression is more strongly associated with hopelessness than are most other mental disorders and symptoms.

The potential role of hopelessness in the generation of stress suggests an interpersonal elaboration to Abramson et al.'s (1989) hopelessness theory of depression. According to the hopelessness theory, hopelessness produces depression, and hopelessness, in turn, is produced by stress impinging on a negative cognitive style (e.g., pessimism; cf. Wagner et al., 1998 study on pregnant teenagers).

The addendum to hopelessness theory is depicted in Figure 3.1. The highlighted aspects represent the suggested elaboration to the theory. Specifically, Figure 3.1 shows that hopelessness, once developed—perhaps as a result of the operation of negative cognitive style activated by stress— (a) leads directly to depressive symptoms; (b) leads indirectly to depressive symptoms by generating interpersonal stress; and (c) in generating stress, provides more "grist" for negative cognitive style's "mill," thus propagating the sequence and perpetuating depressive symptoms.

The sequence depicted in Figure 3.1 is recurrent and self-sustaining (i.e., feeds back on itself), and thus may shed light on why depression is chronic. This process of stress generation is particularly relevant to two of the three forms of depression chronicity discussed in chapter 1. First, current

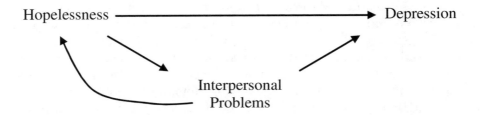

Figure 3.1. Suggested elaboration of the hopelessness theory of depression.

depression, however it is caused, may lead to increased hopelessness and thus to generated life stress. Stress has been shown to expand episode duration. Second, on remission of current depression, subclinical depressive symptoms may remain, which may also foster hopelessness (and have other effects, such as hampering problem solving), induce interpersonal stress, and thus reestablish depression (i.e., relapse).

By contrast, with regard to strictly defined recurrence in which a substantial symptom-free period has occurred, it cannot be claimed that the process shown in Figure 3.1 is fully self-sustaining. Under conditions of recurrence, there has existed a time when depressive symptoms were not there to exert influence. To self-sustain, symptoms need to be present to exert their self-propagating influence (although there may be at least one exception to this rule, as elucidated in chap. 8 on blame maintenance).

RELEVANCE TO REMISSION

In addition to explaining chronicity, a powerful explanation of depression's properties should produce insight as to why depression remits. Without a kind of "breaking mechanism," processes like those depicted in Figure 3.1 spiral infinitely downward. Of course, "infinite downward spirals" exist in the form of depression-related suicide as well as chronic forms of depression (e.g., dysthymia). But most depressions remit (even if most recur; Bothwell & Scott, 1997)—what is the breaking mechanism? Some speculations are offered, none of which have been thoroughly investigated; they thus represent a potentially fruitful avenue for future research.

First, once hopelessness and depression develop, the individual with depression may socially withdraw. Although social withdrawal certainly has costs (Joiner, 1997), it also confers the benefits of distance from interpersonal criticism. During a phase of social withdrawal, the individual may initially become more symptomatic as a result of the lingering effects of previous interpersonal strife and the current experience of loneliness. But with time, the effects of previous relationship strife may fade and the ongoing experience of loneliness may compel him or her to access alternative, underused, and (perhaps) healthier sources of social support that, in turn, may instill hope and encourage recovery. It is interesting in this context to reemphasize that stress generation behaviors appear to be most active during depression-free times; depression may thus shut down stress generation activities, and sow the seeds for recovery (Hammen, 1999).

Although we are not aware of research on the topic, a couple of extrapolations for treatment may be relevant (but we again caution that these are speculative). First, if depression and hopelessness do lead to a slowing down of stress-generating behaviors, this may provide therapists a "window of opportunity" in which to explicitly connect patients' previous patterns of interpersonal behaviors with their current depressed state. Moreover, healthier sources of social support, and appropriate skills training to cultivate them, may be presented to patients as a means to facilitating recovery (and avoiding relapse). Second, the finding that stress generation occurs with greatest intensity during depression-free times underscores the notion that skills such as interpersonal problem solving, assertiveness, and the like may be most effective at preventing relapse if they become highly ingrained through repetition and practice during treatment. Finally, and in spite of our presentation of the possibility that social withdrawal decreases interpersonal stress and thereby reduces depressive symptoms, we do not think it is reasonable to encourage social isolation among depressed persons. To the extent that it occurs naturally, it may reduce relationship strife; however, substantial evidence indicates that the presence of social support can play an important role in recovery from depression (e.g., McLeod, Kessler, & Landis, 1992).

A related possibility with regard to remission is that severe hopelessness and depressive symptoms serve as a powerful distress signal with both negative and adaptive qualities. Much has been made of the negative stimulus value of this signal, and with reason, insofar as one main point of this chapter is that hopelessness generates stress, and one main point of the literature on depression and the response of others is to explain depressed people's negative interpersonal impact (e.g., Coyne, 1976a; Joiner, Alfano, & Metalsky, 1992).

Nonetheless, the communication value of hopelessness and depression may also be adaptive in that it recruits interpersonal solace. In their sociophysiological model, Price and Gardner (1999) argued that depression-related states and behaviors represent forms of an "involuntary subordinate strategy," that arose as a means to cope with losses in social competition, and that functions to send useful communications to others. For example, one function of the involuntary subordination strategy is to communicate to rivals and superiors a "no threat" signal (which discourages aggression from others) and to communicate to allies an "out of action—can't help you" signal (which encourages them to fend for themselves). Depression may thus serve as a type of alarm signal, and like most alarm signals, may be unpleasant but useful in that it communicates distress and need to others.

Indeed, anecdotally, many people who have recovered from depression remark that they "found out who their real friends were," through their response to the distress signal of depression. Joiner et al. (1992) obtained some empirical support for the view that people with tolerant, supportive, or emotionally empathic interpersonal styles were less rejecting than others, even toward people most vulnerable to rejection (i.e., high reassurance-seeking, depressed people). The heightened support of tolerant others—including mental health professionals—may thus serve to break the cycle depicted in Figure 3.1, and may represent one explanation as to why depression remits. In the context of treatment, this notion also accords with well-known findings that the relationship between treatment provider and patient, or *therapeutic alliance*, is crucial to the successful progression of treatment (e.g., Krupnick et al., 1996).

It must also be remembered that positive life events occur, to some degree or another, in everyone's lives. Should a hopeless or depressed person fortuitously experience a positive event (e.g., supportive phone call from an old friend), the experience may foster improvement, especially if the event is attributed to stable and global causes (e.g., "my old friend really cares about me;" Needles & Abramson, 1990). This, too, may represent one explanation of why depression remits. Again, from a treatment perspective, this notion is consistent with effective behavioral techniques such as pleasant events scheduling (although the positive event is hardly "fortuitous" in this case; Lewinsohn & Libet, 1972).

SUMMARY

In summary, there is accumulating evidence that depressed people actively generate their own stress, especially interpersonal stress. There are several possibilities as to how depression-prone people generate stress: Dysfunctional mate selection, impaired interpersonal problem solving, and the pernicious interpersonal effects of increasing hopelessness represent potential mechanisms. Stress generation processes appear relevant to two of the three forms of depression chronicity, in that they may expand the length of depressive episodes and maintain risk of relapse. The perspective also sheds some light on why depression remits (e.g., when depressed, people may cease stress-generating activities).

In the next five chapters, five other processes potentially involved in depression chronicity are described. Each can be seen as first-order, specific instances of the stress-generation concept. For example, *negative feedback-seeking* (defined as the tendency to directly or indirectly invite criticism from other people and viewed as motivated by self-verification strivings; e.g., Swann, 1990), described next in chapter 4, represents a specific mechanism by which depression-prone people contribute to such stressors as relationship dissatisfaction and dissolution. Similarly, *excessive reassurance-seeking* (defined as the tendency to repeatedly and persistently demand assurance from others as to one's lovability and worth, even after such is provided; e.g., Joiner, Metalsky, Katz, & Beach, 1999), described in chapter 5, also directly contributes to interpersonal stress. *Interpersonal conflict avoidance* (chap. 6; defined as the anxious avoidance of self-assertion situations), also sows the seeds of stress generation. It has already been mentioned that depression and anxiety appear to covary; chapter 6 makes the case that anxious avoidance may serve to perpetuate depression.

The two remaining self-sustaining interpersonal processes are less directly implicated in stress generation but nonetheless may serve to perpetuate depression. Research on *self-handicapping* and *inoculation* indicates that depressed people may gain self-protective and other rewards for depressive cognition and behavior. These rewards serve to maintain depressive cognition and behavior, and thereby increase depression chronicity (chap. 7). The final process, *blame maintenance*, is a truly interpersonal phenomenon, in that other people, not the depression-prone person, are maintaining blame of the depression-prone person, somewhat independent of the latter's actions. Insofar as interpersonal strife (e.g., perceived criticism from close others; Hooley & Teasdale, 1989) is a quite strong predictor of depression chronicity, it would be unsurprising if blame maintenance were implicated in the persistence and recurrence of depression (chap. 8).

4

NEGATIVE FEEDBACK-SEEKING

I am not stuck up and am in my place. The moth and the fish-eggs are in their place, the bright suns I see and the dark suns I cannot see are in their place, the palpable is in its place and the impalpable is in it place.

—Walt Whitman

A fellow is more afraid of the trouble he might have than he ever is of the trouble he's already got. He'll cling to trouble he's used to before he'll risk a change.

—William Faulkner

Consider the following exchange between me (Joiner) and a patient:

Patient: I did bad things as a kid; never been a nice person; there's nothing nice about me.

Me: Hmm. . . [*doubtful look*].

Patient: It's true; it is true.

Me: I'm not sure I see it.

Patient: People don't think I'm good; only those who can tolerate a lot like me. This is *true*.

Me: Still not sure I see it.

Patient: Well, perhaps you will. . .you know, there is no need to make me feel better; I just want you to be honest.

During this session, I had the distinct feeling that this patient wanted me to see things his way, and that when I demurred, this only intensified his wish to persuade me. This would not be very unusual, except that his efforts at persuasion were geared toward his own self-denigration.

Why? Why would someone demand cooperation in his or her own devaluation? Perhaps the previously noted excerpts from Whitman (1892) and

41

Faulkner (1932) provide a clue. Maybe people get used to things being "in their place," even when this includes their own low estimate of their place. And maybe people are afraid of change, "cling[ing] to trouble he's used to before he'll risk a change," in Faulkner's words. In what follows, we provide an overview of self-verification theory, which formalizes these possibilities into a theory relevant to self-concept, motivation, and interpersonal behavior. Once we have summarized the theory and several attendant issues, we turn to the relevance of this line of thought for depression chronicity.

SELF-VERIFICATION THEORY

Social psychologist William Swann (1990, 1996) formalized the possibilities that people stay in their place and prefer "trouble to change" into a theory, termed *self-verification theory*. This theory proposes that people strive to attain and preserve predictable, certain, and familiar self-concepts. Further, the theory indicates that people accomplish this by actively seeking self-confirming interpersonal responses from those in their social environment.

A key and perhaps counterintuitive implication of the theory is that there is no difference in the self-verification needs between people with positive self-concepts and people with negative self-concepts. It is interesting to note that we are quite used to people desiring positive responses from others; it seems somehow normal to desire warmth, praise, positive evaluations, and so forth. And, according to self-verification theory, it *is* normal, because the vast majority of people have positive self-concepts. For people with positive self-concepts, self-verification involves seeking warmth, praise, etc. But, according to the theory, people with negative self-concepts appear to desire self-confirmation too, which means seeking criticism and the like from those around them (i.e., negative feedback-seeking). Swann, Stein-Seroussi, and Giesler (1992) suggested that people with negative self-concepts are motivated to do this, even at the cost of receiving unpleasant feedback from those around them.

What exactly are people up to when they seek self-verifying feedback? What specifically motivates them? Swann, Stein-Seroussi, et al. (1992) argued that a sense of familiarity, predictability, and control (Whitman's "being in place") is one important motivational source for self-verification strivings. That is, even if negative, one's self-concept is one's self-concept, changes to which are likely to rock the boat indeed. If you radically changed your self-views, it would take a lot of getting used to, both for you and for those who are used to your "old self." Faulkner's words endorse self-verification theory; there is something reassuring about standing pat, even if one is standing in "trouble."

There may also be something to seeing things as they are, even if they are negative. In this regard, consider the words of ancient Greece's Xenophon (2004, p. 153):

> And this too is plain, is it not: that through self-knowledge men meet with countless blessings, and through ignorance of themselves with many evils? Because, the man who knows himself knows what is advantageous to himself; he discerns the limits of his powers, and by doing what he knows, he provides himself with what he needs and so does well; or, conversely, by holding aloof from what he knows not, he avoids mistakes and thereby mishaps. And having now a test to gauge other human beings he uses their need as a stepping-stone to provide himself with good and to avoid evil.

But surely, if things are bad, especially if the self-concept is negative, it would be best to be deceived. Joiner and Kistner (2005) conducted two studies on this question among undergraduate men and women, and some potentially surprising findings emerged. They assessed the degree to which undergraduates' views of themselves corresponded with others' views of them (in this case, their dormitory roommates' views of them). Then, Joiner and Kistner evaluated whether the amount of correspondence between these views was associated with several indices of emotional distress (e.g., depressive and anxious symptoms). Results from the two studies suggested that high correspondence was associated with fewer symptoms, whereas lack of correspondence was related to more symptoms.

It is not surprising that certain types of correspondence were associated with well-being. For example, for those who view themselves positively and are viewed by roommates positively, low scores on symptom measures would only be expected. What was surprising was that correspondences of any type seemed to relate to well-being, and discordances of any type were associated with high symptoms scores.

That is, people with relatively negative self-concepts seemed protected from symptoms if roommates confirmed their negative self-views! This finding is consistent with the perspective that being truly understood by others is conducive to good mental health (cf. psychotherapeutic models, such as psychoanalytic self psychology [e.g., Kohut, 1984] that emphasize the curative effects of empathy). The result is also consistent with the interpretation of self-verification theory that self-consistent information, regardless of its valence, is soothing, and self-discrepant information, even if positive, is unsettling.

Also of interest and also somewhat surprising was the finding that positive distortions ("self-enhancement"), too, were associated with relatively more symptoms. That is, students whose own self-views outpaced the views that others held of them experienced relatively more emotional distress, despite their positive self-views. To the degree that positive distortions have been considered as mentally unhealthy (and, among others, Taylor & Brown,

1988, framed them as markers of mental health), they have usually been viewed as features of personality disorder, especially narcissistic and antisocial personality disorders (cf. Asendorpf & Ostendorf, 1998; Colvin, Block, & Funder, 1995). Although excessive self-enhancement may indeed characterize these personality conditions, results from my studies suggested that it also is associated with emotional distress. It is interesting to note that narcissistic personality symptoms (and even antisocial personality symptoms) are frequently associated with depressive symptomatology (Fava, Alpert, Borus, & Nierenberg, 1996). In summary, on the basis of these results, Joiner argued that Xenophon (as well as Swann, Faulkner, and Whitman) had it right all along: Interpersonal realism may be adaptive, whereas a distorted view, even if positive, may represent a manifestation of maladjustment.

Katz and Joiner (2002) have extended this line of thinking to relationship quality. They conducted three studies on heterosexual dating partners and same-sex roommates. In Study 1, people in stable dating relationships were most intimate with and somewhat more committed to partners when they perceived that partners evaluated them as they evaluated themselves (even if negative). In Study 2, men reported the greatest esteem for same-sex roommates who evaluated them in a self-verifying manner (even if negative). Results from Study 2 were replicated and extended to both male and female roommate dyads in Study 3. Therefore, with regard to both relationship quality and well-being, it appears that being known is at least as important as being praised.

Swann and colleagues (i.e., Giesler, Josephs, & Swann, 1996; Swann, 1990, 1996; Swann, De La Ronde, & Hixon, 1994; Swann, Griffin, Predmore, & Gaines, 1987; Swann, Pelham, & Chidester, 1988; Swann & Read, 1981a, 1981b; Swann, Stein-Seroussi, et al., 1992; Swann, Wenzlaff, Krull, & Pelham, 1992; Swann, Wenzlaff, & Tafarodi, 1992) have been by far the most active researchers in this area, and have conducted an array of experiments to document that self-verification theory has explanatory power regarding people's self-concepts, motivations, and interpersonal behaviors. In a typical study, for example, experimenters determine levels of self-esteem of potential research participants in pretesting sessions. Then all participants, whatever their self-esteem, are presented with a choice—they may interact with another interviewer who tends to provide warm feedback to research participants, one who tends to provide somewhat critical feedback to participants, or one who is relatively neutral. Among those with a positive self-concept, a huge majority elects to visit with the interviewer who tends to be warm and positive. Among those with a negative self-concept, however, a substantial proportion elects to see the "negative" interviewer, despite the equal availability of other, less negative interviewers. When asked about their choice, negative self-concept people often respond that they believe the negative interviewer is likely to understand them more fully and accurately.

In related research, it has been demonstrated that feedback that matches one's self-concept is more "attention-grabbing," more memorable, more rewarding, and more believable (Swann et al., 1987; Swann & Read, 1981a, 1981b; Swann, Stein-Seroussi, et al., 1992). In addition, a growing body of research suggests that people are more satisfied with and intimate in self-verifying relationships (Ritts & Stein, 1995; Schafer, Wickrama, & Keith, 1996; Swann et al., 1994).

DYSFUNCTIONAL MATE SELECTION

In chapter 3 on stress generation, we suggested that one means whereby stress can be generated is to choose badly when it comes to romantic and other important relationships. In fact, in Hammen's research, some evidence of the fact of dysfunctional mate selection emerged, in that depressed women tended to gravitate toward men who themselves were prone to psychopathology (an interesting avenue for future research is to examine assortative mating from the other perspective—that is, what is it about men with psychopathology, including antisocial behavior patterns, the leads them to "choose" depressed women?). Why might depressed people gravitate toward such partners? One possibility is that people select mates whom they view as similar to themselves (Newcomb, 1961), although this fails to explain why people with different forms of psychopathology tend to connect (e.g., a depressed person with an antisocial partner). Self-verification theory provides potentially another insight into the why of dysfunctional mate selection. That is, perhaps people choose badly as a by-product of choosing people who may see them as they see themselves. For people with negative self-concepts, this would mean choosing people who are likely to verify the negative self-view. If this occurs, a possible therapeutic implication for working with depressed people with a history of relationship problems is that change in negative self-views must precede attempts to change relationship patterns. Consider the case of Joe as an example.

Joe presented for treatment with symptoms of depression. On conducting a thorough interview, it became clear that Joe had had depression of varying intensity for several years (i.e., he met diagnostic criteria for double depression; chap. 2). Prior to seeking treatment, Joe had recently ended a 2-year relationship with a woman. Joe seemed inclined to discuss his relationship history in therapy, and his therapist agreed that would be a profitable route to pursue. Joe described how he was initially attracted to his "ex" because he "felt alive" around her. That is, she was exciting, flashy, and spontaneous ("lived on the edge"), and being around her tended to bring him at least temporary relief from his feelings of anhedonia and lethargy. Her freewheeling nature, frequent partying, and spending sprees sometimes made Joe feel uneasy, but he explained that he was willing to tolerate those excesses to enjoy the benefits of their relationship. Joe also indicated that she was verbally abusive to him at times, calling him "pathetic" or saying that he was "as exciting as watching the grass grow." Nevertheless, she moved in with Joe after a short time of dating. What had initially seemed like a good idea to him turned sour when Joe's house became the default location for her rowdy parties and Joe's savings account almost ran dry after she convinced him to foot the bill for an extravagant lifestyle. Eventually, Joe discovered that she had also maintained other romantic relationships while living in his house. With much hesitation and difficulty, Joe asked her to leave.

After several weeks in therapy and little symptom change, Joe arrived at his session with a different, and noticeably more cheerful, countenance. He discussed how he met a lady at a bar the previous week and how they had already been out twice. As the therapist listened to him, she immediately noticed the similarities between Joe's ex and his new romantic interest: both were intense, loud, and energetic; and both indicated to Joe that he was "stable," if not somewhat dull.

As is evident from this example, Joe was repeating the romantic pattern that previously caused him grief. What's more, Joe's partners were a "good fit" in his opinion because they confirmed his own self-views, while providing an initial lift from his depression. To the extent that Joe continued to view himself as "pathetic" or "boring," and continued to experience depressive symptoms, he was likely to experience one bad relationship after another. Recognizing this pattern, Joe's therapist wisely addressed his low self-esteem in treatment by emphasizing his positive qualities and working together to develop plans for improving areas that he identified as weaknesses.

So does this pattern of self-verification in relationships occur often? In one study on this issue, Joiner (1994), compared dormitory roommates who chose to live together with roommates who were assigned together by the university housing agency. He reasoned that if self-verification processes were at play, then those who chose one another should be more self-verifying with one another, as well as more satisfied with one another, as compared with those who were assigned to live together. Consistent with the research of Swann et al. (1994) Joiner found that those who chose to room together provided each other with more self-confirming ratings, and reported more relationship satisfaction, than those assigned together. This appeared to apply to roommate pairs in which one member had low self-esteem—that is, for low self-esteem participants, relationship satisfaction was higher if the roommate saw them as the participant saw him- or herself (i.e., negatively).

Joiner (1999a) also applied a similar logic to the depression-related phenomenon of suicide clustering and contagion. Joiner argued that suicide clusters (of a sort) appear to occur, and offered an account of why this may be, using principles drawn in part from self-verification theory.

Two general types of suicide cluster have been discussed in the literature; roughly, these can be classified as *mass clusters* and *point clusters*. Mass clusters are media-related (see also Phillips & Carstensen, 1986); point clusters occur on a local level. Joiner (1999a) concluded that the evidence for mass clusters (e.g., increased suicide in response to a well-publicized suicide) was unclear (Kessler, Downey, Milavsky, & Stipp, 1988) but that point clusters appear to exist. Point clusters involve victims who are relatively contiguous within the same point in space and time. Typically, they occur in an institutional setting (i.e., within a school or a hospital). A well-documented example was reported by Brent, Kerr, Goldstein, and Bozigar (1989). In a high school of approximately 1,500 students, 2 students died by suicide within 4 days. During a 3-week span that included the 2 completed suicides, 7 other students attempted suicide and several others reported suicidal ideation. It is important to note that the researchers found that 75% of the members of the cluster had at least one major psychiatric disorder, which had existed before the students' exposure to the suicides (i.e., they were vulnerable to begin with). Also of importance, victims' close friends appeared to develop suicidal symptoms more readily than students who were less close to victims—social contiguity was an important factor.

Haw (1994) reported a point cluster of several suicides among patients of a psychiatric unit. The patients had severe, chronic mental illness (e.g., schizophrenia), and most had ongoing therapeutic contact with the psychiatric unit. The author reported that the point cluster's occurrence may have stemmed from patients' valid perceptions that the future of the hospital was uncertain and that their access to medical staff was decreasing and ultimately threatened.

Why do clusters like those reported by Haw (1994) and by Brent et al. (1989) form? Contagion—the social or interpersonal transmission of suicidality from one victim to another—has been suggested as one possibility. But Joiner argued that with regard to many things, including disasters, accidents, and even illnesses, it is easy to imagine point clusters of victims for whom contagion of any sort is simply not operative.

As an example, consider the victims of the Chernobyl nuclear disaster. These unfortunate people were point-clustered, not because of any type of contagion among them, but because they were simultaneously exposed to radiation. In cases such as Chernobyl, the point-clustering of victims may be seen as the simultaneous effects of some pernicious, external influence, such as radiation, on a prearranged, contiguous group of people, such as those working at or living near the Chernobyl plant.

Joiner suggested that four sets of findings, taken together, indicate an alternative view to the usual contagion explanation. First, consistent with self-verification theory and with research on dysfunctional mate selection, people form relationships assortatively—that is, people who possess similar qualities or problems, including suicide risk factors, may be more likely to form relationships with one another. Second, severe negative life events represent risk factors for suicidality (and the suicidal behavior of a friend or peer qualifies as one of a large array of severe negative life events). Third, good social support (e.g., healthy family functioning) protects people from developing suicidal symptoms. Fourth, there exist several person-based risk factors for suicidality (e.g., personality disorder or other psychiatric disorder).

On the basis of these four lines of research, we suggest the possibility that people who are vulnerable to suicide may cluster before the occurrence of any overt suicidal stimulus (i.e., suicide point clusters may be, in a sense, prearranged by assortative processes), and, when a cluster is impinged on by severe negative events, including but not limited to the suicidal behavior of one member of the cluster, all members of the cluster are at increased risk for suicidality (which risk may be counteracted by good social support).

To illustrate, consider the two point clusters mentioned earlier. In the one described by Haw (1994), victims were assortatively related (through contact with the same psychiatric unit) on the basis, at least in part, of shared suicide risk factors (e.g., chronic mental illness). Vulnerable people were thus clustered (through contact with the agency), were exposed to severe stress (potential for dissolution of the agency; lack of access to important caregivers; for some, suicides of peers), and may not have been well buffered by good social support (those with chronic mental illness often have low social support; a main source of support may have been the agency, which was threatened).

Or, consider point clusters within high schools. Here, the prearrangement of clusters may occur in one or both of two ways. First, vulnerable adolescents may gravitate toward one another on the basis of mutual interests, compatible qualities, or similar problems (including vulnerability to and experience of psychopathology). In fact, Robbins and Conroy (1983) reported a cluster in which two adolescent suicides were followed by five attempts (all subsequently admitted to hospital) and one hospital admission for suicidal ideation. Of the six hospitalized adolescents, all had known each other, and all visited each other during their hospitalizations. Assortative relating appeared to play role in this cluster. A second possibility is that those students who for whatever reason (assortative or not) are socially contiguous to an adolescent who completes or attempts suicide experience suicidality at lower thresholds than those not socially contiguous to the victim (Brent et al., 1989). The mere occurrence, then, of suicidality in one adolescent may automatically arrange a potential cluster.

In an effort to provide further empirical support for these possibilities, Joiner (2003) conducted an analogue study among college roommates (both women and men). In some ways, college roommates are not ideal for the study of suicidal symptoms because, among other reasons, such symptoms are nonexistent or quite low in the usual group of undergraduates. An advantage, however, of the study of roommates is that it provides a type of natural laboratory to study issues involving assortative relating because, in many large universities, a sizable proportion of roommates are randomly assigned to each other (by the university housing agency) and the rest assortatively choose to room with each other. In the analogue study, Joiner expected that suicidal symptom levels would be more similar among roommate pairs who chose to live together than among those randomly assigned together. Furthermore, Joiner predicted that suicidality levels would be particularly similar among pairs that chose one another and who, by their own reports, had been experiencing negative life events that impinged on the roommate relationship. Results supported the view that prearranged clusters (here, assortatively arranged by choosing to live together) would share suicide-related features (here, similar symptoms), and that clustered suicidality would be especially likely in pairs that had been impacted by negative events.

The example of suicide clusters, then, may represent a specific example of dysfunctional relationship selection. This process fits well with a tenet of self-verification theory—people may gravitate toward others on the basis, at least in part, of the potential for others to affirm them.

Allowing that relationship choice may operate, at least in part, following assortative principles, so what? Does who you end up with really affect who you are and who you become?

In response to these questions, it is interesting to consider two issues. First and most obviously, those who end up in abusive relationships are clearly affected; here, relationship choice makes an enormous difference. And incidentally, neither we nor self-verification theory imply that people enjoy the pain of abusive relationships and therefore seek them out. That is, self-verification theory is not talking about masochism. Rather, the theory points out the intractable dilemma of people with low self-esteem. If they choose (by whatever means, conscious or not) affirming relationships, relationship dysfunction, including abuse, may be in the cards. If they choose healthier relationships, they may have to grapple with the feeling that these relationships, despite their healthy qualities, do not provide them with self-confirmation. This represents a very difficult problem that has obvious effects on people's well-being.

A second perspective on the impact of relationship choice comes from the research of Drigotas, Rusbult, Wieselquist, and Whitton (1999) on the charmingly named Michelangelo phenomenon. The Michelangelo phenomenon involves one's relationship partner as the "sculptor" of one's ideal self. On this view, one's relationship partner has considerable influence over whether one progresses toward—or retracts from—the person one ideally would like to be. The means of influence include things like enacting behaviors so that the best (or worst) is drawn out in one's partner. For example, to bring out the best in one's relationship partner, one could steer a group conversation toward topics about which the partner is particularly knowledgeable or animated. In summary, self-verification motives may explain whom one chooses in the first place; processes like the Michelangelo phenomenon may explain how this choice affects later functioning and well-being.

Despite its counter-intuitive view of the motivations of people with low self-esteem, self-verification theory has accrued substantial empirical support, including from studies looking at assortative relating issues. But, except for the patient excerpt that opened the chapter and the discussion of the depression-related phenomenon of suicide clusters, the applicability of self-verification theory to depression and its chronicity has not been discussed. The next section turns to this topic.

SELF-VERIFICATION: RELEVANCE TO DEPRESSION AND ITS CHRONICITY

Swann and colleagues have applied self-verification theory to depression among undergraduate men and women (Swann, Wenzlaff, Krull, & Pelham, 1992; Swann, Wenzlaff, & Tafarodi, 1992). They proposed that depressed people elicit interpersonal rejection because they gravitate to persons who evaluate them negatively. Consistent with this view, Swann, Wenzlaff, Krull, et al. (1992) found that depressed students sought more negative feedback from others, and were more rejected by others, as compared with nondepressed students (cf. Joiner, Alfano, & Metalsky, 1992, 1993; Joiner & Metalsky, 1995).

Similarly, we conducted two studies that demonstrated that undergraduates who expressed an interest in negative feedback and who received it were vulnerable to increases in depressive symptoms. In the first, students who indicated a desire to receive roommates' negative feedback—and who actually received it—were vulnerable to increases in depressive symptoms (Joiner, 1995). In the second, students who indicated a desire for negative feedback, and subsequently received a grade on a midterm exam that fell within their own personal "failure" range, displayed an increase in depressive symptoms (Pettit & Joiner, 2001a). Thus, there is growing evidence that people with depressive symptoms actively seek self-verification (i.e., negative feedback), often receive it, and may become depressed as a result.

However, this work has been done primarily with undergraduate students, relatively few of whom experience clinical levels of depression. Does the same pattern hold for those with more severe forms of depression? Research on the long-term relationship of self-esteem and depression indirectly suggests that the answer is yes. Consistent with the view that negative self-verification strivings make up a self-sustaining process implicated in depression chronicity, low self-esteem—the source of negative feedback-seeking—has been shown to be a predictor of depression chronicity. For example, Bothwell and Scott (1997) assessed depressed inpatients upon hospital admission, and then again 2 years later. Low self-esteem was a predictor of persistent depression, even when considered together with such clinical variables as severity of symptoms at admission (see also Miller, Ingham, Kreitman, & Surtees, 1987).

We, as well as others, have directly investigated the relevance of negative feedback-seeking to depression. For instance, Giesler et al. (1996) examined self-verification theory among clinically depressed participants. These researchers reported that 82% of clinically depressed adults chose unfavorable over favorable feedback, compared with 64% of nondepressed, low self-esteem participants, and 25% of nondepressed, high self-esteem participants. There appears to be something about clinical levels of depression that "ups the ante," even as compared with people with low self-esteem in the absence of other depressive symptoms.

Joiner, Katz, and Lew (1997) conducted a study on self-verification among youth psychiatric inpatients. They found that level of depressive symptoms was significantly associated with interest in negative feedback, as was depressive diagnostic status. Interest in negative feedback was also related to peer rejection, but only within relatively longer peer relationships, suggesting that negative feedback-seeking takes time to affect others. This result is consistent with Swann et al.'s (1994) proposition that self-verification is most consequential for relatively stable relationships as well as Coyne's (1976b) hypothesis that depressed people are caught up in a gradually deteriorating interpersonal context. Results like these indicate that the more stable and intimate the relationship, the more room there is for self-verification processes to operate.

Therefore, it appears that self-verification processes, such as seeking negative feedback from others, are involved in depression. But how might they be involved in chronicity? As demonstrated by the findings of Geisler et al. (1996), depressed people display a strong tendency to invite negative feedback. Negative feedback-seeking, in turn, clearly plays a role in generating interpersonal stress (e.g., criticism, rejection), as demonstrated by a number of empirical studies (e.g., Swann, Wenzlaff, Krull, et al., 1992). Depression may perpetuate itself as a function of encouraging negative feedback-seeking. That is, people with depressive symptoms may solicit negative appraisals (and get them), and the receipt of negative feedback may serve to maintain or amplify their depression. In this way, negative feedback-seeking represents a possible interpersonal mechanism for increased episode duration. Our studies on feedback-seeking as a vulnerability to depression (Joiner, 1995; Pettit & Joiner, 2001a) are consistent with this view. Namely, we found that requests for negative feedback, if honored (i.e., negative feedback provided), predisposed people to future depressive reactions.

With regard to the other two forms of depression chronicity, relapse and recurrence, negative feedback-seeking may also be relevant. In a relapse scenario, in which subclinical depressive symptoms may remain, these symptoms may encourage negative feedback, which in turn may generate stress, and thus facilitate a plunge back into clinical depression. In this sense, a treatment emphasis on full remission (i.e., to the point that no or very few depressive symptoms remain), and particularly on developing more positive self-views and skills for coping with stress, is crucial to avoid the pitfall of relapse.

With regard to strictly defined recurrence, in which a substantial symptom-free period has occurred, if low self-esteem exists, it may re-establish other depressive symptoms to clinical levels through negative feedback-seeking and consequent interpersonal stress. This would be consistent with the idea that episodes of depression scar self-esteem, such that those who experience depression display lower self-esteem even when recovered, which in turn promotes negative feedback-seeking. As is the case with scars on personality, however, the limited empirical evidence to date has not supported the notion that depression permanently erodes self-esteem (Butler, Hokanson, & Flynn, 1994; Lewinsohn et al., 1994; Lewinsohn, Steinmetz, Larson, & Franklin, 1981). We elaborate on this more in chapter 10.

Nevertheless, naturally occurring changes in self-esteem may precede the reintroduction of negative feedback-seeking. Consistent with this notion, we found that negative life events led to a subsequent drop in self-esteem, which in turn served as the driving force behind a greater desire for negative feedback (Pettit & Joiner, 2001b). As we have already argued, the presence of negative feedback-seeking, along with the reception of such feedback, would consequently place individuals at a greater risk for (re)developing depressive symptoms. In sum, negative feedback-seeking likely plays a role in each of the three forms of depression chronicity.

It is interesting to note that, as discussed in chapter 11, many of these same processes may be involved in the depression-related syndrome of *bulimia nervosa*, a persistent and recurrent disorder itself (Joiner, Heatherton, & Keel, 1997). Research indicated that despite serious concerns about body appearance, body shape, and weight, bulimic women were interested in the very feedback that would aggravate these concerns (i.e., negative feedback about physical appearance, weight, and so forth). Moreover, interest in negative feedback appeared to serve as a risk factor for development of later bulimic symptoms (Joiner, 1999b). Women who expressed interest in negative feedback at one point in time were likely to experience an increase in bulimic symptoms when they were assessed several weeks later.

SELF-VERIFICATION: RELEVANCE TO REMISSION

Clearly, negative feedback-seeking propagates depression chronicity. But can self-verification theory provide insight into why depression spontaneously remits? As in the last chapter, a similar speculation is offered, which represents a potentially fruitful avenue for future research. That is, as a depressed person becomes more symptomatic and begins to shut down, they may also stop negative feedback-seeking, giving the interpersonal effects of previous negative feedback-seeking time to fade. As these stressors remit, so may depressive symptoms. It would be interesting to determine if people in the depths of depression do less negative feedback-seeking than those with subclinical symptoms. (We are not aware of any research to date on whether severely depressed people seek negative feedback less than mildly and moderately depressed people.) In addition, it may be the case that an increase in self-esteem (which appears to drive feedback-seeking) resulting from a positive life event may actually change the valence of feedback-seeking from negative to more positive. As previously discussed, a drop in self-esteem appears to increase one's desire for negative feedback (Pettit & Joiner, 2001b); in theory, a rise in self-esteem may produce the opposite effect (i.e., increase one's desire for positive feedback), which may in turn promote a decrease of depressive symptoms.

SUMMARY

In summary, the need to maintain a sense of predictability and control may have untoward consequences for those with negative self-views. As originally described by Swann, Wenzlaff, Krull, et al. (1992), depressed persons may solicit appraisals that confirm their negative self-views, but do so at a high affective cost. Moreover, they often seek out others who are most likely to provide self-confirming feedback. If they receive the requested negative feedback, the result is likely more severe and lengthier depression. To the extent that self-views and negative feedback-seeking behaviors are stable, this interpersonal process may also hold explanatory power for relapse and recurrence of depression. As described in the next chapter, another interpersonal variable—excessive reassurance-seeking—appears to have similar effects as negative feedback-seeking, but through different means and motives.

5

EXCESSIVE REASSURANCE-SEEKING

We open this chapter with a general illustration of the importance of interpersonal connectedness in health and well-being. Then we discuss excessive reassurance-seeking, which we view as an attempt to maintain or increase connectedness. The problem with excessive reassurance-seeking, though, is that it may backfire by alienating others and maintaining and prolonging depressive symptoms.

INTERPERSONAL CONNECTEDNESS: PERCEIVED BURDENSOMENESS AND SUICIDALITY AS AN EXAMPLE

For a number of theorists, smooth interpersonal functioning has been framed as essential to health and well-being. For example, as discussed in the last chapter, Swann (1990) proposed that people value a smooth interpersonal life to such a degree that they strive to maintain "their place," even if this means seeking negative feedback.

Indeed, feeling valued by and connected with others is so important that we recently wondered whether suicidal behavior may represent, at least in part, an attempt to escape the feeling that one is a burden on loved ones. Suicidal patients often explain their suicidality in altruistic terms. That is, they may believe that they are a burden on their loved ones and that their death will be a relief for loved ones in that the burden will be removed. For example, a suicidal patient explained to me (Joiner) that his suicide would benefit his child because the pernicious influence of having a very depressed parent would be removed. Rationally identifying the ways that this father was very connected to and deeply valued by his child, as seen in the following excerpt, was important in therapeutically resolving his suicidal symptoms.

Me: You seem deeply concerned about your child. What really would be best for him? Let's go through pros and cons. What would be the positives for him if you died?

Patient: Like I said, he wouldn't be burdened by my depression.

Me: How specifically would that be a positive, in day-to-day life?

Patient: He wouldn't have to see me be a failure, wouldn't have to worry about what was wrong with me.

Me: Any other positives?

Patient: That's about it I guess.

Me: What about the negatives? What would be the cons for your son if you died?

Patient: He would miss me, miss having a father. I guess even a depressed father is better than a dead one. He might wonder why I did that, why I left him.

Me: How would that affect him day-to-day?

Patient: He wouldn't have a father to turn to when he's in trouble or needs advice; simple things like homework or later, things like girlfriends or work.

Me: Any other negatives?

Patient: He and I would both miss out on sharing his future—when he gets married, when he has kids, things like that.

Me: We've briefly been through pros and cons; what do you think?

Patient: The pros have it overall. I still believe I'm not a great parent, but doing my best for my son is better than giving up.

Me: Your list of pros and cons suggests that you're really important to your son.

Fortunately, by discussing the pros and cons of his suicide in terms of his son's well-being, this man changed his initial belief that his death would benefit his son. Nevertheless, the idea of altruistically motivated suicide has a long and rich history. It was a central notion in Durkheim's (1897) theorizing on suicide (i.e., self-sacrifice for the greater good among those deeply connected to their society). And there are interesting examples dating back to antiquity. For example, Lycurgus, who was to ancient Sparta what Thomas Jefferson was to the modern United States, exacted the promise from his people that they would maintain his laws until his return. He then departed to the Delphic oracle where, after checking with the oracle that his laws were good for his people (the oracle said yes), he starved himself to death, thus delaying his return indefinitely and assuring the perpetuity of his laws (or so he imagined).

More recently, researchers have found that among terminally ill patients a wish to hasten death (cf. euthanasia) is associated with a greater perception of being a burden on others (Kelly et al., 2003). Some evolutionary-psychological theorists have even asked whether suicide may have some adaptive value. On the surface this seems unlikely—how could ending one's life and one's reproductive potential be adaptive?

A model proposed by DeCatanzaro (1995) suggests that perceived liability to one's own gene pool is a precursor of completed suicide. This perspective argues that a *sense of* burdensomness toward kin may erode self-preservational motives, which in turn, fosters suicidality. (Let us be clear that we do *not* argue that suicide is in any way desirable; indeed, together with Rudd et al. [1996], we have worked hard to reduce it.) In tangential support of this perspective, DeCatanzaro obtained the predicted correlation between perceived burdensomeness toward family and suicidal symptoms, within several different samples (e.g., community participants, psychiatric participants). That is, persons with higher levels of suicidal symptoms felt that they were a greater burden on their family than those with fewer suicidal symptoms.

But how can we provide more persuasive support for this perspective? We reasoned that a compelling test of this view would involve the following features: (a) those who completed suicide would be compared with those who attempted suicide—a very stringent comparison; (b) the comparison would involve not only a sense of burdensomeness but also key variables already emphasized in the suicide literature (e.g., hopelessness, general emotional pain, interpersonal anger, and the like); and (c) the result would be that completers differ from attempters on the dimension of burdensomeness, but not on other dimensions.

Joiner et al. (2002) accomplished this by comparing the suicide notes left by those who completed with those who attempted suicide. A group of raters, initially blind to the hypotheses of the study and blind to whether passages were from completers or attempters, read each of the suicide notes and rated each (reliably) on the dimensions of burdensomeness, hopelessness, emotional pain, and interpersonal anger.

An interesting pattern of results emerged. Consistent with the possibility that perceived burdensomeness on others is a precursor to completed suicide, the burdensomeness dimension was the only one to significantly correlate with the variable reflecting completer versus attempter status. Even though things like hopelessness and emotional pain have been framed as essential in the suicide literature, they did not differentiate completers from attempters, whereas burdensomeness did. The direction of the correlation between burdensomeness and completer versus attempter status was such that completers endorsed more burdensomeness than did attempters. Moreover, the correlation between burdensomeness and completer versus attempter status was significantly greater than the correlations between the other rated dimensions and completer versus attempter status. In an additional study of suicide notes from those who died by suicide (no attempters in the sample), sense of burdensomeness predicted more lethal means of suicide (e.g., guns are relatively more lethal than overdose).

On the basis of these findings, Joiner et al. (2002) suggested the possibility that feeling valued (i.e., not a burden) by loved ones is so deeply important that in certain cases, people may even go to the lengths of suicide to avoid the perception that he or she burden their loved ones. Obviously, however, everyone who worries that he or she may be a burden does not consider suicide. In response to concern that one is not interpersonally valued or connected, many people simply ask others if this is the case. This seems a sensible solution; the problem is that if relying on others in this way becomes exaggerated, others may become annoyed or even rejecting.

Joiner et al. (2002) were intrigued by the association they found between feelings of burdensomeness toward loved ones and wanted to explore it in more depth. In particular, they wondered if the social nature of burdensomeness might be experienced differently across cultures and, if so, how that might affect the relation between burdensomeness and suicide. To address this question, they examined suicide notes left by individuals in a much more collectivistic society—the People's Republic of China (Pettit et al., 2002). Of note, the studies mentioned earlier included suicide notes from the United States and Germany, both highly individualistic societies. Examining the burdensomeness model of suicide in cultures with very distinct conceptualizations of the self and interpersonal relations speaks to the universality of the model.

In stark contrast to earlier findings, Pettit et al. (2002) found that those who were judged to be lowest on burdensomeness were the most likely to use more lethal means of suicide! How do we interpret this discrepancy in findings? It could be that burdensomeness is simply not that relevant to suicide, although that seems to be an unsatisfactory explanation. Rather, the discrepancy may be accounted for by striking differences in the cultural orientations of the samples. As made reference to, cultural individualism or collectivism refers to how individuals in societies see their role in relation to others. In individualistic cultures such as the United States, people see themselves as unique individuals, separate from their group, and value independence, achievement, and personal goals over in-group goals (Gudykunst, 1998). Collectivistic cultures such as the People's Republic of China, however, see individuals as members of a larger group. They value harmony and foster in-group goals, values, and needs (Kim, Sharkey, & Singelis, 1994). Although both individualistic and collectivistic cultures have in-groups, persons in collectivistic cultures tend to belong to more stable in-groups (usually their families), which are quite influential over them.

Within this cultural framework, a degree of burdensomeness (albeit mild) may actually reflect a sense of mutual obligation and duty to others, rather than carrying a negative connotation associated with draining the resources of one's family. Perhaps an underlying, mild sense of burdensomeness toward loved ones is constant within a highly collectivistic society and, therefore, is not explicitly expressed in the context of interpersonal communications such as suicide notes. That is, a low level of burdensomeness may be a naturally following consequence of the interdependent self-conceptions and connections to loved ones found in collectivistic societies. In contrast, the complete lack of burdensomeness in such a society may be a sign of detachment and isolation. A sense of detachment could be a tremendous stressor for an individual with an interdependent self-construal in which the self is defined by its relationship to others. Thus, this sense of disconnectedness may disrupt a person's sense of self and, consequently, be related to lethality of suicide. From this perspective, a moderate amount of burdensomeness in a collectivistic society might serve a protective function from suicidal behavior, as it represents attachment and mutual accountability to others.

As is evident from the foregoing discussion of perceived burdensomeness, interpersonal dependency and its relation to psychopathology is a complex issue that is highly influenced by cultural contexts. Despite cultural differences, however, it seems safe to conclude that when interpersonal relations go awry, the consequences are often damaging—and at times destructive.

EXCESSIVE REASSURANCE-SEEKING AS A SPECIFIC FORM OF INTERPERSONAL DEPENDENCY

The relation of interpersonal dependency to depression also has a long history. In much of the early theorizing about interpersonal dependency, depression, and depressed people's relationships, there was a distinctly hostile tone toward depressed people. Consider, for example, this sampling:

Their complaints are really "plaints" in the legal sense of the word . . . everything derogatory that they say of themselves at bottom relates to someone else . . . they give a great deal of trouble, perpetually taking offence and behaving as if they had been treated with great injustice.

—Sigmund Freud (1917/1951, p. 11)

These persons, in their continuous need of supplies that give sexual satisfaction and heighten self-esteem simultaneously, are 'love addicts.'

—Otto Fenichel (1945, p. 387)

By demonstrating their sufferings they try to obtain the 'narcissistic supplies' which they need, or they may exploit the depression for the justification of the various aggressive impulses toward external objects, thus closing the vicious circle.

—Edward Bibring (1953, p. 46)

Most of the time the husband tried to reassure his (depressed) wife of her competence…Sometimes he would become quite irritated and demand that she 'grow up' and act her age.

—Myrna M. Weissman and Eugene S. Paykel (1974, p. 93)

We wish to insist on the important and little realized fact that the depressed person…is always truly aggressive toward others through the very medium of the manifestation of his depression. His suffering is an accusation. His sense of incurableness is a reproach. His demands are perhaps humbling, but devastating. His depression is tyrannical. He wallows in suffering, whilst trying to enmesh his object in it as well.

—Sacha Nacht and Paul-Claude Racamier (1961, p. 486)

These clinicians (especially Nacht & Racamier, 1961) are frustrated and exasperated with depressed people. It was against this backdrop of wonder and frustration that Coyne's (1976b) account of depressive interpersonal behavior was proposed.

Coyne's interpersonal theory of depression (1976b) proposed that in response to doubts as to their own worth or as to whether others truly care about them, initially nondepressed individuals may seek reassurance from others. Others may provide reassurance, but with little effect, because potentially depressed people doubt the reassurance, attributing it instead to others' sense of pity or obligation. Potentially depressed people thus face a very difficult problem: They both need and doubt others' reassurance. The need is emotionally powerful and thus may win out (at least temporarily), compelling the potentially depressed individuals to again "go back to the well" for reassurance from others; even if received, however, the reassurance is again doubted, and the pattern is repeated. Because the pattern is repetitive and resistant to change, the increasingly depressed persons' significant others become confused, frustrated, and irritated and thus increasingly likely to reject the depressed persons and to become depressed themselves.

As the disruption of depressed persons' interpersonal environments occurs, the now depressed persons' symptoms are exacerbated. The theory thus describes an interpersonal process involving the gradual worsening of depressive symptoms within the crucible of close relationships, with implications for the causes, maintenance, exacerbation, consequences, treatment, and prevention of depression.

Together with our colleagues, we have engaged in a program of research geared toward empirically testing some implications of this theory. We have argued that excessive reassurance-seeking constitutes the theory's main ingredient in that it serves as a type of interpersonal vehicle that transmits the distress and desperation of depression from one person to another, with untoward consequences for all (e.g., Joiner, Alfano, & Metalsky, 1992). In this research, excessive reassurance-seeking is defined as the tendency to excessively seek assurances from others that one is lovable and worthy, and to persist in the asking even after such assurance has already been provided.

Our emphasis on excessive reassurance-seeking has produced two primary lines of research, one having to do with depression's *consequences*, the other, with depression's *causes*.

EXCESSIVE REASSURANCE-SEEKING AS AN EXPLANATION OF DEPRESSION'S CONSEQUENCES

The association between depression and social functioning is well-documented; as emphasized in chapter 2, depressed people often face negative interpersonal outcomes (see also Segrin & Dillard, 1992, for a review). But there are a few studies in which people have not reacted as negatively to depressed persons (e.g., King & Heller, 1984; McNiel, Arkowitz, & Pritchard, 1987).

We wondered whether depression might be associated with interpersonal problems, but particularly under certain interpersonal conditions (e.g., when the depressed person is excessive in reassurance-seeking). Our thesis was that the aversive properties of depression may not be interpersonally aversive unless clearly and repeatedly signaled to other people. Moreover, we suggested that a signal that implicates others in the development of the problem (e.g., "you don't *really* love me anymore, do you?"), as well as overtaxes others by demands to solve the problem, would be interpersonally disruptive. In our view, excessive reassurance-seeking is this signal. We have focused on two categories of consequences: interpersonal rejection and "contagious" depression.

Interpersonal Rejection

Along with our colleagues, we have conducted studies in which people who report depressive symptoms are negatively evaluated by significant others, but only if they are also excessive in reassurance-seeking. For example, Katz and Beach (1997a) studied women involved in heterosexual dating relationships. They found that women with depressive symptoms were negatively evaluated by their dating partner, but only if they were high in reassurance-seeking. (And there were negative evaluations of dating partners—it appears that being in a dating relationship is no safeguard against negative evaluation or reporting of negative evaluation to researchers!)

Benazon (2000) reported a replication of the rejection effect among a sample of married dyads, each with one clinically depressed member. Excessive reassurance-seeking on the part of the depressed member predicted the partner's negative evaluation of the depressed member, even beyond variance contributed by a very strong correlate of negative spousal evaluation, marital dissatisfaction.

Joiner and Metalsky (1995; see also Joiner et al., 1992; Joiner, Alfano, & Metalsky, 1993) obtained results among college men and women and their same-gender roommates that converge with those of Katz and Beach (1997a). Specifically, students who experienced depressive symptoms were negatively evaluated by their roommates, if the student was excessive in reassurance-seeking. Joiner and Metalsky (1995) found that the same did not hold for anxious students—they were not likely to be negatively evaluated by roommates, even if excessive in reassurance-seeking. On this basis, Joiner and Metalsky argued that there is something special about the interpersonal effect of depression specifically (as opposed to symptoms generally). It may be that depressive symptoms, as opposed, for example, to anxious symptoms, are particularly "heavy" on others, in that they convey a sense of desperation, burden, and hopelessness that others have difficulty responding to. Excessive reassurance-seeking amplifies this signal. Consider the following hypothetical scenario between two male college roommates:

Nondepressed Roommate:	Hey, we need one more guy to join us before we can sign up for the intramural basketball league—are you in?
Depressed Roommate:	I don't know, you know, I'm pretty tired. You guys would probably regret having me on your team, anyway. Do you think I'm good enough?
Nondepressed Roommate:	Yeah, man—it's just intramurals; it's not like Michael Jordan and Yao Ming are out there.
Depressed Roommate:	I don't have much energy to get up and down the court. You've seen me shoot—do you think I could knock down some shots in a game?
Nondepressed Roommate:	Probably.
Depressed Roommate:	I don't know, it's so hard for me to focus or concentrate these days . . . I'd probably miss wide-open shots, and then you guys would hate me for losing the game. Do you really think I'm good enough?
Nondepressed Roommate:	Look, man, I'm not a basketball talent scout. I just need a 'yes' or 'no' from you.

Depressed Roommate: See, you're already getting frustrated with me.
Imagine how mad you would be if I blew a game.
There's no way I'm taking that risk.

As is evident in this example, the depressed man wanted his roommate to reassure him that he was good enough to be an accepted member of the team, and his roommate initially provided that assurance. But the depressed man's repeated requests for reassurance, along with his expressions of pessimism (connected to his depressive symptoms), led to increasing frustration in his roommate. The consequence, unfortunately, was that the depressed man felt rejected and made a decision that would further decrease his social and physical activities.

In addition to couples and college roommates, Joiner (1999b) extended these findings to an even younger population. Among a group of psychiatric inpatients between the ages of 7 and 17 years, those who frequently sought reassurance reported interpersonal difficulties, particularly when also experiencing depressive symptoms. Here again, specificity was noted: It was depressive symptoms specifically, not emotional distress in general, that appeared to drive the effect. This is not to say that a measure of reassurance-seeking and clinginess represent pathology among children. In fact, it is quite normal for children to demonstrate a degree of clinging behavior to their parents. Whereas children may naturally express a greater degree of reassurance-seeking than adults, extreme excesses do serve as a vulnerability to depression.

Taken as a whole, these studies are consistent with our view that depression, when "delivered" to significant others through excessive reassurance-seeking, may generate interpersonal difficulty. Research on another interpersonal consequence, contagious depression, is described next.

Contagious Depression

One need not have a background in the mental health profession to understand that our moods are influenced by those around us. For centuries, writers have noted the interpersonal impact of others on our mood. Take, for example, the following passages from the Biblical book of Proverbs:

An anxious heart weighs a man down, but a kind word cheers him up.
—New International Version (Prov. 12:25)

Pleasant words are a honeycomb, sweet to the soul and healing to the bones.
—New International Version (Prov. 16:24)

As Solomon, the author of these proverbs, noted approximately 3,000 years ago, the expression of positive emotions has the capacity to induce positive moods in others. Likewise, he implied that displays of negative emotions have the power to produce the opposite effect:

Better a dry crust with peace and quiet than a house full of feasting, with strife.

—New International Version (Prov. 17:1)

Better to live in a desert than with a quarrelsome and ill-tempered wife.

—New International Version (Prov. 21:19)

The notion that irritable or depressed persons have an adverse effect on those in their immediate surroundings has existed for millennia. It was taken a step beyond common knowledge in the 1960s, when Schachter and Singer (1962) conducted a study on the interpersonal transmission of mood. In their seminal investigation, Schachter and Singer divided participants into four groups: (a) those who received an injection of epinephrine and were informed that they might experience symptoms of physiological arousal, (b) those who received a placebo injection and were told they might experience symptoms of physiological arousal, (c) those who received an injection of epinephrine without being told about possible symptoms, and (d) those who received a placebo injection and were not informed about possible side effects. Next, they placed each participant in a room with a confederate (i.e., an actor) who overtly expressed either elation or anger. They found that individuals who experienced physiological arousal from the epinephrine but were not informed about potential side effects, endorsed and expressed emotional feelings similar to the emotionally laden behaviors of the confederate with whom they interacted. For example, participants aroused by epinephrine, but unaware of the cause of their arousal, reported feeling happy if they were placed with a confederate acting cheerfully, or reported feeling angry if placed with a confederate displaying symptoms of anger. However, participants who were informed about the cause of their arousal were less likely to adopt the emotional state of their counterparts. Schachter and Singer (1962) summarized their findings with the following statement:

> Given a state of physiological arousal for which an individual has no immediate explanation, he (sic) will label this state and describe his (sic) feelings in terms of the cognitions available to him (sic). To the extent that cognitive factors are potent determiners of emotional states, it should be anticipated that precisely the same state of physiological arousal could be labeled "joy" or "fury" or "jealousy" or any of a great diversity of emotional labels depending on the cognitive aspects of the situation. This attribution defines what we refer to as emotion, and also determines the relative intensity and valence of the physiological arousal. (p. 398)

In this groundbreaking work, Schachter and Singer (1962) provided preliminary evidence that mood may indeed be transmitted from one person to another. Since then, numerous other studies have been conducted on *mood contagion*, focusing on specific moods, behaviors, and processes under which mood contagion occurs (e.g., mimicry of nonverbal behaviors; Hatfield,

Cacioppo, & Rapson, 1993). Particular emphasis has been placed on contagious depression. Joiner and Katz (1999) reviewed the literature on contagious depression, and concluded that 40 findings from 36 separate studies provided substantial overall support for the proposition that depressed mood, and particularly, depressive symptoms, are contagious.

On the basis of two studies, we believe that excessive reassurance-seeking may be implicated in depression contagion. Katz, Beach, and Joiner (1999), in a study of college students and their dating partners, reported that partners' depression levels significantly corresponded, even controlling for relationship satisfaction. Furthermore, partners of those who reported both high levels of reassurance-seeking and of depressive symptoms were especially likely to report substantial depressive symptomatology themselves. In a study of college roommates, Joiner (1994) reported a very similar finding: Even controlling for negative events that may affect both members of a roommate pair, one roommate's depression level prospectively predicted the other's, particularly if reassurance-seeking was high. This effect applied to depressive symptoms, not merely to general emotional distress.

Contagious depression is thus a reasonably well-documented phenomenon. Moreover, excessive reassurance-seeking may explain, in part, when depression will be interpersonally transmitted. Taken together with research on interpersonal rejection, the work on contagious depression suggests that the joint operation of depressive symptoms and excessive reassurance-seeking disaffects significant others, by distancing them actually (e.g., ending the relationship) or functionally (e.g., emotional unavailability due to frustration or to contagious depression).

EXCESSIVE REASSURANCE-SEEKING AS A VULNERABILITY FACTOR FOR DEPRESSION

It is clear that excessive reassurance-seeking leads to some of the undesirable consequences of depression, such as interpersonal rejection or the development of depression in others. But does excessive reassurance-seeking play a role in causing depression? The notion of causality is troublesome in the context of nonexperimental psychopathology research, but we can say with greater certainty whether a behavior or condition serves as a vulnerability factor for psychopathology. Garber and Hollon (1991) developed a quite useful heuristic for establishing the presence of a risk factor, focusing on three necessary criteria for putative vulnerability factors. First, a vulnerability factor and the syndrome in question should *covary* (i.e., be related to one another). Second, a vulnerability factor should temporally precede the syndrome. And third, the relationship between a vulnerability and an outcome should be nonspurious (e.g., it should not be better accounted for by a third variable). With regard to excessive reassurance-seeking and depression, we examine each of these criteria in turn.

Covariation

In all samples studied to date, a significant correlation between excessive reassurance-seeking and depression has emerged. These samples include over 3,000 participants from a variety of settings (e.g., general college students, Air Force cadets, various clinical samples, women in heterosexual dating relationships; Joiner & Metalsky, 2001), thus supporting the universality of the association. It should be noted, however, that there is not a 1:1 correspondence between reassurance-seeking and depression. Instead, the two variables are only modestly correlated.

Why isn't the association between excessive reassurance-seeking and depressive symptoms higher? One would only anticipate a strong correlation if excessive reassurance-seeking were hypothesized to be a necessary or sufficient cause of depression. However, excessive reassurance-seeking is hypothesized to be a contributory cause rather than a necessary or sufficient cause of depressive symptoms. Modest correlations between excessive reassurance-seeking and depression are thus expectable, in that excessive reassurance-seeking is viewed as one contributory cause working in tandem with other causes (e.g., interpersonal stress, negative partner reactions) to induce depression.

Temporal Antecedence

High reassurance-seeking at one point in time may represent a harbinger for the development of depressive symptoms at a later point in time, consistent with the criterion of temporal antecedence. Joiner and Schmidt (1998) tested this prediction in a study of 1,005 Air Force cadets (predominately men) who were undergoing basic training. Participants completed measures of excessive reassurance-seeking and depressive symptoms before basic training and again completed symptom measures following basic training. Consistent with the criterion of temporal antecedence, baseline levels of reassurance-seeking were significantly predictive of increases from baseline to follow-up in depressive symptoms.

Consistent with earlier remarks about contributory versus sufficient and necessary causes, three studies have taken a diathesis–stress approach to the relation between excessive reassurance-seeking and future depression, framing stress and reassurance-seeking as interactive, contributory causes of depressive symptoms. For example, Joiner and Metalsky (2001) showed that high reassurance-seeking college students, when faced with the stress of an unsatisfactory grade on a midterm exam, exhibited depressive reactions, whereas low reassurance-seeking students did not. Similarly, we found that high reassurance-seeking students, when paired with a roommate who viewed them negatively, experienced increased depressive symptoms, but low reassurance-seeking students did not. Others studies have obtained very similar findings: High reassurance-seeking women, when in a dating relationship with a man who viewed them negatively, reported increases in depressive symptoms, but low reassurance-seeking women, even if in a devaluing relationship, did not experience depression increases (Katz et al., 1999).

Potthoff, Holahan, and Joiner (1995), too, found that excessive reassurance-seeking was a contributor, together with interpersonal stress (e.g., disagreements with friends), to subsequent depressive symptoms. Using structural equation modeling techniques, these researchers reported that latent variables corresponding to excessive reassurance-seeking and to interpersonal stress were contributors to prospective increases in depression.

Taken together, these studies support the contention that excessive reassurance-seeking satisfies the criterion of temporal antecedence in its relation to depressive symptoms as a contributory cause. Note that none of these studies examined clinical forms of depression, leaving open the question of whether excessive reassurance-seeking is relevant regarding more severe forms of depression. We address this question (at least in part) in the following section on nonspuriousness.

Nonspuriousness

Unlike the criteria of covariation and temporal antecedence, which are clearly defined and have specific statistical tests associated with them, the criterion of nonspuriousness makes up a broader category. Briefly, the criterion is a succinct way of saying that one needs to rule out as many alternative explanations as possible for the relation between the proposed vulnerability factor and the syndrome in question.

An important form of nonspuriousness is diagnostic specificity (Hollon, Kendall, & Lumry, 1986); that is, that the relation between a hypothesized causal factor and a psychopathological syndrome not be attributable to the relation of either the hypothesized factor or the syndrome to a distinct clinical phenomenon. For example, the hypothesis that excessive reassurance-seeking is a risk factor for depression would be undermined if it were shown that excessive reassurance-seeking and depression were related merely because both are related to anxiety.

This instance of nonspuriousness informed three studies conducted by Joiner and Metalsky (2001). In the first of these studies, undergraduates who received a diagnosis of major depression were compared with those who received other clinical diagnoses, and to those who received no diagnosis. Consistent with the view that diagnostic specificity may characterize the relation between excessive reassurance-seeking and depression, depressed undergraduates obtained significantly higher reassurance-seeking scores than undergraduates with other diagnoses, and those with no diagnosis. This same result held when depressed undergraduates were specifically compared with anxiety-disordered undergraduates.

In a study of almost all male (94%) VA psychiatric inpatients, Joiner and Metalsky (2001, Study 1) obtained similar findings: Patients with a diagnosis of depression obtained higher reassurance-seeking scores than other patients, including those diagnosed with schizophrenia and severe anxiety disorders. In a study of youth psychiatric inpatients (Joiner & Metalsky, 2001, Study 2), the same result occurred, this time in a comparison of depressed youth and those with externalizing disorders such as conduct disorder, attention-deficit/hyperactivity disorder, or their co-occurrence. Taken together, these three studies present good evidence of some specificity of excessive reassurance-seeking to depression, in keeping with the criterion of nonspuriousness.

Joiner and Schmidt (1998) combined the criteria of temporal antecedence and nonspuriousness in their study of Air Force cadets in basic training. As noted, in keeping with the criterion of temporal antecedence, high reassurance-seeking cadets were more vulnerable to prospective increases in depressive symptoms than were their low reassurance-seeking counterparts. This same result did not apply to increases in anxious symptoms. Consistent with the criteria of both temporal antecedence and nonspuriousness, excessive reassurance-seeking served as a risk for future depressive symptoms, but not for future anxious symptoms.

In summary, research to date lends good support to the view that excessive reassurance-seeking may represent one contributory cause of depression. With regard to the criteria of covariation, temporal precedence, and nonspuriousness, our program of work on excessive reassurance-seeking has yielded positive findings.

WHERE DOES EXCESSIVE REASSURANCE-SEEKING COME FROM?

Now that we have seen that excessive reassurance-seeking exists, we turn to its origins. The developmental origins of excessive reassurance-seeking remain obscure, but a few speculations are offered to spur future research. First, excessive reassurance-seeking may be more common among those high in the (partly) genetically determined personality traits of both neuroticism and extroversion. Indeed, these two traits capture much of the essence of excessive reassurance-seeking, which includes affiliative elements (cf. extroversion), as well as elements of self-doubt, nervousness, and the like (cf. neuroticism). It is interesting to note that we have data showing that excessive reassurance-seeking is positively correlated with both shyness (cf. neuroticism) and sociability (cf. extroversion; Joiner & Metalsky, 2001). The link with shyness may be interesting to explore in light of the work of Gray (1987) and Kagan and Snidman (1991) on behavioral inhibition. One might expect, for example, that behaviorally inhibited children are more likely than others to develop an interpersonal style characterized by excessive reassurance-seeking. Furthermore, other elements of excessive reassurance-seeking are also partly heritable, including low perceived affection (Hur & Bouchard, 1995) and low perceived support (Bergeman, Plomin, Pederson, McClearn, & Nesselroade, 1990).

Second, it is possible that family-of-origin experiences are relevant in understanding the development of excessive reassurance-seeking. In particular, Cummings (1994; see also Cummings & Davies, 1999) demonstrated that lack of felt emotional security is implicated in developmental psychopathology and is related to exposure to marital conflict in the home. Just as lack of felt emotional security may be linked to a learning history in the family of origin, so too might tendencies toward excessive reassurance-seeking. For example, work on emotional insecurity suggests that children who grow up in homes characterized by high marital conflict are more likely (a) to display heightened fear, distress, and vigilance in interpersonal settings; (b) to regulate and overregulate their exposure to high negative affect; and (c) to develop insecure representations of family and interpersonal relations (Davies & Cummings, 1998). Although the link between lack of emotional security in childhood and excessive reassurance-seeking has not been examined empirically, the early development of fear and distress in close interpersonal relations, as well as an insecure representation of interpersonal relations, may translate into the thoughts and fears that drive reassurance-seeking. More important, excessively seeking reassurance from others may represent an overregulation of exposure to negative affect in relationships. In other words, people may seek assurances to an excessive degree as a means of promoting positive emotional experiences in their close interpersonal relations. Unfortunately, however, it often backfires.

The more proximal precursors of heightened reassurance-seeking may be negative life events and associated increases in anxiety and decreases in self-esteem. Joiner, Katz, and Lew (1999) hypothesized that the occurrence of negative events engenders a sense of concern and uncertainty about one's self (cf. self-esteem) and about the future (cf. anxiety). In response to increased anxiety and to the threat to self-esteem, people may engage in reassurance-seeking, to assuage their sense of doubt about the self and about the future. Results supported the view that negative life events predicted an increase in reassurance-seeking as a function of increases in anxiety and decreases in self-esteem.

Even more proximally, excessive reassurance-seeking may represent, in part, a quest for certainty. Uncertainty about the self and the world may be a prime motivation for excessive reassurance-seeking (Joiner, Katz, et al., 1999). Such uncertainty could lead to preference for more revealing, "diagnostic" questions of others (Hildebrand-Saints & Weary, 1989), as well as a greater tendency toward perseverative questioning of others (cf. the *excessive* component of excessive reassurance-seeking). In this scenario, minor indications of partner dissatisfaction may induce perseverative questioning, leading to withdrawal and rejection by significant others.

For example, imagine the following scenario in which Jim and his girl-friend Theresa have been talking about their favorite movies. Theresa yawns and looks away at one point in the conversation, and Jim wonders if she is tired of talking with him.

Jim: You seemed bored. Do you enjoy talking with me like this?

Theresa: Of course I enjoy it—why would you think I don't?

Jim: Well, you seemed like you weren't into the conversation, or that you just wanted it to end. That made me start to wonder if you really enjoy when we talk. Do you?

Theresa: Sure I enjoy our conversations; I wouldn't be with you if I didn't.

Jim: Really? You're not just saying that, right?

Theresa: No, Jim.

Jim: I don't know. . .it just seemed like you were getting bored listening to me talk. Deep down inside are you starting to get tired of me?

Theresa: [Exasperated] What is it with you, Jim? I already told you how I feel. You can either believe me or not.

What Jim wanted from this conversation was to be reassured that Theresa liked him and enjoyed his company. Unfortunately, the excessive nature of his questioning led her to become frustrated with him and essentially drew their conversation to an unpleasant end.

IS REASSURANCE-SEEKING NECESSARILY A BAD THING?

We have been careful to use the term *excessive reassurance-seeking*, to emphasize a key distinction between this variable and one involving the acquisition of social support, which has been shown to be protective vis-à-vis health problems (e.g., Collins, Dunkel-Schetter, Lobel, & Scrimshaw, 1993). We suggest that there is a considerable difference between the routine and adaptive solicitation of social support across distinct situations, and the repeated and persistent seeking of reassurance within the same situation, even when reassurance has already been provided. This distinction is borne out by the positive association between support-seeking and health in the social support literature, and the negative association between excessive reassurance-seeking and mental health in our program of research.

RELEVANCE TO CHRONICITY AND REMISSION

How might excessive reassurance-seeking lead to and propagate depression? Research is still needed in this area, but we present a couple of promising possibilities. First, high reassurance-seeking may promote depression because people who engage in this behavior become demoralized as their reassurance-seeking does not produce hoped-for results. That is, the high reassurance-seeking person struggles to gain others' comfort but becomes disappointed and discouraged with their responsiveness. A second possibility is that as depression mounts, excessive reassurance-seeking becomes difficult for significant others who withdraw from or reject the reassurance-seeking person, which in turn, encourages more symptoms still. This relates back to the interpersonal consequences of excessive reassurance-seeking that we discussed earlier in the chapter. Ongoing reverberations of depression, reassurance-seeking, and interpersonal problems thus appear to be self-perpetuating, perhaps accounting, in part, for the chronic nature of depression (i.e., lengthy and recurrent depressive episodes).

With regard to episode duration, it is easy to imagine how both dissatisfaction with others' assurances and withdrawal from others might exacerbate and maintain depressive symptoms within a given episode. To the extent that reassurance-seeking remains stable even as depressive symptoms improve, it may also represent a relatively persistent vulnerability for relapse and recurrence of depression.

In contrast to the empirical attention devoted to the intrapsychic and interpersonal consequences of excessive reassurance-seeking, less is known about how it may relate to the remission of depression. We offer the following as potential pathways from reassurance-seeking to remission, while underscoring the need for systematic research in this area. As discussed in the previous two chapters, increasing severity of depression tends to dampen social behaviors or all sorts (both maladaptive and adaptive). In this sense, further declines into depression may mute interpersonal behaviors to the point that individuals no longer solicit assurances from others. Without the aversive interpersonal experience of receiving excessive requests for reassurance, others may come to the aid of depressed persons, thereby solidifying social support and reducing depressive symptoms.

Another possibility is that depressed persons may simply begin to accept (at least some of) the assurances provided by others. In this scenario, either a change in others' behaviors or a change in depressed persons' perceptions may occasion the acceptance of comfort as genuine, which presumably would cut down on interpersonal friction and boost self-esteem. We expect that if this indeed happens, it likely initially occurs within certain domains of depressed persons' lives, and gradually spreads to other areas. For instance, a depressed man may maintain that he has deficiencies in a number of areas but eventually agree with his spouse's assurances that he is a loving, caring father. The positive emotions and attendant behaviors from viewing himself as a "good dad" may spill over into other areas of his life, leading to an upward spiral of emotions and behaviors. In the context of therapy, such a process may go as follows:

Therapist:	. . . so you've identified your caring, attentive behaviors toward your children as a sign that you're a pretty good dad?
Patient:	In that regard, yes.
Therapist:	And your wife helped you arrive at that conclusion?
Patient:	Yes, you know, she would tell me how good I was with the kids, how devoted I was as a father, and things like that. I guess I didn't pay much attention to it before, but I've noticed it more recently.
Therapist:	And that's something you take pride in.
Patient:	Well, yes. I have my fair share of problems, but at least I can say that I'm doing okay as a father.
Therapist:	Good, I'm glad to see you acknowledge your strengths. I wonder if there are other things you do well that you 'didn't pay much attention to before'?
Patient:	People at work are always saying that I'm good at. . .

In this example, the man's frequent reassurances from his wife eventually "stuck" with him and opened the door for considering other areas from which he could derive positive self-esteem. To the extent that he does so, his depression is likely to improve.

SUMMARY

In this chapter we described excessive reassurance-seeking and its relation to depression chronicity. We argued that excessive reassurance-seeking is implicated as a potential contributory cause of depressive symptoms and is involved in generating negative interpersonal outcomes, such as interpersonal rejection and contagious depression. These negative interpersonal outcomes likely increase depressed persons' sense of demoralization and hopelessness, increase the level of dependency (and strain) on remaining relationships, and may intensify reassurance-seeking among depressed persons' limited social supports. The result is likely the maintenance or, worse yet, the exacerbation of depressive symptoms. In the next chapter, we explore how interpersonal dependency needs compel another behavior implicated in the propagation of depression: conflict avoidance.

6

INTERPERSONAL
CONFLICT AVOIDANCE

To avoid criticism do nothing, say nothing, be nothing.
—Elbert Hubbard

In the previous three chapters on self-propagatory processes in depression, we focused on active behaviors emitted by depressed persons (i.e., stress generation, negative feedback-seeking, and excessive reassurance-seeking). In this chapter, we focus on a passive, but still damaging, set of behaviors that similarly contributes to the prolongation of depression.

General avoidance often weaves its way through the fabric of depressed persons' lives. One of my (Pettit's) first clinical supervisors proposed that avoidance captures the true essence of depression. He argued that depression, at its root, is simply the opposite of participation. Although this is surely an overly broad and simplistic conceptualization of depression, it highlights the idea that depressed people are often passive recipients of life, rather than active participants in life. Moreover, depressed persons tend not only to inertly accept life's occurrences but also to commonly avoid behaviors or situations that may be perceived as unpleasant.

But isn't this something that we as human beings all do? Avoiding unpleasant situations seems like a natural means by which to maximize enjoyment and minimize distress. To a certain extent, that is true. Consider the case of an individual who avoids attending social gatherings at a particular friend's house because of highly allergic reactions to the friend's cat. In this case, the avoidant behavior serves an adaptive function; namely, it promotes physical well-being and prevents the discomfort associated with a severe allergic reaction. The negative consequences resulting from this avoidance behavior are a possible reduction in social activities and missing out on the enjoyment derived from such social gatherings. Assuming the individual has a range of social contacts and activities, however, avoiding the gatherings at one friend's house would not be expected to produce interpersonal or emotional distress.

In the case of depressed persons, however, avoidant behavior may hold more pernicious consequences. For one thing, depressed persons often have less developed social networks (e.g., Costello, 1982), which magnifies the effects of missing out on the social activities that are present in their lives. (Of note, this is similar to how limited social resources intensify the effects of reassurance-seeking and negative feedback-seeking on existing relationships; see also chaps. 4 and 5.) But more important, the aversive effects of avoidance in the context of depression are largely related to the nature of the avoidance engaged in by depressed persons.

As mentioned earlier, depressed persons often exhibit generalized problems with social avoidance. What's more, evidence suggests that depression is frequently preceded by anxiety of some form (e.g., Kovacs, Gastonis, Paulauskas, & Richards, 1989). Anxiety, of course, is characterized by avoidance of some feared object, cognition, or event. Although anxiety and general social avoidance certainly play a role in depression, a more specific form of social avoidance appears more pertinent to the propagation of depression: Avoidance of interpersonal conflict. We argue that depression is characterized, and even propagated, by a pattern of interpersonal conflict avoidance.

INTERPERSONAL AVOIDANCE IN THE CONTEXT OF DEPRESSION

It is well-known that depression is associated with a number of factors related to interpersonal avoidance. Four such factors (i.e., low assertiveness, social withdrawal, general avoidance, and shyness) have specifically been identified as interpersonal characteristics of a large number of depressed individuals.

Low Assertiveness

Ball, Otto, Pollack, and Rosenbaum (1994) found that a lack of assertiveness was a predictor of major depression, even controlling for a very strong clinical predictor, past history of depression (see also Youngren & Lewinsohn, 1980). Low assertiveness, in essence, is driven by an individual's desire to avoid interpersonal conflict. Two characteristics of assertive behaviors may be of great difficulty to depressed persons. First, asserting oneself requires active engagement with others, which forces the depressed person to overcome feelings of general social anxiety, in addition to overcoming the lethargy and indifference that retard activity in general among such individuals. Second, and more important, assertive behaviors entail making explicit requests of others. Social conventions dictate that requests naturally merit a response, be it positive or negative, and it is at this point that the interpersonal stage for potential disharmony is set. To reach this point, one must conquer general social anxiety and place himself or herself in a position that allows for the possibility of negative, rejecting responses from others. This latter possibility appears to be the sticking point for many depressed persons. That is, depressed persons overcome social inhibition and inertia but are often unwilling to knowingly make themselves vulnerable to interpersonal rejection (although they often engage in behaviors that unknowingly place themselves at greater risk of rejection, such as excessive reassurance-seeking). Later in this chapter, we discuss the reasons for, as well as the benefits and drawbacks of, an interpersonal approach that limits opportunities for social rejection.

Social Withdrawal

As alluded to previously, social withdrawal has also been associated with depression and related disorders. It is not surprising, therefore, that clinical manifestations of social withdrawal have been linked to the range of depressive disorders. One such disorder is social phobia, which involves a marked and persistent fear of social or performance situations in which embarrassment may occur (American Psychiatric Association, 1994). Pini, Cassano, Simonini, and Savino (1997) found that social phobia, an avoidance-related syndrome, was more highly associated with major depression than closely related disorders, even dysthymia and bipolar disorder. Others report that social phobia is associated with more chronic forms of depression. For instance, Sanderson, DiNardo, Rapee, and Barlow (1990) found that over 20% of social phobics also met criteria for dysthymia. Hence, it appears as though depression and social withdrawal frequently co-occur, although it is not yet possible to draw a causal relationship between these two variables. It is interesting to note that social phobia is driven by the same fear that limits depressed persons' willingness to engage in assertive behaviors: fear of interpersonal rejection.

Generalized Avoidance

Another similar disorder linked to depression is *avoidant personality disorder*. The *Diagnostic and Statistical Manual of Mental Disorders*, (4th ed.;

American Psychiatric Association, 1994) defines avoidant personality disorder as "a pervasive pattern of social inhibition, feelings of inadequacy, and hypersensitivity to negative evaluation . . ." (p. 664). As can be seen through its definition, avoidant personality disorder is strikingly similar to social phobia. It is distinguished, however, by a more chronic course and a more pervasive influence. That is, avoidant personality disorder may affect more areas of an individual's life than social phobia. Consequently, avoidant personality represents a general lifestyle of avoidance, particularly in interpersonal relationships. Alpert, Uebelacker, McLean, and Nierenberg (1997) reported an association between avoidant personality and depression. Furthermore, they found that depressed people with avoidant personality disorder were more likely than other depressed people to report an early age of depression onset. As mentioned earlier, early age of onset is a marker of depression chronicity. Thus, evidence suggests that (a) a general level of interpersonal avoidance is frequently associated with depression and (b) high levels of such avoidance may be associated with a chronic course of depression.

Work from our own lab further buttresses the relationship between general interpersonal avoidance and depression. We found that avoidance was strongly and negatively related to positive affect (Joiner, Pettit, et al., 2001). The significance of this finding is that a large research base supports the notion that positive affect is a distinctive component of depression (e.g., Clark & Watson, 1991; Mineka, Watson, & Clark, 1998). Although not definitive by itself, the strong association seen between general avoidance and positive affect in this study increases our confidence that these two phenomena are intertwined.

Shyness

A final relationship illustrating the interpersonally evasive nature of depressed people is the connection between shyness and depression. Shyness is a relatively common phenomenon; eminent social psychologist Philip Zimbardo has conducted several general population surveys, finding that approximately 40% of the population currently classified themselves as shy, and 80% of the population reported being shy at some point in their life. Shyness, represented by tension and inhibition in social situations (Cheek & Buss, 1981), has a relevant life course when one considers the chronic nature of depression. Like depression, shyness is a chronic phenomenon (even more so than depression), and may be considered an enduring personality disposition. Kagan and Snidman (1991) argued that shyness emerges before the first year of life, and it appears to remain stable throughout the course of one's life.

Reports have also indicated that shyness is associated with depression (Alfano, Joiner, Perry, & Metalsky, 1994; Anderson & Harvey, 1988), as well as many of its symptoms (e.g., low self-esteem; Cheek & Buss, 1981; Jones, Briggs, & Smith, 1986) and correlates (e.g., negative cognitive style, Alfano et al., 1994; loneliness, Cheek & Busch, 1981; Jones et al., 1986). In addition to simply being related to depression, a moderate amount of evidence suggests that shyness serves as a vulnerability factor for depression. Research focused on personality traits has identified shyness as one of a number of characteristics that may place an individual at risk for future depressive episodes. For example, VanValkenberg, Winokur, Lowry, Behar, and VanValkenberg (1983) found that depressed women retrospectively reported shyness as a personality trait present prior to the occurrence of depressive episodes. Similarly, Nystrom and Lindegard (1975) reported that a number of traits, including shyness, may serve as a predisposing factor to depression. To more fully understand the circumstances under which shyness may serve as an antecedent of depression, Joiner (1997) conducted a study examining the interaction of shyness and social support as it relates to depressive symptoms. As expected, Joiner found that shy undergraduate students were prone to increases in depressive symptoms. This finding, however, did not apply to all shy people in the study; depressive symptom increases occurred among shy people only in the absence of social support, and it occurred as a function of loneliness. That is, shy individuals with an adequate amount of social support (i.e., not lonely) did not exhibit increases in depressive symptoms. Hence, shyness alone does not appear to be a vulnerability factor for depression. In the context of a constricted interpersonal environment, however, shy individuals are more likely to become depressed than their non-shy counterparts.

CONFLICT AVOIDANCE

As we have briefly illustrated through these four features associated with depression, depressed persons often experience generalized problems with social avoidance. Moreover, at this point, we have at least some evidence to support the notion that social avoidance temporally precedes the development of depression. Nonetheless, we believe that interpersonal avoidance per se, despite its clear relevance to depression, is not necessarily the key component placing persons at risk for depression or propagating current depressive symptoms. Rather, we make a more narrow distinction and highlight the role of interpersonal conflict avoidance in depression, as opposed to generalized avoidance. There are at least three reasons to emphasize interpersonal conflict avoidance, as opposed to generalized avoidance.

First, we draw on the previously demonstrated relationship between depression and assertiveness. As demonstrated by Ball et al. (1994), assertiveness is often quite difficult for depressed people. Assertiveness is a necessary component of successful conflict negotiation. It goes beyond mere interpersonal contact (and consequently, generalized interpersonal avoidance) and often requires the individual to assume a confrontational position. Furthermore, assertive actions expose one to the possibility of a variety of negative responses from others, such as anger, hostility, and rejection. Avoiding assertive behaviors thus allows the individual to escape the discomfort of receiving negative reactions from others. It also, however, lessens the individual's chances of obtaining desired outcomes, a point we return to later.

Second, it is likely that generalized avoidance is subserved by conflict-related cognitions (Youngren & Lewinsohn, 1980). That is, beliefs or expectations that interactions will lead to unpleasant outcomes may underlie pervasive patterns of avoidance. For example, a person holding the belief that self-expression will lead to humiliation will most likely avoid situations in which this expected experience may occur (Gilbert, 1997). Other cognitions associated with the potential negative effects of conflict may produce comparable behavioral inhibitions.

Third, the argument has been presented that behaviors and states corresponding to depression may have developed as a means of avoiding social conflict. Price, Sloman, Gardner, Gilbert, and Rohde (1994) argued that depression-related states and behaviors represent evolved forms of a primordial "involuntary subordinate strategy." Price et al. contended that the involuntary subordinate strategy arose primarily as a means to cope with social competition and conflict, particularly losses therein. Out of this framework, the primary function of depression is to resolve interpersonal conflicts by presenting a "no threat" signal to others. Recent animal research has provided a degree of support for this proposition. In work with cynomolgus monkeys, Shively, Laber-Laird, and Anton (1997) manipulated the social status of a group of females, such that previously dominant monkeys became subordinate to formerly subordinate monkeys. This reduction in social status produced behavioral and hormonal reactions corresponding to depressive reactions among humans. Behaviorally, these monkeys exhibited fearful scanning of the environment, and more important, decreased social affiliation. These behavioral changes suggest that the newly subordinate monkeys were engaging in interpersonal avoidance. Similarly, the monkeys' hormonal activity transformed, and they began hypersecreting cortisol. Research has demonstrated that hypersecretion of cortisol occurs more frequently among depressed humans (e.g., Asnis, 1981; Volsan & Berzewski, 1985). Other studies of animal social hierarchies and avoidance provide results consistent with those of Shively et al. (e.g., Jones, Stoddart, & Mallick, 1995). Although these results alone do not speak to how depression developed over time, they are nonetheless consistent with the notion that depressive behaviors may function as a means of interpersonal avoidance, and more specifically, interpersonal conflict avoidance.

CONTRIBUTING FACTORS IN
INTERPERSONAL CONFLICT AVOIDANCE

Clearly, then, there are reasons to believe that interpersonal conflict avoidance and depression are intertwined. Furthermore, the role of interpersonal avoidance, particularly of conflicts, in propagating depression is also readily drawn from the links between the two phenomena. Three aspects of interpersonal conflict avoidance demonstrate how this behavioral pattern feeds the chronicity of depression: loss, decreased social reinforcement and social support, and negative reinforcement.

First, interpersonal conflict avoidance, or interpersonal submission, involves loss. By submitting to others and avoiding assertive behaviors, individuals stand to lose in a number of areas. Avoidant people may lose status, material possessions, rights, and, potentially, their freedom. Overall, interpersonal submission involves the loss of opportunities of virtually any kind. Animal studies such as that reported by Shively et al. (1997) clearly demonstrate the link between submission and the loss of status and material resources. Jones et al. (1995) also found evidence of this connection, as consistently subordinate and recently subordinate (i.e., formerly dominant) marsupial sugar gliders had significantly less access to colonial resources. Of course, the relationship between avoidance and loss is not entirely straightforward. That is, although avoidance often leads to loss, there are times when it keeps one from experiencing a loss (e.g., not challenging your boss may keep you from losing your job). Certainly, there are instances in which conflict avoidance is prudent. On the whole, however, a pattern of routinely avoiding conflict in interpersonal relationships makes it more likely than one will routinely experience losses.

Loss, in turn, has been viewed as an important trigger of depression. Sloman (2000) described the role of loss in depression in a theoretical treatise of how biopsychosocial factors lead the "involuntary defeat strategy" (formerly referred to as "involuntary submission strategy") to produce depression in response to loss. Empirical studies demonstrate that depression may be triggered by a variety of losses: job loss (e.g., Catalano, Aldrete, Vega, Kolody, & Aguilar-Gaxiola, 2000), loss of a loved one (e.g., miscarriage; Klier, Geller, & Neugebauer, 2000), material loss (e.g., Ennis, Hobfoll, & Schroeder, 2000), loss of physical abilities (e.g., De Leeuw et al., 2000), and loss of social status (e.g., Edelstein, Kalish, Drozdick, & McKee, 1999). Analogously, Lewinsohn, Pettit, Joiner, and Seeley (2003), in a study involving a large number of depressed adolescents and young adults, found that almost 90% of depressive episodes were triggered by an external event, and that a large proportion of these events involved loss of some form, be it relational, material, occupational, or otherwise.

Given the activating influence of loss on depression, interpersonal avoidance (which has already been presented as a cause of loss) may be a precursor to depressive episodes as well as a contributor to the maintenance of depression. Thus, loss appears to be one mechanism through which interpersonal conflict avoidance may propagate depression.

Furthermore, recent evidence suggests that current depression also predicts perceived loss of social support and resources, particularly among women (Bansal, Monnier, Hobfoll, & Stone, 2000). In this case, being depressed actually increases the chances that one will perceive future losses. This is essentially the reverse of the sequence of events previously described, in which loss precedes depression. Not only does loss, a consequence of interpersonal avoidance, lead to depression; but depression also leads to the perception of loss. The bidirectional nature of this relationship provides even more support for the notion that interpersonal avoidance, through loss, propagates depression. (Bansal et al. hypothesized that the association between depression and future loss of social support was stronger among women because they may be more likely to define social support in emotional terms, whereas men may be more likely to define social support in instrumental terms [i.e., social support is needed to complete a task; Belle, 1987].)

A second way in which interpersonal avoidance propagates depression chronicity occurs through the diminution of social contact. Social contacts provide social reinforcement, or positive interactions with others. Lack of social reinforcement, in turn, appears to be linked to depression. Several researchers, most notably Lewinsohn and Rehm, (e.g., Lewinsohn & Libet, 1972; Rehm, 1977) have persuasively argued that a lack of positive reinforcement acts to maintain depression. Similarly, low social support has been implicated in the onset and maintenance of depression (Joiner, 1997; Roos & Cohen, 1987). Even more conclusive evidence of the long-term, deleterious effects of diminished social contact comes from research demonstrating that low social support predicts depression chronicity (Brugha, Bebbington, MacCarthy, & Stuart, 1990; Lara, Leader, & Klein, 1997). Consistent with these findings, evidence indicates that the presence of social support actually speeds recovery from depression (McLeod, Kessler, & Landis, 1992).

In the context of our earlier illustration of depression as a lack of participation, it is easy to imagine how a dearth of positive social interactions and a meager social support structure propagate depressive states. In this scenario, depressed individuals have little or no encounters outside of their own depressive, bleak worldview.

Consider the case of Mauricio. Mauricio was a young man who sought treatment at our clinic. In our first meeting, Mauricio slowly—and with much prompting—opened up and told me what led him to seek treatment at our clinic. He described persistent feelings of lethargy, boredom (i.e., anhedonia; see also chap. 1), and most painful of all, social isolation. When directly questioned, he endorsed sadness and bouts of crying, as well as fleeting thoughts that he would "be better off dead." He described his one previous romantic relationship, and the pain he had experienced since it ended approximately 1 year prior to our meeting. He reported that he had little contact with others outside of his immediate family. Moreover, he indicated that his relationships with immediate family members were strained because of his irritability toward them and frequent episodes of "snapping" and yelling at them. It is interesting to note that this pattern of being overly reserved or acquiescing with strangers, but extremely negative and antagonistic toward close relatives or romantic partners, is quite common among people who are depressed. Mauricio indicated that he had always been somewhat shy and did not feel comfortable approaching people or starting conversations. He also felt as though he couldn't think of anything to say when interacting with others, or that his statements sounded "dumb" to him after he made them. This feeling of social awkwardness was particularly troubling to him, because he longed for close relationships, but believed that others did not want to be around him.

Mauricio was caught in a cycle in which his lack of social reinforcement intensified and maintained his depression, and his depressive symptoms interfered with his development of improved social relations. Fortunately, with practice in social skills and assertive behaviors, as well as Mauricio's willingness to take interpersonal risks, his depression and his interpersonal relations improved.

A third way in which interpersonal avoidance propagates depression chronicity is through the well-studied mechanism of negative reinforcement. Negative reinforcement, in short, functions to strengthen a response through the removal of an aversive stimulus. For instance, phobias are maintained by the rewarding anxiety-reducing effects of avoidance (Reiss, 1980). A comparable pathway occurs in the lives of interpersonally avoidant individuals. By dodging interpersonal communication, particularly conflict, individuals have a means for escaping the anxiety associated with such encounters. In this case, the response (i.e., avoidance) is strengthened because an aversive stimulus (i.e., interpersonal conflict) has been removed as a result of the response (i.e., avoidance). Thus, interpersonal avoidance is propagated by the relief of evading a feared interpersonal conflict.

The link between interpersonal avoidance and depression chronicity, unfortunately, has not received a great deal of attention from researchers. Nevertheless, at least one study provides direct evidence for the association between interpersonal avoidance and depression chronicity. Parker, Hadzi-Pavlovic, Brodaty, and Boyce (1992) found that the absence of childhood timidity and shyness was positively related to outcome among depressed adults. That is, individuals without these traits were more likely to have a longer remission from depression and fewer relapses of depression.

RELEVANCE TO REMISSION

Through the pathways of loss, decreased social reinforcement and support, and negative reinforcement, then, conflict avoidance is implicated in the persistent nature of depression. But what about the reverse process; namely, the occurrence of spontaneous remission of depressive symptoms among those high in interpersonal conflict avoidance?

To the extent that the losses associated with conflict avoidance are temporary, one might posit that depressive symptoms would also be temporary. That is, a loss (e.g., failure to be promoted in a job) that is contributed to by low assertiveness is likely to be followed by an exacerbation of depressive symptoms. As things stabilize over time (e.g., acceptance of unchanged work status), however, depressive symptoms may naturally subside or at least decrease to subthreshold levels. Subsequent experiences of loss may hold explanatory power for the relapse or recurrence of depression.

A related possibility involves positive environmental changes that occur in spite of depressed persons' low assertiveness. Although less frequently occurring than among nondepressed persons, depressed, unassertive people nonetheless get job promotions, become involved in relationships (usually initiated by others), and the like. Insofar as these events are perceived as positive gains (as opposed to losses) and function to increase social support, it would not be surprising if they also lead to a reduction in depression. Consistent with this notion, daily positive events are associated with more positive affect and improved functioning among depressed people (Nezlek & Gable, 2001; Peeters, Nicolson, Berkhof, Delespaul, & deVries, 2003). An interesting question for research to explore is whether the mechanism by which this occurs is increased social reinforcement.

RECONCILING CONFLICT AVOIDANCE AND STRESS GENERATION

At this point, the question may reasonably be asked, "If depressed people avoid interpersonal conflict, how is it that they generate stress in the context of interpersonal relationships?" Indeed, the material presented in this chapter may initially appear to contradict that of earlier chapters (e.g., excessive reassurance-seeking [chap. 5]). However, upon further reflection on the nature of the behaviors described thus far and the context in which they often occur, it becomes clear that interpersonal conflict avoidance accords quite well with behaviors such as negative feedback-seeking and excessive reassurance-seeking.

Although this is an area in need of more empirical research, we consider it unlikely that depressed persons view behaviors such as reassurance-seeking or negative feedback-seeking as conflict-promoting behaviors. That is, seeking assurances from others is likely viewed as a means to draw others closer, to receive empathy and support from others, and to verify that one's relationship is harmonious (e.g., "they really *do* love me"). And that is typically the case, when done in small amounts. When it becomes excessive, however, it tends to push others away. We speculate that depressed people who feel a greater need for assurances may be less accurate judges of when "enough" becomes "too much." The end result, as we described in chapter 5, is that an approach that initially led to feelings of connectedness now leads to feelings of frustration. Consider the following excerpt from a therapy session I (Pettit) had with a man who excessively sought reassurance from his girlfriend:

> *Patient:* . . . And I asked her if she found me as attractive as those guys on T.V. At first, she just looked at me like I was crazy or something, then she said that she finds me very attractive. But it didn't seem genuine, you know, so I was like, "Do you really think I'm in as good of shape as them?" And then I asked if she found me as attractive as Steve, her ex-boyfriend. Then she started to get upset, and asked me why I always force her to compare me with other guys. . .
>
> *Me:* How were you hoping she would respond? Put another way, what did you want to get out of that situation?
>
> *Patient:* I just wanted to know that she finds me attractive, that she loves me as much as I love her.

As is evident from this short excerpt, this patient sought assurances to feel closer to his girlfriend; he had difficulty recognizing that the excessive nature of his requests actually produced, rather than quelled, conflict.

Likewise, we presented material in chapter 4 that depressed people (and others) tend to seek out relationship partners who view them as they view themselves. As such, behaviors such as negative feedback-seeking may actually reduce, rather than promote, conflict. That is, to the extent that others' views of depressed persons accord with the depressed persons' self-views, soliciting and receiving negative feedback entails little conflict (e.g., "I think I'm a lousy cook; Janice agrees that I'm a lousy cook; Janice really knows me and is honest with me"). In contrast, when others provide appraisals that do not accord with depressed persons' self-views, the interpersonal stage is set for conflict (e.g., "I think I'm a lousy artist; Janice says I'm a good artist; Janice either doesn't know me well or isn't being honest with me"). Thus, negative feedback-seeking is quite consistent with a general avoidance of interpersonal conflict. The downside, as we described in chapter 4, is that negative evaluations maintain or worsen depressive symptoms, even if they do initially reduce interpersonal friction.

SUMMARY

In summary, then, depression is associated with interpersonal avoidance, occurring in the forms of low assertiveness, social withdrawal, generalized avoidance, and shyness, among others. Avoidance propagates depression through loss of social and material reinforcement and of social support. Furthermore, avoidance propagates itself through the mechanism of negative reinforcement and is implicated in expanding depressive episode duration (e.g., current depression's association with low assertiveness leads to withdrawal, loss of social support, and thus exacerbated depression) and inducing relapse when subclinical depressive symptoms remain. Regarding recurrence on full remission, it is not at all clear that depression is erosive in the sense that it leaves a residual avoidant interpersonal style. Nonetheless, formerly depressed people are at heightened risk for avoidant pathology (Angst, 1996). Such pathology, in turn, heightens the risk for future depression (Ball et al., 1994). Avoidance may propagate strictly defined recurrence, then, through its association with both past and future depression. In the next chapter, we examine another propagatory feature of depression that is also driven largely by fears of social evaluation.

7

SELF-HANDICAPPING

Always acknowledge a fault. This will throw those in authority off their guard and give you an opportunity to commit more.

—Mark Twain

Up to this point we have emphasized the role of depressed persons in soliciting information from others about their own attributes. In the case of negative feedback-seeking, depressed persons actively seek out information that confirms their already low self-concepts. In the case of excessive reassurance-seeking, depressed persons desire and repeatedly ask for assurances as to their worth, but reject others' attempts to assuage their concerns. As we have demonstrated, both of these behaviors have deleterious interpersonal consequences that ultimately prolong the depressive experience. In this chapter, we shift the focus from the depressed person's requests for information to the depressed person's self-presentation. As will become apparent as we progress through this chapter, depressed persons often put Mark Twain's witty advice into action (even in the absence of a fault) and reap harmful consequences.

DEPRESSED PERSONS' SELF-PRESENTATION

In general social settings depressed persons can often come across in a number of unflattering ways: distant, apathetic, shy, hostile, clingy. These presentations undoubtedly stem from an interaction of individual personality traits (e.g., introverted–extroverted) and social determinants (e.g., familiarity with others). But the question remains as to whether depressed persons—regardless of general personality styles—display consistent self-presentational behaviors in a specific type of situational context: social evaluation. By social evaluation, we are simply referring to situations in which others are likely to form some impression or make some judgment about a person. Social evaluations can be as formal as a yearly job performance evaluation, or can be as informal as a brief conversation about the clothes one is wearing. Unfortunately, the self-presentational behavior of depressed persons in social evaluation settings is an understudied area. Nonetheless, extrapolations from social psychology, combined with a handful of studies on depressed persons, suggest that such individuals may indeed display characteristic behavior patterns in the context of social evaluation.

Research by Alloy and Abramson (1982) indicates that depressed persons are less likely to display defensive, self-enhancing behaviors in an effort to cast themselves in a favorable light. In a series of studies assessing participants' perceptions of control over events, they found that nondepressed persons consistently overestimated their ability to influence the outcome of uncontrollable events. It could thus be said that nondepressed persons typically display an "illusion of control." In contrast, depressed persons accurately estimated their ability to influence the outcome of such events. This, along with other similar findings, led to the early conclusion that depressed persons hold a "sadder but wiser" perspective on their abilities. A different pattern began to emerge, however, when researchers investigated perceptions of control in situations in which persons really did have an impact on the outcome. In these cases, the illusion of control and the sadder but wiser effects tended to disappear, as nondepressed persons became more accurate predictors and depressed persons become less accurate at predicting their level of control over events (e.g., Pacini, Muir, & Epstein, 1998). Thus, depressed persons may be better able to judge their level of (non)control on noncontingent laboratory tasks but likely to underestimate their ability to affect outcomes in controllable, real-world settings. Why would depressed people sell themselves short in their daily environments? The answer to this question is complex, for sure, but research on a phenomenon called *self-handicapping* indicates that depressed people may gain self-protective and other rewards for depressive cognition and behavior. These rewards serve to maintain depressive cognition and behavior, and thereby perpetuate depression.

Self-handicapping, a concept with origins in the field of social psychology, refers to placing obstacles in the way of one's performance on tasks so as to furnish oneself with an external attribution when future outcomes are uncertain (Leary & Shepperd, 1986). That is, in the anticipation of a possible failure or a poor performance of some sort, people may either claim to have some limitation or actually produce a limitation that provides an explanation in the event that they perform poorly. Self-handicapping is a frequently occurring phenomenon and is not limited to depressed people. Consider, for example, a man in his late 30s who, after pressure from his cowork-ers, agrees to join the company softball team. Concerned with how others will evaluate his performance, he repeatedly mentions "it's been years since I've held a bat" and "my back just isn't what it used to be." In the event that he plays poorly in the game, he (and others) can attribute his performance to a lack of recent practice and to back pain. Conversely, if he plays well, he deserves extra praise because his performance has occurred in spite of the limitations he cited. In this instance, the self-handicapping serves as a rela-tively benign way to reduce concerns of social evaluation and to maintain one's favorable self-image. Now let us turn to a slightly more extreme ex-ample. Consider a young lady who must pass an audition to gain admission into an honors music program at her university.

Concerned with her ability to perform well in the honors program, and others' evaluations of her if she does not, she occupies herself with other tasks and fails to prepare for the audition. Upon auditioning, she now has a ready explanation if she performs poorly (i.e., her failure to prepare), and she appears all the more talented if she passes the audition despite not practic-ing. Notice that in this case, the young lady not only claims a handicap (as did the man in the earlier example) but also produces an actual handicap by not preparing for the audition. Before we discuss the relevance of self-handicapping to depression chronicity, let us review some general character-istics of the phenomenon.

WHEN DOES SELF-HANDICAPPING OCCUR?

A series of studies by Baumgardner (1991) found self-handicapping, in general, appears to occur in one of two situations. First, it may occur when people have experienced a failure privately and hold concerns about that failure becoming public. An example is relevant here. Continuing our previ-ous example of the man playing softball, perhaps he formerly played softball with a different group of people and repeatedly struck out. On the basis of that prior "failure," which is private in the sense that his current coworkers do not know about it, he is likely to self-handicap so that a poor performance will not be attributed to a lack of skill on his part. People may also self-handicap when they have experienced a success publicly yet doubt their abil-ity to maintain that success. Studies have demonstrated that people who engage in this second form of self-handicapping may put forth less effort on tasks or even engage in substance use prior to performing the task. Continu-ing the example of the woman who failed to prepare for her audition, perhaps she has previously had success as a musician and received praise for her per-formances. Concerned that she will not be able to maintain her successful track record, and therefore lose the praise of others, she exerts little effort in preparing for her audition. Consequently, a poor performance will not be attributed to her abilities as a musician but, rather, to her busy schedule and lack of time to prepare.

As is evident from our examples, two forms of self-handicapping exist: *claimed* and *acquired* (these have also been referred to as *self-reported* and *behavioral*, respectively). Claimed handicaps are likely more common than acquired handicaps. An individual's willingness to acquire a handicap appears to depend on the interpersonal payoff of the handicap. More specifically, claimed handicaps occur when people believe that the handicap will explain their poor performance. Acquired handicaps, however, occur when people (a) believe the handicap will explain their poor performance and (b) believe that the handicap will lower others' future expectations. Both forms of self-handicapping are likely relevant to depression, as we discuss in the following section.

SELF-HANDICAPPING IN THE CONTEXT OF DEPRESSION

Unfortunately, relatively little research attention has been devoted to self-handicapping among depressed persons. One may wonder how applicable self-handicapping behavior is to depression for a couple of reasons. First, it is conceptualized as a way to enhance or preserve self-esteem, which, on the surface, does not appear to be as important to depressed persons as it is to nondepressed persons. That is, depressed persons are often self-denigrating, which would seem contrary to the notion that they seek to enhance their self-esteem (although appearances may be deceiving in this case!). Second, evidence suggests that self-handicapping, at least behavioral self-handicapping, occurs more frequently among men than women, which is in contrast to the higher rates of depression seen among women. Self-reported, or claimed, handicaps occur at similar rates among men and women.

What might explain these two apparent discrepancies? The answer may depend partially on a misperception of depressed persons and partially on traditional ways of conceptualizing the motives of self-handicapping. (It is also important to note that self-handicapping occurs among nondepressed as well as depressed persons). Although depressed persons may come across as not overly interested in preserving their public image, research suggests that persons with low self-esteem (as are most depressed persons) are actually more concerned with protecting the self (Baumeister, Tice, & Hutton, 1989). To the extent that self-handicapping protects the self, then those with low self-esteem are more likely to do it. Likewise, some have suggested that doubts about one's ability to make a desired impression on others may drive self-handicapping (Arkin & Baumgardner, 1985). As is clear from behaviors such as negative evaluations of their own social influence and the presence of excessive reassurance-seeking, depressed persons lack confidence in their ability to make desired impressions on others. Hence, the notion that depressed persons seek to enhance their self-image is actually quite consistent with empirical data. The ways in which they go about it, however, often backfire.

The gender discrepancy seen with behavioral, but not claimed, self-handicapping may result from methods used to measure self-handicapping. Typically, self-handicapping has been measured in the context of performance on paper-and-pencil tests of ability. It is unclear whether the gender difference would also apply to other domains, such as social performance evaluation. This is ultimately a question that will have to be resolved empirically.

Despite these two concerns, empirical evidence confirms that depressed people are more likely to self-handicap than others. This trend toward self-handicapping appears to emerge in youth, as data suggest that young adolescents with depressive symptoms are more likely to engage in such behaviors (Greaven, Santor, Thompson, & Zuroff, 2000). (Note that this is also around the same time that the prevalence of depression begins to increase.) In addition to being more pervasive among depressed persons, self-handicapping may also possess some unique qualities among depressed persons. One way in which self-handicapping appears to be unique among depressed persons is in the use of depressive affect and cognitions to explain failures and lower others' expectations of them. Baumgarder (1991) provided support for this notion, finding that depressed persons completing a task were more likely than nondepressed persons to endorse negative mood if they were told that negative mood often impedes performance on the task. That alone is not surprising, given that depressed persons actually do experience more negative mood. What was surprising was that depressed and nondepressed persons were equally likely to report negative mood when they were not told that negative mood hinders performance. Thus, depressed persons were only more likely to report negative mood when it served as a "legitimate" handicap on performance.

In a similar study, Rosenfarb and Aron (1992) found that another symptom of depression, self-critical thoughts, was endorsed at a greater rate by depressed women when they were led to believe that such cognitions could serve as excuses for poor performance. Although these studies only investigated two symptoms of depression, one can readily imagine how other symptoms such as fatigue, anhedonia, and sleep disturbances could be used as claimed or real handicaps to performance. Consider the following example from a conversation I (Pettit) had with a depressed patient who failed to complete a homework assignment that we established in the previous session:

> Me: What do you think might be interfering with your completing the homework assignment?

> Patient: It's because I don't fall asleep until late, and then I'm so tired that I stay in bed till three or four in the afternoon.

> Me: In our previous meeting, we talked about how you have tended to avoid trying things because you're concerned

that others might judge you or see you as deficient. I wonder if that same pattern might be operating with regard to
the homework assignments?

Patient: I don't think so . . . I really want to do them, but I'm sure
I won't be able to do them well when I'm so tired.

Granted, this patient really did have difficulty sleeping at night, as do
many depressed persons. However, his ability to carry out the homework
assignment was not contingent on sleeping through the night. My impression was that his reticence to complete the assignment stemmed more from
his fear of social evaluation than from sleep disturbance—an impression that
was supported by his self-handicapping in multiple areas of life. The patient
did complete the homework assignment prior to the next session but noted
that he could have done a better job on a full night's rest. This brief example
of how depressive symptoms (i.e., sleep disturbance) might be used as a handicap leads us into the next section.

FUNCTIONS OF SELF-HANDICAPPING

Given that claimed and acquired self-handicaps occur in particular settings, let us turn to the question of why it occurs. That is, what functions
does the behavior serve? And, relatedly, what are the consequences of such
behavior? Most researchers have highlighted the self-protective functions of
self-handicapping, and this attention appears to be justified. As described
earlier, self-handicapping reduces threats to one's self-esteem by providing
an explanation for poor performances. Failures no longer reflect poorly on
one's abilities or worth but, rather, stem from a less threatening source such
as low effort or an uncontrollable circumstance. It is also important to note
that self-handicapping operates on both intrapsychic and interpersonal levels. That is, the handicap provides the individual a cognitive explanation of
the failed performance and also provides an explanation to others who may
be privy to the failure. Jones and Berglas (1978) also highlighted the self-
enhancing function of self-handicapping. In addition to providing an external attribution for failure, barriers to performance increase the likelihood of
internal credit for success (i.e., self-enhancement). Consequently, individuals who self-handicap apparently benefit regardless of whether they succeed
or fail.

The self-protective nature of self-handicapping raises an important issue with regard to depression. Why is it that a behavior enacted with the
purpose of protecting or enhancing self-esteem is actually associated with
depressed mood? Intuitively, it seems as though behaviors that protect self-
concept would reduce, rather than maintain, depression. The answer to
this question likely involves two phenomena, both of which occur at the

interpersonal level. As discussed earlier, people self-handicap in the social arena with the goal of promoting a more positive image. Ironically, self-handicapping tends to have the reverse effect! Rhodewalt, Sanbonmatsu, Tschanz, Feick, and Waller (1995) provided initial evidence of this notion, finding that that the performance of persons who made excuses prior to and during a task was evaluated more negatively than the performance of those who offered no excuses. Moreover, this was the case even when the performance was objectively equal across the excuse and no-excuse groups. Hence, the negative evaluation was unrelated to actual performance but, rather, resulted from the perception that people were making excuses for their performance. It is important to emphasize that this negative evaluation was made after briefly observing a stranger. Although the effects of more chronic self-handicapping have not been investigated, it is likely the case that individuals grow tiresome of and becoming increasingly rejecting toward those who habitually engage in self-handicapping behaviors (cf. blame maintenance, chap. 8).

I (Pettit) saw a relatively mild form of this occur in therapy with a college student. The student, Sasha, reported a variety of depressed and anxious symptoms. Sasha excelled in academics but struggled in interpersonal relationships. After a few meetings, I picked up on Sasha's efforts to focus our conversations exclusively on academic evaluations, such as tests, papers, and the like. Sasha routinely prefaced her discussion of these evaluations with statements to the effect that she knew very little about the academic area, was too busy to study, or did a project at the very last minute. Nevertheless, she typically obtained very high marks—and always had an excuse ready when she obtained "low" grades (e.g., less than an A). Sasha came to recognize that her peers tended to react negatively when she discussed academics but had great difficulty pinpointing why that was the case. Although I never spoke with her peers, I suspected that her frequent and often exaggerated self-handicapping, combined with her high grades, rubbed more than a few peers the wrong way. Part of our work in therapy focused on helping Sasha to accept her good and bad performances as just that (performances), not as indications of her worth as a person.

A second potential explanation of the paradoxical effects of self-handicapping may lie in another function—and corresponding consequence—of the behavior. In addition to reducing self-esteem threats, self-handicapping also lowers expectations of others (and arguably, the self). Lowered social expectations likely seem attractive for many depressed persons, at least initially. They reduce demands on an already overwhelmed and fatigued system, they allow depressed persons to devote less energy to tasks and relationships, and so on. In this sense, depressed persons benefit from the reduced social demands that accompany their depressive cognitions and behaviors. On the basis of the principles of operant conditioning, it is easy to imagine that the rewarding, or reinforcing, properties of such behaviors would increase the likelihood that these behaviors will be repeated in future social settings. But as long as these thoughts and behaviors protect the self and reduce social demands, then they are beneficial to depressed persons, right? Unfortunately, the answer appears to be "no." As previously mentioned, individuals who are perceived as making excuses are typically viewed more negatively. Furthermore, lower social expectations presage lower social opportunities, which by itself is a bad prognostic sign for depression. Consider the following example from one of my (Pettit's) interactions with a depressed patient.

Patient: My boss offered to let me take the lead on the new project. Man, I couldn't believe it.

Me: Congratulations! How did you respond?

Patient: Well, I told her not to expect too much since it's not my specialty, and then she turned around and gave it to my coworker because he has more experience in that area. Can you believe that?

Me: You seem surprised by that turn of events.

Patient: Yeah, I didn't think she would just up and change her mind like that. But it's probably for the best . . . I don't have enough energy these days to do that sort of thing, anyway.

In this case, the patient's self-handicapping likely led to the loss of a career-advancing opportunity, which further intensified her depressed mood. Of note, it was "beneficial" in the sense that it removed the immediate pressure associated with taking on greater job responsibilities. In the long run, however, the career-damage and negative evaluations resulting from these types of behaviors increase depression's chronic course.

What is more, these behaviors (and their negative consequences) are hardly limited to job settings. They occur in the context of familial relationships, friendships, romantic relationships, and even during encounters with strangers. Although further empirical research on the interpersonal sequelae of these behaviors is needed before firm conclusions are drawn, they likely reduce opportunities for positive social engagement, increase antagonistic behaviors from others, and reconfirm depressed persons' views that they are socially inept. The end result, tragically, is continued and exacerbated depression. As self-handicapping behaviors continue to occur as depression lifts, relapse and recurrence would not be surprising.

A primary task in therapy with the patient just described (and something we routinely do with depressed patients in general) was to explicitly connect her specific behaviors in specific situations with specific outcomes. A systematic approach such as the cognitive–behavioral analysis system of psychotherapy (McCullough, 2000) is ideal for linking patients' thoughts and actions to identifiable outcomes; less formal approaches of asking patients to identify "what they thought" and "what they did" in specific instances may also be useful.

RELEVANCE TO REMISSION

In the manner just described, self-handicapping may propagate depression, thereby partially explaining its chronic course. How then, could self-handicapping behaviors relate to remission of the disorder? Empirical investigations have not yet tackled this question, but we offer some possibilities and encourage future research into the mechanisms by which self-handicapping might pull people out of depression.

First, recall one of the primary functions of self-handicapping: to protect one's self-esteem. Although we have argued that self-handicapping may lead to a withdrawal of social opportunities, it also provides a nonthreatening explanation for failures and disappointments. Moreover, successes remain attributed to the person's own abilities, as they occur in spite of the handicap. To the extent that depressed persons who self-handicap begin to attribute failures to external causes and successes to internal causes, then it would not be surprising to see a reduction in depressive symptoms. Indeed, a highly effective treatment for depression, cognitive therapy, systematically examines and modifies patients' attributions of successes and failures in manner consistent with what naturally occurs in self-handicapping (although the emphasis is on realistically evaluating causes of successes and failures, not developing handicaps to explain behaviors).

Second, and as previously noted, self-handicapping may reduce environmental stressors and demands, at least temporarily. Such reductions may afford overwhelmed depressed persons the opportunity to "regroup," fortify their resources and coping skills, and ease back into their predepression levels of functioning. This is more likely the case for time-limited self-handicapping that may occur with milder, stress-precipitated depressive episodes. Chronic self-handicapping, in contrast, likely reduces social opportunities and pushes away interpersonal resources.

AN EXTREME CASE OF SELF-HANDICAPPING: SELF-DEFEATING PERSONALITY DISORDER

When taken to an extreme, chronic behavioral self-handicapping may significantly hinder interpersonal relations and lead to the development of maladaptive behaviors such as alcoholism and substance dependence. This, by the way, may provide some insight as to why men have been observed to engage in more behavioral self-handicapping, yet experience lower rates of depression. Men are more than twice as likely than women to be diagnosed with alcohol or substance abuse disorders (e.g., Kessler et al., 1994).

The habitual placement of obstacles in the way of one's path to success is similar to what some have referred to as *self-defeating personality disorder* (SDPD). SDPD, the subject of diagnostic controversy, refers to a pervasive pattern of setting oneself up for failure, rejecting the help of others, rejecting opportunities for pleasure, and responding negatively to positive personal events. We found evidence to support the existence of SDPD: Its symptoms were distinct from other related syndromes, its symptoms predicted distress and impairment beyond other personality disorders, and its symptoms did not appear to be biased against women (i.e., did not occur with substantially greater frequency among women; Cruz et al., 2000). Although the behavioral pattern associated with SDPD obviously extends beyond self-handicapping, parallels can be seen with regard to stacking the deck against oneself for success. It is not surprising that SDPD is associated with chronic depressive symptoms.

SUMMARY

Empirical data regarding the relationship of self-handicapping to depression are sparse. Nevertheless, we have provided an initial overview of how such behaviors may operate in the context of depression. By lowering social expectations, self-handicapping is relevant to depression chronicity to the extent that they decrease opportunities for social interaction and advancement. Likewise, those who are viewed as making excuses for their behaviors are more likely to receive negative evaluations from others.

In contrast, self-handicapping may offer a partial explanation for the spontaneous remission of depression. In these instances, the short-term beneficial effects of self-handicapping, such as reducing behavioral demands, may allow less severely depressed persons to fortify their coping resources and return to normal levels of functioning. We encourage future research to focus more extensively on the interpersonal effects of self-handicapping, particularly with regard to depression.

8

BLAME MAINTENANCE

In chapter 6 we discussed the pervasive pattern of interpersonal avoidance exhibited by people who are prone to depression and also explained how this behavioral pattern exacerbates and extends the chronic nature of depression. Despite their tendencies toward interpersonal avoidance, however, depressed persons need to communicate with others; communication is a necessity of life and is ultimately unavoidable. Humans have a strong desire for social acceptance. For example, extensive evidence supports the idea that humans are motivated to achieve and maintain relatedness with others. In fact, the desire to feel included in a social network is so well documented that social psychologists Baumeister and Leary (1995) concluded that wanting to be accepted and valued by others constitutes a basic human need.

Baumeister and Leary (1995) discussed the far-ranging repercussions of the need to belong, including, for example, the deleterious health consequences that can result from insufficient social belongingness. In their analysis, Baumeister and Leary asserted that humans' need for belongingness is driven by evolution. Belonging to a group maximizes numerous survival and reproductive benefits that living on one's own could not offer.

An adequate level of social support, therefore, is said to act as a buffer against physical and mental health problems. People who belong to a supportive, caring network of relationships are people with sound minds and bodies. Conversely, an insufficient level of social support renders the individual vulnerable to a plethora of ill effects. Individuals who do not engage in friendly, positive interactions on a frequent basis are also more likely to experience emotional distress, mental anguish, and physical illness (Baumeister & Leary, 1995).

Numerous empirical studies bear out this notion. As one example, consider the following study of the importance of social support among elderly men and women (Blazer, 1983). Blazer measured three dimensions of social support and related them to mortality risk: (a) roles (e.g., marital status, children), (b) frequency of interaction (e.g., telephone calls, visits), and (c) perceptions of social support (e.g., lonely when with people, contact with a confidant). The parameter most strongly associated with mortality risk was individuals' subjective perceptions of social support (roles and frequency of visits were less predictive of mortality). In addition to the absence of social support, "social undermining" (e.g., negativity, active conflict) was found to be predictive of mental health change (Vinokur & Van Ryn, 1993).

In addition to demonstrating the need for social connection, a distinction has also been made between the quantity and quality of contact between two individuals. Baumeister and Leary (1995) concluded that the need to belong is satisfied only when both aspects are present, such that (a) the individual has a relational bond with another that involves their frequent contact, and (b) interactions within the relationship are positive and relatively nonconflicted. Indeed, empirical research supports the importance of both amount of contact and quality of interactions in healthy functioning.

As we discussed in chapter 6, depressed persons are often low on the quantity dimension of interpersonal contact. We have also demonstrated in several chapters how the quality of depressed persons' relationships may be inadequate. In chapter 3, for example, we argued that depressed people, in general, have a penchant for selecting dysfunctional partners, displaying impaired interpersonal problem-solving skills, and adopting a hopeless attitude toward unfulfilling relationships. In chapters 4 and 5, respectively, we proceeded to discuss the negative feedback-seeking style of depressed persons, as well as reassurance-seeking and its destructive interpersonal aftermath. Given this lengthy list of deleterious relationship characteristics, what impact do depressed people have on others?

As we discussed in chapter 5, depressed individuals often have a negative impact on significant others, such as eliciting rejection from others through excessive reassurance-seeking or inducing depression in others (i.e., contagious depression). In this chapter, we focus on the former circumstance and explore the mechanisms by which negative evaluations and interpersonal rejection transpire.

MENTAL REPRESENTATIONS AND THE EFFECTS OF DEPRESSION

Over the past 3 decades, research has accumulated to paint a picture of severely maladaptive interpersonal effects of depression. Although the majority of work regarding depression has adopted an intrapsychic focus, early work by Coyne (1976b) addressed the interpersonal as well as the intrapersonal aspects of depression. His work on the nature of depression first pointed to the behaviors of depressed individuals as an important source of their social exclusion, particularly emphasizing the role of communication in producing negative evaluations from nondepressed others. Joiner, Alfano, and Metalsky (1992) extended this work, demonstrating that excessive reassurance-seeking is one factor contributing to this rejection. Thus, excessive reassurance-seeking among depressed people provides a broad explanation for negative evaluation and rejection from others.

Nevertheless, this still does not explain the intrapsychic processes within the significant other that build the bridge from a companion's excessive reassurance-seeking to rejection of that person. That is, what goes on in the course of excessive reassurance-seeking that leads to negative evaluation and rejection?

Sacco (e.g., Sacco, 1999; see also Sacco & Dunn, 1990) tackled that question, arguing that depressed people's relationship partners develop mental representations of them that become relatively autonomous and that bias subsequent perceptions of their depressed partners. To study this phenomenon, Sacco and Dunn presented undergraduate students with one of two hypothetical responses to a commonly used measure of depressive symptoms (the Beck Depression Inventory; Beck & Steer, 1987). One set of responses reflected those of a mildly to moderately depressed person, and the other represented those of a nondepressed person. Next, they presented students with hypothetical events involving the depressed or nondepressed person, and asked the students a series of questions about the extent to which they thought the person played a role in the occurrence of those events. It is interesting to note that students were more likely to attribute the depressed person's failures to internal, controllable causes, whereas the nondepressed person's failures were judged to result more from external, uncontrollable factors. Students also considered the causes for failures to be more stable and have a wider impact on the depressed person's life, as compared with the nondepressed person. The reverse pattern was seen for successful events. That is, successes were judged to result from external, uncontrollable factors among the depressed person but internal, controllable factors for the nondepressed person.

Both of these processes are important—depressed persons not only are blamed more for negative events but also are given less credit when positive events occur! Sacco and Dunn (1990) carried their investigation a step further and found that the hypothetical person's depression status predicted attributions made about that person, which in turn predicted emotional responses to that person (angry and concerned), which in turn predicted how willing students were to help or interact with the person. These striking effects are not limited to responses to brief vignettes of hypothetical persons.

Similar attributional and affective responses to events have also been demonstrated among spouses of currently or formerly depressed wives (Sacco, Dumont, & Dow, 1993).

As if these attributions and emotional reactions to depressed people were not enough, the story does not end there. Once formed, the mental representations remain stable, regardless of whether the depression has remitted. These representations are, of course, initially influenced by depressed people's actual behavior, especially while in depressive episodes. However, once developed, such representations take on an autonomous quality in that they selectively guide attention and expectancies to confirm the representation. Furthermore, these social cognitive processes may occur spontaneously and outside the awareness of the perceiver (Lewicki, Hill, & Czyzewska, 1992).

Fiske (1993) discussed the phenomenon of person perception in broader terms and proposed that people infer meaning from social information by abstracting relevant structures (most commonly traits, stereotypes, and stories). She further argued that the automatization of social constructs maximizes cognitive efficiency. This may explain the stability of mental representations regarding depressed individuals. That is, once a mental representation of the depressed person is formed, it becomes an automatic "default" descriptor of that person. Although this process makes information processing more rapid and efficient, it also maintains the negative perception of a depressed person, regardless of whether the depression is current or in remission.

In addition to the automatic, unconscious nature social cognitive processes, it appears that negative behaviors, as compared with positive behaviors, may be particularly salient to such processes. Pratto and John (1991) found that negative behaviors were more likely than positive behaviors to draw attention. Ybarra and Stephan (1996) extended this research, finding that negative behaviors that were attributed to the person (rather than the situation) were more likely to be remembered. This finding suggests that a memory bias exists such that negative, dispositionally attributed behaviors are recalled more easily than behaviors attributed to environmental contingencies. Similarly, representations of negative behaviors, once solidified, are more difficult to alter than representations of positive behaviors (Rothbart & Park, 1986). To compound the implications of the negative memory bias, such representations tend to gain momentum with use, in that they disproportionately influence social cognition relative to actual subsequent behaviors of the represented person (Sherman & Klein, 1994). It is clear that negative impressions are readily formed and attended to, but are resistant to change.

It should now be apparent that people readily and unconsciously develop long-lasting, autonomous, default mental representations of depressed persons and that these representations likely develop in response to negative, as opposed to positive, behaviors. But what is the content of such representations? Evidence to date suggests that others view the self-presentational motives of depressed people as realistic, but negative (Gurtman, Martin, &

Hintzman, 1990). That is, depressed people are not perceived as trying to present an overly negative or overly positive image of themselves. Rather, they are perceived as accurately describing a life full of problems and negative emotions.

This finding is consistent with the notion of *depressive realism* that we discussed in chapter 7 (Alloy & Abramson, 1988). Depressive realism refers to findings that depressed people are more accurate judges of successes and failures than nondepressed people, who tend to overestimate their successes and capacities for future success. It appears as though this depressive realism effect may be interpersonally transmitted, such that nondepressed others likewise view depressed persons as accurate judges of their competencies but still find interactions with depressed persons aversive. As alluded to previously, the aversive nature of these interactions appears to relate to both the quantity and the quality of negative content embedded in such interactions.

Further evidence of congruence between depressed persons' self-views and others' perceptions of them comes from studies of attributional styles. Returning to the findings from Sacco and Dunn (1990), these investigators found that others were likely to view depressed persons' failures as the result of internal, relatively permanent characteristics and that depressed persons would be likely to fail again. Failures not only were attributed to enduring traits of depressed persons but also were viewed as under the control of depressed persons (i.e., the depressed person could have avoided the failure if they had really tried). This is strikingly similar to depressed persons' characteristic self-blaming attitude. They attribute their own failures to internal, stable, and global factors (Abramson, Seligman, & Teasedale, 1978; Sweeney, Anderson, & Bailey, 1986). Consider the following excerpt from an interaction that I (Pettit) had with a depressed patient:

Patient: I've been even more depressed the past couple of days, because I haven't heard back about that job I interviewed for.

Me: Getting that job was important to you.

Patient: Yeah, but I'm not surprised. I never make a good impression. People can see that I don't have what it takes to be successful.

In just two short sentences, this depressed patient communicated a wealth of clinical information. First, the patient concluded that his own incompetence (an internal factor) was the reason he had not heard back from the potential employer. Second, the word *never* indicates that he considered his ineptness to be constant, or stable. Finally, by extending his statement to include "people" in general, rather than the specific employer, he displays the belief that his incompetence affected all areas of his life (i.e., it is global).

This patient's, as well as most depressed persons', attributions are clearly saturated with self-directed blame. To compound matters, others tend to adopt the same negative, blaming attributions and behaviors toward depressed persons. Tragically, this very thing happened with the family of the patient described above. When I met with him and his spouse together, it was clear that she, too, bought into the notion that he did not have what it took to be successful. Although trying to be sensitive to him, her comments reflected the sentiment (and resentment) that he was incompetent in work-related matters, that he would never obtain meaningful, stable work, and that she would have to bear the burden of supporting a family without his help.

RELEVANCE TO AND IMPLICATIONS FOR DEPRESSION CHRONICITY

The implications of this research on person schemata for depressed individuals and depression chronicity are potentially important. The largely immutable nature of others' rejecting views is consistent with the chronic nature of depression. That is, both depression and negative views from others tend to be long in duration and rather unresponsive to changes. So, are others' negative views simply to be considered concomitant to their companion's depressed mood? There is reason to believe that although they may be originate from partners' depression and depression-related behaviors (e.g., reassurance-seeking), negative views are more than concurrent "symptoms" of depression. Primarily, negative views remain stable even after depression has remitted. Hence, it appears that depression is erosive regarding others' views of formerly depressed people, in that negative depressive behaviors (e.g., self-degradation, self-injury, complaining, loss of interest and energy, excessive reassurance-seeking, negative feedback-seeking) instill in others a person schema that negatively biases subsequent perceptions and is difficult to alter. If so, with regard to others' perceptions, the depressed person encounters an intractable problem: Continued negative behaviors only serve to maintain others' negative views; positive changes, because they do not match others' schemata, may be unnoticed or misattributed, leaving others' negative schemata unaffected.

This last point is of interest when combined with the theoretical underpinnings of self-verification theory (see also chap. 4). To briefly review, the depressed person rejects information that is not consistent with his or her negative self-view, while seeking information that confirms the negative self-concept. Once a negative other-view of the depressed individual has been formed by a significant other, information that is not consistent with this representation is also discarded, although data confirming such a view becomes increasingly salient. Thus, the depressed person focuses exclusively on devaluing information, and the significant other similarly develops a perspective causing him or her to emphasize the negative qualities of the depressed, or even formerly depressed, partner. Consequently, neither the depressed person nor the significant other is able to recognize positive qualities of the depressed person.

Others not only fail to recognize positive attributes but also alter their interaction styles with the depressed person. There is evidence that others' negative views subserve the communications they emit to the negatively represented person. For example, the literature on attributions and relationship functioning has documented a connection between negative attributions and blaming communications (e.g., Bradbury & Fincham, 1990). Bradbury and Fincham have thoroughly investigated the relation—probably causal in nature—between attributions, communication, and satisfaction among marital dyads. In short, negative attributions lead to blaming communications and decreased relationship satisfaction. Given the high probability of negative evaluation and rejection of depressed partners, the application of this finding (i.e., negative attributions lead to blaming communication) to depressed persons is easily made.

Blaming communications, in turn, represent a specific instance of the array of interpersonal indicators shown to predict depression chronicity. Examples of such indicators that predict depression chronicity include perceived criticism (Hooley & Teasdale, 1989), low social support (Lara, Leader, & Klein, 1997), and impaired relationships (Miller, Ingham, Kreitman, & Surtees, 1987), among others. A great deal of evidence implicates perceived criticism as a contributor to depression. For instance, perceived criticism appears to play a prominent role in the effect of social interactions on depression, even serving as a stronger predictor of depressive symptoms than factors such as low social support (Franks, Shields, Campbell, & McDaniel, 1992). Moreover, the large body of literature on expressed emotion in families (e.g., Hooley, 1987) has also demonstrated that critical and hostile messages from family to patient worsens prognosis. This appears to be the case not only with depression but also with a number of other psychological disorders as well (e.g., schizophrenia, Lopez, Nelson, Snyder, & Mintz, 1999; bipolar disorder, Miklowitz, Simoneau, Sachs-Ericsson, & Warner, 1996; attention-deficit/hyperactivity disorder, Paris & Baker, 2000; eating disorders, van Furth et al., 1996). Moreover, low social appraisal from others longitudinally predicts a variety of factors related to mental and physical health, including depression, anger, physical aggression, physical illness, cigarette–alcohol use, and lower self-esteem (Joiner, Vohs, & Schmidt, 2000).

Perceived criticism and hostile communications also tend to predict poor response to treatment for some disorders and relapse of depression (e.g., Chambless & Steketee, 1999; Uehara, Yokoyama, Goto, & Idha, 1996). Furthermore, research suggests that interpersonal communication patterns of critical expressed emotion remain relatively stable over short periods of time (Paris & Baker, 2000), and it is not yet known whether these communications are stable over longer periods. The influence of perceived criticism on depression chronicity, in conjunction with the temporal stability of critical communications, may explain to a large degree the chronic nature of depression.

Consistent with our argument that negatively biased mental representations of depressed individuals lead to interpersonal rejection, several authors have speculated that attributional processes underlie expressed emotion (e.g., Hooley, 1987). Hooley and Licht (1997) found empirical support for this notion, as critical spouses were more likely to attribute depressed patients' symptoms and negative behaviors to factors that were controllable by and personal to the patients. Their attributions also indicated that they held their depressed spouses responsible for their difficulties (see also Brewin, MacCarthy, Duda, & Vaughn, 1991). Expressed emotion, therefore, is likely due in part to a poor understanding of the disorder. Moreover, it appears that family attributional processes may serve as the initial link in a chain that leads to interpersonal strife and eventually fans the flame of depression chronicity.

RELEVANCE TO REMISSION

Perhaps more so than any of the other self-propagatory processes described thus far, it is hard to imagine how blame maintenance can explain the phenomenon of spontaneous remission. Indeed, as we have described, blame maintenance essentially assures that others will continue to hold negative views of depressed persons, regardless of the depressed persons' presentations. As such, it is much easier to view it as a propagating or maintaining factor in depression, rather than as relevant to remission. Nevertheless, it is plausible that at least some aspects of blame may promote positive changes among depressed persons. Although the following is purely speculative, it may be that some depressed people are motivated and activated by the blaming communications of others. We imagine that this would be most likely to occur among those who are less severely depressed and still have resources to draw on (e.g., energy, at least some optimism). In the event that depressed persons actively respond to others' criticisms, they may derive some satisfaction simply from being more active and more productive. Furthermore, if significant others respond positively to depressed persons' efforts, they may increase the likelihood that depressed persons will continue to engage in such active behaviors (i.e., positive reinforcement). The result may be an upward spiral of activation and reduced interpersonal friction with significant others.

We emphasize that these are all big "ifs," and research is more consistent with the notion that this sequence does not frequently happen. Moreover, when depressed persons' efforts to address the complaints of others are met with continued rejection and negativity—as is likely the case—persistence of depressive symptoms is often the result. Despite this grim pic-

ture, not all hope is lost; we discuss potential ways to combat blame maintenance in chapter 13 on therapeutics.

SUMMARY

As we demonstrated in this chapter, the phenomenon of blame maintenance is directly implicated in depression chronicity. We noted that versions of both erosive and self-propagatory processes appear to be involved,
but with an important difference as compared with other processes described
in this book. That is, blame maintenance operates with regard to others'
views and communications, not to the depressed person's own characteristics. Regarding erosion, depressed persons' actual negative behaviors may
erode others' views of them. Regarding self-propagation, once developed and
elaborated, others' negative views persist, in the sense that they actively guide
subsequent social cognition and are self-maintaining and resistant to change.
Unlike other self-propagatory processes described here, blame maintenance is
clearly relevant to all forms of depression chronicity. Once initiated, the process is independent of current symptomatology (i.e., operative in episode, immediately following remission and well after remission) and thus may expand
episode duration, produce relapse in the vulnerable period immediately following remission, or induce strictly defined recurrence well after remission.

9

STABLE VULNERABILITIES

In the preceding chapters, we discussed six interpersonal processes by which depression may propagate, or maintain, itself. As should be clear by this point, these processes likely play a significant role in explaining why depression can be such a chronic condition. Nevertheless, we do not make the claim that erosive and self-propagatory processes account for all aspects of depression chronicity. An additional factor, not mentioned thus far, is the presence of persistent, stable vulnerability factors that maintain risk over time. In chapter 1, we introduced the idea that certain characteristics or manners of perceiving and relating to the world may serve as persistent vulnerabilities to depression. Furthermore, such factors may be implicated in the propagation of existing depression.

Examples of persistent vulnerabilities may include genetic and neurobiological risk factors as well as cognitive style risk factors. In fact, at least two of the self-propagatory processes reviewed in previous chapters—excessive reassurance-seeking and interpersonal avoidance—probably have stable qualities (shyness clearly does; Kagan, Reznick, & Snidman, 1987). Stable vulnerabilities do not necessarily act alone. That is, they can cooperate with self-propagatory processes to perpetuate depression, such the case in which current depression exacerbates preexisting tendencies (e.g., avoidance, excessive reassurance-seeking) that in turn, generate stress and contribute to expanded episode duration and relapse risk.

In this chapter, we focus primarily on stable psychological risk factors, as opposed to genetic or neurobiological vulnerabilities. Stable psychological vulnerabilities can be divided into three categories: cognitive, interpersonal, and personality–characterological (we recognize that these three areas likely have genetic and neurobiological underpinnings but have labeled them as *psychological* vulnerabilities for ease of discussion). These vulnerabilities offer theoretical accounts for the onset of depression but cannot completely explain the causes of depression. In this chapter, however, we demonstrate how these stable psychological vulnerabilities may incorporate and interact with various propagating factors that we discussed in chapters 3 through 8. Through their connections with propagating factors, these vulnerabilities to depression may prolong the course of depression.

Before we discuss the role of propagating factors among stable vulnerabilities to depression, it is important to note that vulnerabilities could provide one explanation for depression's chronic course in the absence of propagating factors. In particular, the long-standing nature of depression, with various depression-free episodes interspersed between times of depression, may occur simply as a result of interactions between stable vulnerabilities and negative life events. That is, in the presence of negative life events, persistent vulnerabilities may be activated to the point that they induce a depressive episode. After a change in environmental circumstances (e.g., reduction of stress) or a fortification of coping skills, the depressive episode may remit. However, as long as the vulnerability remains, negative events may send an individual into a downward spiral of depression.

This notion is consistent with the majority of theories of vulnerabilities to depression, as well as to psychopathology in general. That is, most theories are diathesis–stress models, positing that a given vulnerability serves as an underlying diathesis to illness, and an external stressor such as a negative life event triggers the diathesis into an increase in symptoms of the illness. In addition to the theoretical concordance of vulnerability–event interactions, empirical data indicate that depressive episodes are usually precipitated by an identifiable negative event. In fact, in a study of the characteristics of major depression among adolescents and young adults, Lewinsohn, Pettit, Joiner, and Seeley (2003) found that specific life events were identified as precipitants of depressive episodes about 90% of the time! Although they did not examine the interaction of vulnerabilities with life events, the overwhelming percentage of depressive episodes that occurred following a negative life event is at least consistent with diathesis-stress models.

Nevertheless, the fact remains that not all depressive episodes are precipitated by negative events. There remains a subset of depressions that seem to more or less "come out of the blue," occurring for seemingly no recognizable reason. These depressions may occur as a result of the vulnerabilities themselves, the scarring effects of a previous depressive episode (see also chap. 1 for an in-depth discussion of this process), or an interaction between vulnerabilities and erosive processes.

STABLE COGNITIVE VULNERABILITIES

Perhaps the most thoroughly researched vulnerabilities to depression stem from theories regarding mental representations of environments and events, more commonly referred to as *cognitions*. The notion of cognitive vulnerabilities to depression emerged from the theoretical framework that humans actively interpret and construct mental representations of the world around them, including social contacts. A central line of empirical work in this area comes from Abramson and Alloy's hopelessness theory of depression.

Hopelessness

According to the hopelessness theory (Abramson, Metalsky, & Alloy, 1989), the tendency to attribute negative events to stable and global causes represents a diathesis that, in the presence but not the absence of negative life stress, increases vulnerability to depression. Furthermore, the theory specifies the mechanism by which negative attributional style (i.e., the tendency to attribute negative events to stable, global causes) leads to depressive symptoms. Specifically, those who possess a negative attributional style and who encounter negative life events are predicted to become hopeless, and as a function thereof, become depressed.

Past research on adults and adolescents has provided support for each of the elements of the hopelessness theory. Several reports have shown that the diathesis–stress component is associated with increases in depression (e.g., Metalsky, Joiner, Hardin, & Abramson, 1993), and some have demonstrated that such increases are mediated, at least in part, by hopelessness (Hankin, Abramson, & Siler, 2001; Metalsky & Joiner, 1992). To date, the most compelling evidence in support of the theory derives from the Temple–Wisconsin cognitive vulnerability to depression project (e.g., Alloy & Abramson, 1999). These researchers selected a group of currently nondepressed young adults— some of whom possessed a negative attributional style and some of whom did not—and followed these participants for over 2 years to determine who became depressed. At the 2-year follow-up, the rate of current major depression among those with a negative attributional style was 22%, and the corresponding rate among those with a positive attributional style was 3.4%. In a very important supplemental analysis, these authors showed that this same difference emerged when participants with a previous history of depression were excluded; the results were thus not explained by any association between negative attributional style and past history of depression. It is interesting to note that there were no differences between the negative and positive attributional style participants with regard to anxiety disorders, consistent with the theory's claim that it is specific to depression, even as compared with closely associated mental disorders. Subsequent research supports the specificity of the model to depression, not anxiety (e.g., Hankin, Abramson, Miller, & Haeffel, 2004).

Recent work from Alloy et al. (2001) identified potential antecedents to the development of a "depressogenic" cognitive style (i.e., negative attributional style). In an investigation of parental characteristics, Alloy et al. found that mothers of individuals with a depressogenic cognitive style were more likely to exhibit negative inferential styles and dysfunctional attitudes. Furthermore, both mothers and fathers of such individuals provided more stable, global attributional feedback for negative events in their child's life and provided more negative consequence feedback for negative social events in their child's life. Finally, low levels of emotional acceptance and warmth from fathers were more prevalent among individuals displaying a depressogenic cognitive style.

Gibb et al. (2001) identified another precursor to a depressogenic cognitive style: childhood emotional maltreatment. Higher levels of self-reported childhood emotional maltreatment were predictive of the later development of a depressogenic cognitive style. In contrast, lower levels of childhood physical maltreatment were associated with a depressogenic cognitive style. Although the mechanism by which developmental emotional maltreatment leads to a depressogenic cognitive style is unknown, individuals possessing this style may have internalized their adverse environments and the negative cognitions espoused by their abusers.

As these two studies illustrate, parental characteristics and the interpersonal dynamics of the parent–child relationship may play a key role in the development of a relatively stable vulnerability to depression: negative attributional style. Most likely, many other variables contribute to the development of this vulnerability, and it is overly simplistic to assert that parenting factors alone produce a negative attributional style. Nonetheless, the role of childhood environments in the development of later depression cannot be discounted.

In addition to being a stable vulnerability factor itself, hopelessness likely interplays with self-propagatory processes to promote the persistence of depression. Take, for example, Wagner, Berenson, Harding, and Joiner's (1998) findings on teenage pregnancy and depression: All of the pregnant girls, pessimistic and optimistic alike, generated the considerable stressor of teenage pregnancy. But only the pessimistic girls, because of the relatively enduring personality trait of pessimism, reacted to the generated stress with postpartum depression. Furthermore, once the diathesis of a negative attributional style has developed, the negative interpersonal consequences of hopelessness may serve as stressors themselves, which maintain and intensify the depressive experience. In this sense, the negative interpersonal effects of hopelessness may be, at least in part, the mechanism that makes negative attributional style a stable vulnerability for depression.

Imagine, for example, a hypothetical scenario in which one of the pessimistic adolescents in Wagner et al.'s (1998) study developed postpartum depression. For the purposes of this example, let us assume that the father of the baby and the adolescent girl's family rallied together with her to assume supportive, mutual roles in caring for the child (although this is often not the case among teenage parents, unfortunately). As the young mother struggles with depression and the trials of caring for an infant, they (i.e., the infant's father and her family) initially assist with the caregiving and make supportive statements such as "we'll get through this tough time," "I'm here to help," and "we're in this together." After being repeatedly met with pessimistic responses from her (e.g., "my life is over," "everything is messed up now," "you can't do anything to make this better"), however, their supportive and caring approach cools considerably. As a result, she feels isolated, unloved, and as though she alone bears the child-rearing burden. Hence, despite her desire (and need) for support during this difficult time of stress and transition, the expression of hopelessness served to distance those closest to her, increasing the likelihood that her depression will continue. It is clear that therapeutic work in this case could focus on increasing the girl's optimism, working with significant others to better understand the effects of postpartum depression and how they can best support her, and clarifying roles of various family members with regard to child care.

Sociotropy

A second, albeit similar, major cognitive model of depression maintains that dysfunctional attitudes (e.g., "I am nothing if a person I love doesn't love me") represent vulnerability factors that interact with negative life events to contribute to the development of depressive symptoms (Beck, 1976). This happens as a function of the development of stream-of-consciousness negative automatic thoughts about the self, world, and future (i.e., the negative cognitive triad). Within this line of research, a distinction between *sociotropic* dysfunctional attitudes (i.e., excessive neediness vis-à-vis other people) and *autonomous* dysfunctional attitudes (i.e., perfectionistic expectations regarding achievement) has emerged (Beck, Epstein, & Harrison, 1983). The validity of this distinction, however, is controversial (Coyne & Whiffen, 1995).

According to Beck's theory, individuals displaying sociotropic dysfunctional attitudes often find themselves distraught over issues of interpersonal intimacy, social neediness, and dependency. As such, one expects that sociotropic cognitions form the mental basis of overt behaviors such as excessive reassurance-seeking (see also chap. 5), negative feedback-seeking (see also chap. 4), and interpersonal conflict avoidance (see also chap. 6). Moreover, sociotropy and autonomy represent personality dimensions in Beck's theory, and this characterization is supported by their considerable temporal stability (e.g., Moore & Blackburn, 1996). Consequently, the dimension of sociotropy may represent an enduring pattern of cognitions (and coinciding behaviors) that predisposes people to developing and maintaining depression. This vulnerability not only places individuals at increased risk for developing depressive episodes but also, as we have argued in previous chapters, establishes a cyclical pattern of thoughts and behaviors that makes it exceedingly difficult to come out of a depressed state.

If sociotropic cognitions and maladaptive interpersonal behaviors are indeed related, sociotropic dysfunctional attitudes may serve as stable vulnerabilities to the aforementioned maladaptive behaviors, and consequently, to depression. Moreover, such maladaptive interpersonal behaviors may be the mechanism by which sociotropic cognitions promote depression. That is, interpersonal behaviors such as excessive reassurance-seeking and negative feedback-seeking may mediate the relationship between sociotropy and depression. For example, a man who displays a great deal of dependence on his relationship partner yet feels insecure about the stability of their relationship and whether she will leave him (i.e., is high in sociotropy) may actually drive her away by excessively questioning her loyalty and desire to stay with him. Her termination of the relationship may then serve as a stressor that pushes him into a depressive episode. Although this topic has received little empirical attention, at least one study has provided evidence for this mediational model. To wit, Beck, Robbins, Taylor, and Baker (2001) found that sociotropy, but not autonomy, was related to excessive reassurance-seeking. More important to the present model, excessive reassurance-seeking mediated the relationship between sociotropy and depressive symptoms. Further research on this topic is clearly necessary, but empirical data thus far are consistent with the notion that cognitive vulnerabilities such as hopelessness and sociotropy may have their most pernicious and chronic effects through the interpersonal behaviors that they engender.

Self-Regulatory Perseveration

A third cognitive model that proposes relatively stable vulnerabilities emphasizes failures in self-regulation as a causal factor in depression onset and chronicity (Pyszczynski & Greenberg, 1987). Although this is not a purely cognitive model, the heavy emphasis on self-focused attention places it nearer to the cognitive camp than to other camps. Pyszczynski and Greenberg's model, which draws on findings from social and personality psychology, posits that self-focused attention leads to a self-evaluative process whereby people compare their present state on a particular aspect with their ideal state on that aspect. This is part of a natural self-regulatory feedback cycle whereby an individual monitors and adjusts his or her progress toward specific goals. According to the model, positive affect results when one meets or exceeds the desired standard, and negative affect comes about when one falls short of the aspired standard (Duval & Wicklund, 1972). Moreover, meeting one's standards leads to an exit of the cycle and a subsequent decrease in self-focused attention. However, falling short of one's standards causes the individual to attempt to adjust his or her present self to become more aligned with the ideal self. When the subjective probability of attaining the standard is high, the individual works to achieve this goal. When the subjective probability is low, however, the individual ceases efforts to reduce the discrepancy between the current self and the ideal self and avoids self-focus.

Pyszczynski and Greenberg (1987) expanded on this work, proposing a model wherein a negative life event (i.e., a loss) is likely to increase self-focused attention that in turn activates the self-regulatory cycle. As a result of loss, people sense a negative discrepancy between the real and ideal selves and experience negative affect. The subjective probability of diminishing this discrepancy determines whether people engage in behaviors geared toward that end. Depression onset occurs when this probability is low, yet people continue to engage in the self-regulatory cycle. This perseveration occurs because the loss is central to people's sense of identity. Thus, they are caught in a cycle of self-focus but are unable to regain what was lost. Hence, the increased self-focus leads to an increase in negative affect, self-blame, self-criticism, and the like. As a result, people develop a *depressive self-focusing style* through which they self-focus about negative events but not about positive events. Furthermore, their self-image is altered as a result of the aforementioned processes, and the new, negative self-image is sustained by a depressive self-focusing style.

The relevance of this model to depression chronicity is relatively straightforward. According to the model, depressive episodes are primarily caused and maintained by a failure to exit the self-regulatory cycle. Thus, people continue to focus on the self-standard discrepancy. This leads to a depressive self-focusing style, through which people self-focus and make internal attributions regarding failures but make external attributions regarding successes. Such internal attributions and high self-focus lead to increased (and continued) negative affect, and the negative self-concept becomes firmly established. In this manner, failure to exit the self-regulatory cycle directly leads to depression. But there is also likely an indirect pathway from depressive self-focusing to depression. In this scenario, the increased negative affect and excessive self-focus that result from the depressive self-focusing style may lead to neglect and failure in other areas of people's lives that in turn maintains the self-regulatory process and negative self-focus.

In all likelihood, interpersonal relationships make up one of these other areas—and an important one, at that! Excessive self-focus requires resources that may otherwise be allocated to interpersonal behaviors. At the most basic level, increased focus on the self dictates a decrease in focus on others. It is not surprising that depressed persons often withdraw from social interactions, which only amplifies attention devoted to the self. In the interpersonal relations that are maintained by depressed persons, increased self-focus likely surfaces in interactions. For instance, increased self-focus may lead to reassurance-seeking and negative feedback-seeking, both of which are maladaptive communicative behaviors that focus on the self. That is, following a loss and the consequent failure to meet a self-standard, people likely desire reassurances from others that they are still worthy in some sense. As a result, they engage in the reassurance-seeking process as was described in chapter 5. However, reassurances from others are likely dismissed because they are inconsistent with the failure to meet a self-standard. Such people may also seek negative feedback from others (see chap. 6) because it is consistent with their recent failure to meet a self-standard. The interpersonal fallout and exacerbation of depressive symptoms accompanying these two interpersonal behaviors have already been explained. The important point here is that the excessive self-focus posited in Pyszczynski and Greenberg's (1987) model may promote and maintain depression through its influence in the social arena.

A study we conducted supports the validity of this sequence of events (Pettit & Joiner, 2001b). We had undergraduate students fill out measures of negative life events, self-esteem, and feedback-seeking at two times separated by a 5-week interval. We found that students who experienced more negative life events during the period of the study expressed a greater desire in negative feedback at the end of the study, even when taking into account their initial levels of feedback-seeking. Moreover, the predictive relationship between negative life events and later negative feedback-seeking was accounted for by changes in self-esteem following the negative life event. That is, the negative life events led to a drop in self-esteem that in turn led to a greater desire for negative feedback. Although we did not measure whether the drop in self-esteem corresponded to an increase in self-focused attention, self-esteem has often been framed in terms of the comparison of actual and ideal selves (Higgins, 1987). It therefore seems reasonable to tentatively conclude that negative events disrupt self-concept (and perhaps increases self-focused attention) that in turn promotes maladaptive interpersonal behaviors. These maladaptive interpersonal behaviors then increase the probability of depression.

Consistent with the emphasis on self-focused attention, Nolen-Hoeksema, Morrow, and Fredrickson (1993) proposed that enduring attention to one's own symptoms represents a stable vulnerability to depression. More specifically, these investigators have emphasized the deleterious effects of a ruminative response style. They have argued that the duration of depressive symptoms is influenced by the manner in which individuals respond to their own symptoms. Ruminative response styles involve enduring attention to one's negative emotions; that is, attention is passively and repetitively focused on one's symptoms as well as on the causes, meanings, and consequences of those symptoms (Nolen-Hoeksema, 2000a). It is important to note that ruminative responses inhibit purposeful activity geared toward symptom relief or toward change of one's current situation. Nolen-Hoeksema et al. (1993) have shown that depressed people tend to display ruminative response styles and that such styles expand the duration, severity, and recurrence of depressive episodes (see also Nolen-Hoeksema, 2000b).

How might a ruminative response style interplay with interpersonal self-propagatory factors to encourage depression chronicity? Similar to the material just presented, a speculative possibility is that rumination is the "cognitive motor" that drives behaviors such as excessive reassurance-seeking and negative feedback-seeking. Regarding reassurance-seeking, Joiner, Katz, and Lew (1999) found that dysphoric ideation and mood fueled excessive reassurance-seeking. Insofar as rumination may sustain dysphoric ideation and mood, it may also drive reassurance-seeking. Moreover, uncertainty and doubts are thought to contribute to excessive reassurance-seeking. It is not surprising that ruminators are characterized by uncertainty and a lack of confidence in interpersonal problems (Ward, Lyubomirksy, Sousa, & Nolen-Hoeksema, 2003). Similarly, because rumination may maintain focus on feelings of inadequacy and self-doubt, it may induce negative feedback-seeking.

Thus, high self-focus (ruminative or otherwise) may lead to a serious disruption in interpersonal relationships through (a) social withdrawal; (b) maladaptive, overly self-focused communication patterns (e.g., excessive reassurance-seeking); and (c) interpersonal rejection that stems from these self-focused communication patterns. In this manner, self-regulatory failures marked by increased attention on the self may alter interpersonal relationships, become a stable vulnerability for depression, and therefore promote the chronicity of depression.

Fortunately, and as we discuss in chapter 13, there are multiple avenues for cutting off the life-blood of depression chronicity in such instances. Both cognitive and behavioral techniques could be applied to modify rumination patterns, to increase social activities, or to improve social skills and communication patterns (an ideal approach would likely address all three of these areas during the course of treatment). Moreover, in the context of couples or family therapy, issues of blaming and interpersonal rejection in response to depressive communications could be addressed.

STABLE INTERPERSONAL VULNERABILITIES

It should be quite clear by now that numerous interpersonal factors contribute to the development and maintenance of depression. The stability of some of these factors, such as reassurance-seeking and negative feedback-seeking, is not known. That is, research has not investigated whether these interpersonal behavior patterns fluctuate over time or whether they demonstrate temporal consistency (although initial evidence indicates that feedback-seeking behaviors may fluctuate in response to self-esteem changes; Pettit & Joiner, 2001b). Evidence suggests that other vulnerabilities, however, remain a stable threat to the well-being of their possessor.

Dependency

One such factor is excessive dependency. Interpersonally dependent persons are more likely to be depressed than their nondependent counterparts (American Psychiatric Association, 1994). The *Diagnostic and Statistical Manual of Mental Disorders* (4th ed.; American Psychiatric Association, 1994) classifies an extreme and pervasive pattern of dependency as dependent personality disorder, otherwise know as DPD. Moreover, it lists mood disorders (i.e., depressive disorders) as one of the most common associated features. DPD is described as a "pervasive and excessive need to be taken care of that leads to submissive and clinging behavior and fears of separation . . ." (p. 668), and diagnostic criteria include difficulty making everyday decisions without excessive reassurance from others, difficulty expressing disagreement with others, and going to excessive lengths to obtain nurturance from others, to name a few. Note that these DPD criteria are strikingly similar to some of the behaviors that we argue propagate depression (e.g., reassurance-seeking). So it is not surprising that DPD overlaps considerably with depression.

Shyness

DPD also entails another stable interpersonal vulnerability to depression: interpersonal conflict avoidance (see also chap. 6). The tendency to avoid potentially uncomfortable social interactions is a stable trait, with shyness demonstrating remarkable consistency from early childhood until late adulthood. Indeed, personality researcher Arnold Buss (1991) maintains that shyness is derived from personality traits that appear during the first year of life, persist in later life, and derive at least in part from heredity. Shyness has been implicated as a risk factor for depression. In a study examining the specific role of shyness in producing depressive symptoms, Joiner (1997) found that the combination of shyness and low social support led to increases in depressive symptoms. That is, shyness in and of itself did not promote depression. Those persons with social support were buffered from the development of depressive symptoms. Those without adequate social support, however, were at risk for becoming more depressed. It is interesting to note that this relationship between shyness, social support, and depression was partially mediated by increases in loneliness. Stated differently, the increase in depressive symptoms among shy people with low social support was partially due to the fact that they became more lonely during the course of the study. It is worth noting that these findings were specific to depression; the same process did not lead to an increase in anxious symptoms.

SOCIAL SKILLS DEFICITS

Social skills represent another potential stable vulnerability to depression. As Lewinsohn (1974) described, people who display poor social skills are less likely to obtain positive outcomes and avoid negative outcomes in interpersonal relationships. As a result, they are more likely to become and stay depressed (e.g., Segrin & Dillard, 1992; Segrin & Dillard, 2000). Although the long-term stability of social skills deficits needs to be more thoroughly studied, an impressive amount of evidence suggests that people who are depressed also display poor social skills. As Segrin (2001) outlined, evidence to date supports three possible explanations for the association of social skills deficits and depression: (a) poor social skills are a causal antecedent to depression; (b) the experience of depression produces deficits in social skills; and (c) poor social skills may represent a stable, distal vulnerability, which only leads to depression in the presence of other stressors.

Interpersonal stress generation, as we discussed in chapter 3, may also be considered a chronic interpersonal vulnerability to depression. Although we are not aware of any studies directly addressing the long-term nature of interpersonal stress-generation, the work of Hammen (e.g., Hammen, 1991) suggests that this behavioral pattern represents a relatively stable phenomenon.

Therefore, drawing on the material already discussed in previous chapters, as well as the brief discussion here of dependency, shyness, social skills, and stress generation, the case can be made that certain patterns of interpersonal behaviors serve as stable vulnerabilities to depression. Moreover, they likely interact with self-propagatory processes to further exacerbate and extend depression.

PERSONALITY-BASED VIEWS OF DEPRESSION

As we have argued, depression is often chronic and stable. The fact that it has been theoretically associated with personality, which is also highly stable, therefore comes as no surprise. In fact, the notion that certain stable personality and temperament traits may be linked to depression has existed since antiquity. For example, in his theory of "humors" (bodily fluids), Hippocrates proposed that people with an excess of black bile were more likely to be "melancholic" (Lloyd, 1978). More recently, clinical and personality scientists have associated specific personality components or traits with depression. One such trait, neuroticism (i.e., the tendency toward emotional distress, self-consciousness, and insecurity) has received empirical support as a vulnerability factor for long-term increases in depression (e.g., Henderson et al., 1997). The shyness model previously discussed—which may be linked to neuroticism—may also be viewed as a personality-based model of depression, to the extent that shyness is considered a stable personality trait.

In addition to work implying that depression may be more of a trait-like, personality-based syndrome, as opposed to an episodic disorder, some have argued that a specific *depressive personality disorder* exists. A *personality disorder* refers to "an enduring pattern of inner experience and behavior that deviates markedly from the expectations of the individual's culture, is pervasive and inflexible, has an onset in adolescence or early adulthood, is stable over time, and leads to distress or impairment" (American Psychiatric Association, 1994, p. 629). Personality disorders reflect maladaptive and inflexible manifestations of personality traits, which entail patterns of perceiving, relating to, and thinking about the environment.

Klein and Shih (1998) investigated the validity of depressive personality disorder as a diagnostic category. Although they refrained from providing specific conclusions about its validity, they presented evidence suggesting that it may in fact be a legitimate frame of reference for those who have enduring cases of depression. In their study, they asked five questions that would help to determine the validity of depressive personality disorder. First, they questioned whether depressive personality disorder could be distinguished from *major depressive disorder* (MDD) and dysthymia, another chronic, but low-grade, form of depression. They found that among outpatients with mood disorders, personality disorders, or both, there was a high degree of overlap between depressive personality disorder and dysthymia (i.e., 80% of people with a primary diagnosis of depressive personality disorder were also diagnosed with dysthymia, and 73% of people with a primary diagnosis of dysthymia were also diagnosed with depressive personality disorder). They did not find the same level of overlap between depressive personality disorder and either current MDD or lifetime MDD. Furthermore, depressive personality disorder was only weakly associated with diagnoses of dysthymia and MDD among first degree relatives of the outpatients. Thus depressive personality disorder overlapped considerably with a chronic, milder form of depression (dysthymia), but not MDD.

Second, Klein and Shih (1998) investigated the extent to which depressive personality disorder overlapped with already existing personality disorders. Consistent with the notion that depressive personality disorder represents a valid nosological construct, depressive personality disorder did not overlap exceedingly with existing personality disorders. The greatest overlap was with *avoidant personality disorder* (APD) and *borderline personality disorder* (BPD), but it was still less than 30%. It is interesting to note that the two disorders that were the most empirically similar to depressive personality disorder both involve significant interpersonal tension, even as compared with other personal disorders. For example, APD is highly similar to the pattern of interpersonal conflict avoidance presented in chapter 6. Likewise, BPD frequently involves high levels of interpersonal stressors and impaired problem solving (e.g., Linehan, Camper, Chiles, Strosahl, & Shearin, 1987), both of which are reminiscent of material discussed in chapter 3 on interpersonal stress generation (e.g., Hammen, 1991) and impaired interpersonal problem solving (e.g., Davila, Hammen, Burge, & Paley, 1995). Therefore, depressive personality disorder appears to be distinct from other personality disorders, while still sharing characteristics of those that are replete with interpersonal factors that promote depression chronicity.

Third, Klein and Shih (1998) investigated the relationship between depressive personality disorder and normal dimensions of personality and positive and negative affect. Both positive affect (PA) and negative affect (NA) have been implicated as constituents of depression (Clark & Watson, 1991). The authors found that depressive personality disorder was moderately correlated with the dimensions of NA and PA. Moreover, depressive personality disorder contributed unique information over and above NA and PA to the prediction of a history of a mood disorder. Thus, depressive personality disorder appears to represent more than simply two components of depression.

Fourth, the authors (Klein & Shih, 1998) determined the temporal stability of depressive personality disorder. If it truly represents a personality disorder, it should exhibit considerable stability over many years. Over a period of 30 months (the length of the study), depressive personality disorder demonstrated stability comparable to those of other personality disorders. When estimating probable diagnoses, almost 75% of individuals with a diagnosis of depressive personality disorder at Time 1 would receive a diagnosis of DPD 30 months later. Therefore, depressive personality disorder passes the test of stability.

Finally, Klein and Shih (1998) investigated the ability of depressive personality disorder to predict Axis I depressive status (i.e., MDD and dysthymia) 30 months after baseline assessment. After controlling for baseline MDD, dysthymia, PA, NA, and other personality disorders, depressive personality disorder remained a significant predictor of Axis I depressive status. Thus, these findings suggest that depressive personality disorder has incremental validity over a number of theoretically related variables.

Overall, the work of Klein and Shih (1998) provides compelling evidence for the existence of a depressive personality disorder. The presence of such a category indicates that depression, among some individuals, represents a lifelong pattern of thinking and acting and solidifies the notion of depression as a chronic disorder. Moreover, their work demonstrates that depressive personality disorder serves as a risk factor for the development of full-blown major depressive episodes and chronic, low-grade forms of depression.

Although research on interpersonal processes at work in depressive personality disorder is scarce, initial evidence suggests that it—like other forms of chronic depression—is associated with interpersonal loss (cf. stress generation; Huprich, 2003). This appears to be the case even controlling for the association of state depressed mood and interpersonal loss.

SUMMARY

In this chapter, we reviewed certain models of persistent vulnerabilities to depression, and have proposed possible interpersonal mechanisms by which these characteristics and styles play a role in the development and maintenance of depression. Stable vulnerabilities may be primarily cognitive, such as a depressogenic attributional style characterized by hopelessness, or may be more relevant to interpersonal domains, such as excessive dependency. Other evidence suggests that stable personality characteristics such as neuroticism promote depression, or even that depression itself may take on a personality-like quality (e.g., depressive personality disorder). It can be argued, however, that despite the different domains of stable vulnerabilities, at least part of their contribution to the chronicity of depression occurs through the types of interpersonal behaviors we outlined in previous chapters. In the next chapter, we return our focus to the interpersonal behaviors discussed in chapters 3 through 8, and examine how they may interact to propagate the disorder and erode personal resources.

10

THE COMPLEX INTERPLAY
OF THE FACTORS

To manage a system effectively, you might focus on the interactions of
the parts rather than their behavior taken separately.
—Russell L. Ackoff

In our presentation of six interpersonal processes that lead to the self-
propagation of depression, we devoted a chapter to how each process contributes to depression chronicity. We did this for both conceptual (i.e., they
are distinguishable processes) and presentational reasons (i.e., it is easier to
present and understand one process at a time). Despite our distinction between these processes, we emphasize that they are not mutually exclusive. In
fact, they likely co-occur within depressed persons to further prolong depression. In this chapter, we discuss examples of how these interpersonal processes co-occur with each other and with other erosive processes, and what
the untoward consequences may be.

THE INTERPLAY OF SELF-PROPAGATORY PROCESSES

Fifty-seven possible combinations of the six processes described in chapters 3 through 8 are possible (120 are possible if just one erosive factor is
added to the mix). It is clear that we do not have enough space to discuss all
of these combinations. To focus the discussion, we consider only sets of two

(e.g., negative feedback-seeking and excessive reassurance-seeking) with the additional criterion that such combinations must be either empirically supported or conceptually compelling.

In addition to all the possible combinations of these processes, there are various ways in which they may relate to each other. That is, these processes likely do not co-occur simply by coincidence; rather, they influence and interact with one another. For conceptual clarification, we discuss these combinations along four dimensions: (a) synchrony, (b) compounding, (c) initiation, and (d) erosive–propagatory interactions.

Self-Propagatory Processes as Synchronous

When we refer to the interplay of processes as *synchronous*, we mean that one process may accomplish another. An example outside the domain of psychopathology may be helpful here. Consider the tasks of (a) studying 19th-century English literature and (b) expanding one's vocabulary. These are separate, distinguishable behaviors, yet the former arguably accomplishes the latter to a certain extent. In a similar manner, some of the interpersonal processes described earlier may accomplish others. For example, there is a synchrony between the higher order concept of stress generation, on the one hand, and the first-order instances of negative feedback-seeking, excessive reassurance-seeking, and interpersonal avoidance, on the other hand. Simply put, these latter processes accomplish the former. That is, the very acts of excessively seeking reassurance and negative feedback strain relationships by leaving both partners frustrated. For instance, consider the case of a depressed woman who excessively seeks assurances from her boyfriend as to her own attractiveness then rejects his assurances because they contradict her self-perception as unattractive. The boyfriend is frustrated by the excessive nature of her requests for reassurances as well as confused by the mixed messages he receives. Likewise, the woman remains distressed over her negative self-image and her doubts of her partner's sincerity. Hence, the solicitation of assurances and negative feedback represent forms of stress generation in and of themselves.

Although not hierarchically related in higher-order versus first-order arrangement, negative feedback-seeking and self-handicapping may be viewed as synchronous, in the sense that one may accomplish the other. As one example, the phrase "I'm just no good as a spouse" may both invite confirmation as a bad spouse and reduce others' expectations of future performance as a spouse. It is notable that this same phrase, if properly intoned, may also invite reassurance (e.g., "no, really, like I told you before, you're a *very* good spouse").

Self-Propagatory Processes Compound One Another

In addition to being synchronous, self-propagatory processes may compound the negative effects of other processes. Consistent with the example of simultaneously soliciting and rejecting assurances, we argue that people with negative self-views are caught in a "cognitive–emotional crossfire" between coexisting needs to obtain negative feedback (to fulfill cognitive needs for verification) and reassurance (to fulfill emotional needs for support; Joiner & Metalsky, 1995). In the interpersonal arena, excessive reassurance-seeking and negative feedback-seeking compound one another by creating a particularly confusing and frustrating experience for relationship partners of depressed people. To continue the previous example, the boyfriend responds to his depressed girlfriend's request for assurance about her attractiveness, only to have his response rejected. After repeated occurrences of this request–respond–reject transaction, the boyfriend may feel exasperated to the point of ending the relationship (which would likely leave the woman feeling even more distressed and unattractive). It is interesting to note that this process has been confirmed empirically: Joiner and Metalsky (1995) found that relationship partners of depressed people are particularly likely to evaluate them negatively if they engaged in both excessive reassurance-seeking and negative feedback-seeking.

The effects of excessive reassurance-seeking and negative feedback-seeking on depressed people's relationships may be further compounded by interpersonal avoidance. Insofar as avoidant people often have few relationships on which to rely, the negative effects of excessive reassurance-seeking and negative feedback-seeking may be concentrated on just one or two relationships. Let us expand on the ongoing example and assume that the depressed woman who sought and rejected reassurance from her boyfriend is also avoidant of interpersonal exchanges (a reasonable assumption, and also supported by data showing that excessive reassurance-seeking is positively correlated with shyness; Joiner, 1998). Given her reticence in social settings, she is unlikely to have developed an extensive social network. As such, the majority—if not all—of her need for reassurances about her attractiveness are directed toward her boyfriend rather than being spread out among various friends, acquaintances, and the like. Hence, just as a lens may intensely focus sunlight on one spot, avoidance may focus excessive reassurance-seeking and negative feedback-seeking on one relationship. In this sense, interpersonal avoidance may compound, or intensify, the negative impact of excessive reassurance-seeking and negative feedback-seeking. Namely, the intensity and repetitive nature of these behaviors in a given relationship often leads to frustration, and at times, even depressive symptoms or full-syndrome depression among others (cf. contagious depression). Consequently, relationships may be compromised by the pressure, leaving the avoidant depressed person truly bereft of social reinforcement and support.

To make matters worse, interpersonally avoidant (i.e., shy) people are vulnerable to the experience of loneliness and thus at risk for depression unless buffered by good social support (Joiner, 1997). When maladaptive interpersonal behaviors compromise relationships, shy people are more likely to experience loneliness, less likely to have good social support (their relationship partner is no longer available), and are therefore more likely to become even more depressed.

Self-Propagatory Processes Induce One Another

The idea that one process may produce another needs little elaboration. A relevant example here is the development of blame maintenance (chap. 8). In the chapter on blame maintenance, we argued that others' mental representations of depressed people, originally based at least in part on actual behaviors of the depressed person, become relatively autonomous and negatively bias subsequent social cognition. Each of the other five self-propagatory processes potentially represents a "data source" on which others may draw to initially form negative person schemata. Indeed, research on excessive reassurance-seeking (e.g., Joiner & Metalsky, 1995) and negative feedback-seeking (e.g., Swann, Wenzlaff, Krull, & Pelham, 1992) has shown that these behaviors on the part of depressed people lead others to form negative impressions. It is not hard to imagine that conflict avoidance and self-handicapping processes would also negatively influence others' impressions or confirm negative schemata already in operation (e.g., "he's not up to the task," "she's always making excuses," "he just lets people walk all over him"). Thus, several of the self-propagatory processes may induce blame maintenance.

Similarly, excessive reassurance-seeking and negative feedback-seeking may induce one another (in addition to compounding one another). Specifically, Joiner and Metalsky (1995) hypothesized that these two processes were entrained, such that receipt of reassurance (i.e., positive feedback), because it is discrepant with negative self-views, leads to needs for negative, self-verifying feedback. Negative feedback, in turn, because it is discrepant with emotional needs for support and assurance, leads to needs for reassurance, and so on. Evidence backs up this hypothesis. Joiner and Metalsky found that although excessive reassurance-seeking and negative feedback-seeking are uncorrelated, they were entrained among those with depressive symptoms, such that one leads to the other, which leads to the first, and so on (Katz & Joiner, 2002). The model is that, at least initially, excessive reassurance-seeking leads to positive (if dismissed) feedback from others. This feedback may be dismissed because it is discrepant with the negative self-concept, stimulating needs for self-confirmation in the form of negative feedback. Negative feedback, although confirming, is emotionally painful (cf. Joiner, 1995), arousing needs for reassurance, and so on. A self-sustaining cycle may thus be established, fueled by intrapsychic needs for self-verification and emotional consolation, and played out on the interpersonal stage.

Depressed people, then, may encounter the ironic and intractable problem that satisfaction of one set of needs is at odds with satisfaction of another. Excessive reassurance-seeking and negative feedback-seeking may continually induce one another, leaving the relationship partners of depressed people confused, frustrated, and increasingly likely to negatively evaluate (cf. blame maintenance) and reject (cf. stress generation) the depressed person.

As a final instance of one self-propagatory process inducing another, conflict avoidance may encourage self-handicapping regarding social and interpersonal performance. For example, the statement "I'm just no good at handling conflict" may simultaneously accomplish conflict avoidance, explain current performance deficits, and reduce others' expectations for future performance. Some research exists to support the notion that socially avoidant persons react negatively to success in the social arena: Wallace and Alden (1997) reported that social phobic patients, on experimentally manipulated social success, experienced increased negative affect as well as concerns that others would expect more from them in future social interactions. Avoidant people, then, may be motivated to strategically fail in social situations (cf. Weary & Williams, 1990), so that performance demands, as well as negative emotional states, are reduced. Referring back to our example of the man who self-handicapped on the work softball team, imagine that he was also high in avoidance, to the point that going to bat and being on base were unpleasant experiences. He may be motivated to "strike out" as a means of quickly escaping the social spotlight and quelling others' expectations of him.

Erosive–Propagatory Interactions

The possibility of erosive or "scarring" processes in chronic depression is discussed in chapter 1. In the strictest sense, erosive processes involve the passive loss of personal and psychological resources, such as when a depressive episode erodes neurobiological mechanisms responsible for healthy functioning (Post, 1994). Nonetheless, it is conceivable that erosive processes would set forth self-propagatory processes, in at least three ways. First, erosion of certain domains of functioning (e.g., problem-solving, self-esteem) may lead to active, maladaptive processes such as impaired interpersonal problem solving and negative feedback-seeking. In this way, a passive erosion of resources lays the groundwork for an active self-propagatory process.

Of course, it should be noted that the very existence of erosive processes has not been thoroughly investigated, and when it has, results have been mixed. More specifically, evidence has not supported the notion that the experience of depression leaves a lasting scar on personality, at least as assessed in adulthood (Rohde, Lewinsohn, & Seeley, 1990; Shea, Leon, Mueller, & Solomon, 1996; Zeiss & Lewinsohn, 1988). Nevertheless, some research indicates that depression experienced among children and adolescents may exert a long-term, negative impact on certain cognitive processes. For example, Nolen-Hoeksema, Girgus, and Seligman (1992) found that explanatory styles of depressed children deteriorated (i.e., became more pessimistic–hopeless) with onset of depression and did not later ameliorate, even on remission of symptoms. Work among psychiatric hospitalized youth likewise suggests that a negative attributional style characterized by stable and global causal attributions of negative life events persists even after depressive symptoms remit (Voelz, Walker, Pettit, Joiner, & Wagner, 2003). That is, both during and after depression, youth were likely to view the causes of negative life events as stable (unlikely to change) and global (likely to affect other outcomes in life). Thus, a small body of evidence suggests that the experience of depression in childhood or adolescence may promote the erosion of certain attributional cognitions.

It is interesting to note the discrepant findings on depression scars between samples of adults and youth. It may be the case that children, who are still in their formative years in many respects, are more vulnerable to enduring effects of depression. Nolen-Hoeksema (2000a) elaborated on this notion with regard to cognitive styles. In particular, she speculated that children, who are in the process of developing beliefs about themselves and the world around them, may be permanently affected by extended periods of depression characterized by negative thoughts and negative life events. In contrast, adults' belief systems are more developed and stable and may therefore be more resistant to the long-term cognitive effects of a depressive episode. From this perspective, it seems plausible that erosive processes may be at work when depression occurs during childhood or adolescence but are less likely to occur among depressed adults.

Given that cognitive erosion may occur among youngsters, how might it engender active self-propagatory processes in the interpersonal domain? One possibility is related to our interpersonal elaboration of Abramson's hopelessness theory of depression (see also chap. 3). As readers will recall, we reported on a series of studies in which students with depression experienced increased rejection by their roommates (cf. stress generation) as a function of their hopelessness. As applied to the current discussion, the experience of depression may erode attributional style, which in turn increases the likelihood of interpersonal rejection, possibly through mechanisms such as blame maintenance. In this manner, an erosive process may activate at least two self-propagatory processes (i.e., blame maintenance and stress generation). Still, we urge caution in accepting this particular pathway until it has received proper empirical scrutiny.

Similarly, erosion may be related to self-propagatory processes in that erosion of a domain may itself become a self-propagatory process. An interesting area in this regard involves the interplay and temporal sequencing of interpersonal avoidance and interpersonal stress generation. This idea has been described by Dobson (2000), who noted that because depressed people have likely experienced interpersonal rejection as a result of symptoms and behaviors associated with the disorder, they may be more likely to avoid social contact even after remission of the disorder. Thus, depression (through interpersonal rejection) may erode social functioning, and the erosion may subsequently serve as a self-propagatory factor for continued depression. In this sense, interpersonal avoidance not only may be a self-propagatory process for future depression but also may be an erosive process following the experience of depression.

In addition to promoting maladaptive processes, a third manner by which erosion of a domain of functioning may set forth self-propagatory processes is through *compensatory* behaviors. That is, following a deterioration in one area (e.g., explanatory style), certain behaviors may emerge in an attempt to compensate for its negative impact. However, it is possible that the compensatory behaviors themselves propagate depression. For example, let us assume that depression erodes self-esteem (a very tenuous assumption, although current depression obviously lowers self-esteem). As a result of the scar of low self-esteem, individuals may engage in excessive reassurance-seeking as an attempt to buttress self-esteem. Consistent with that process, Joiner et al. (1997) found that low self-esteem is an antecedent of increases in excessive reassurance-seeking. (This study did not, however, examine whether lowered self-esteem was a scar of former depression). Erosive process, then, to the extent that they exist, may affect depression chronicity through their effects on self-propagatory features.

SUMMARY

In this chapter, we argued that the self-propagatory processes described in chapters 3 through 8 may interact in numerous ways to influence the chronicity of depression. Possible combinations of interpersonal processes may be considered along four dimensions: (a) synchrony, (b) compounding, (c) initiation, and (d) erosive–propagatory interactions. Although an examination of all possible combinations is clearly beyond the scope of this book—and far beyond existing empirical data—we provided relevant examples that are either empirically supported or conceptually appealing. Moreover, we discussed how self-propagatory processes may interact with erosive processes in chronic depression. In the next chapter, we shift our focus from depression to describe how another form of psychopathology, bulimia, may also develop into a chronic and self-propagating disorder through interpersonal channels.

11

APPLICATION TO A DEPRESSION-RELATED DISORDER: BULIMIA

As we have already discussed, depression frequently co-occurs with other forms of psychopathology, including anxiety disorders, substance use disorders, and eating disorders, to name a few. In this chapter, we extrapolate the interpersonal processes described in previous chapters to a specific eating disorder: bulimia. We focus on bulimia for several reasons. First, this is an area of great interest and familiarity to us, as our own research has emphasized bulimia (Joiner, Heatherton, & Keel, 1997; Vohs et al., 2001). Second, the interpersonal processes described thus far have received more empirical attention in the context of bulimia than other commonly occurring problems (e.g., substance use). Third, the co-occurrence of depression among people with bulimia is extremely high, arguably higher than the co-occurrence of depression among people with other disorders.

Psychopathology researchers, clinicians, and neuroscientists have long noted the relationship between depression and bulimia. Indeed, the two disorders overlap considerably. Although most depressed persons do not develop bulimia, the opposite pathway appears to be true. That is, the vast majority of persons with bulimia are also depressed. It is interesting to note that it appears as though at least some of this overlap may be due to the presence of a presumed "core feature" of bulimia: body dissatisfaction. This is particularly the case among women. However, body dissatisfaction may not necessarily be as specific to bulimia as was once thought. Substantial evidence from Joiner, Wonderlich, Metalsky, and Schmidt (1995) and Vohs et al. (2001) indicates that body dissatisfaction is associated with both depression and bulimia (especially among women), but not with other forms of psychopathology like anxiety. Moreover, Joiner, Wonderlich, et al., (1995) found that depression uniquely and singularly predicted the presence of body dissatisfaction, whereas bulimia did not. That is, being depressed was a better indicator of body dissatisfaction than was being bulimic. Findings therefore suggest that body dissatisfaction is as much a feature of depression as of bulimia! It may be the case that body dissatisfaction is associated with bulimia simply because it is associated with depression (and most people with bulimia are also depressed). To be clear, we are not suggesting that these individuals do not experience body dissatisfaction—they most certainly do, as any bulimic patient or clinician who works with eating-disordered patients can attest. Rather, the results suggest that those with bulimia may be dissatisfied with their bodies as a function of the depressed symptoms that so often accompany bulimia. If these results are reliably replicated, it suggests that the presence of body dissatisfaction is not pathognomonic of bulimia, but an associated feature of depression or a mixed depression–bulimia presentation.

Why are depression, bulimia, and body dissatisfaction so highly related? In light of their research showing that bulimic symptoms tend to precede depressed symptoms but not vice versa, Joiner, Metalsky, and Wonderlich, (1995) proposed that bulimic behavior may be an attempt to fight against the depressogenic effects of body dissatisfaction. The onset of body dissatisfaction may occasion a negative emotional reaction that, if left unchecked, may worsen to the point of depression. Bulimic behavior may be viewed as a "solution" to body dissatisfaction and the consequent negative emotions, in that it is thought (wrongly, it turns out) to improve appearance. Of course, this solution backfires, both psychologically and physiologically: Body dissatisfaction is unaffected, feelings of helplessness regarding binge–purge cycles may arise, and physiology is compromised. All of this may work to increase depression. To summarize this proposed model, body dissatisfaction leads to reactive bulimic behavior, and subsequently, the combination of (continued) body dissatisfaction and problematic bulimic behaviors leads to depression. Although we think this model has promise as an explanation of the interrelation of bulimia, depression, and body dissatisfaction, it should be considered speculative until it has been empirically tested.

CHRONICITY OF BULIMIA

Similar to depression, evidence suggests that bulimia may also be a chronic condition, although perhaps not as persistent as depression. For example, Joiner, Heatherton, et al. (1997) found that bulimic symptoms demonstrated relatively high temporal stability over a 10-year period. Moreover, those with bulimia at the onset of the study were 15 times more likely to display bulimia 10 years later than were those who were not bulimic at the onset. Consistent with this evidence for the stability of bulimic symptoms, Fallon, Walsh, Sadik, Saoud, and Lukasik (1991) reported that almost one half of women hospitalized for bulimia nervosa were bulimic several years later. An additional 20% continued to manifest some bulimic symptoms, despite falling short of diagnostic criteria for syndromal bulimia. Studies with community samples also support the persistence of bulimic symptoms, with estimates suggesting that current bulimic symptoms among adults had an average duration of over 6 years since onset (Hay, 2003).

The finding that bulimic symptoms possess relatively high temporal stability is consistent with several possible courses of symptom manifestation. First, it could be the case that the course of bulimic symptoms is chronic, or long lasting. This would be evidenced by episodes that last for months, or even years. Second, bulimic symptoms may follow a relapsing course, in which symptoms improve but rapidly resume in the vulnerable time frame just following remission. Third, the course of bulimia may be recurrent, in that symptoms remit following an episode, a relatively symptom-free period ensues, but symptoms reappear later during a low-risk period. Fourth, representing the most severe possibility, bulimia may be both long lasting and recurrent. That is, the disorder may be characterized by episodes that last for months or years, remit for a time, and then either relapse or recur in the form of additional lengthy episodes. It is currently not clear which of these courses bulimic symptoms are most likely to follow, or if different people experience different trajectories of the disorder. Nevertheless, any of these scenarios represents a pernicious, persistent disorder with serious consequences for one's health and functioning.

INTERPERSONAL EXPLANATIONS OF BULIMIA CHRONICITY

Given the high rate of depression among people with bulimia, the overlap of at least one major feature (i.e., body dissatisfaction), and the similarly chronic courses of the two disorders, an interesting question is whether some of the same interpersonal processes at work in depression also promote the development and maintenance of bulimic symptoms. Although interpersonal processes in bulimia represent an understudied area, several studies provide preliminary answers to this question.

Negative Feedback-Seeking

Negative feedback-seeking has received much attention thus far in our discussion of depression. The extrapolation of such behaviors to the context of bulimia is easy to imagine. For example, consider a bulimic woman who gets caught in a vicious cycle in which she needs the very interpersonal responses that maintain or exacerbate her symptoms. That is, she needs the predictable, consistent environment that results from others' seeing her the way that she sees herself (e.g., overweight, unattractive). As a result of such evaluations, however, she continues, or even ramps up, purging behaviors with the intended goal of improving her appearance and reducing the negative affect that results from her dissatisfaction with her body. An excruciating dilemma thus emerges: Either sacrifice self-confirmation needs and thus escape from bulimia or meet self-confirmation needs at the price of bulimia.

Joiner (1999b) investigated whether this sort of process may occur among undergraduate women. Consistent with the example previously presented, he predicted that women's interest in negative feedback would be associated with body dissatisfaction and bulimic symptoms, such that women who displayed a desire for more negatively valenced feedback would also display more body dissatisfaction and bulimic symptoms. Indeed, bulimic women were more interested in negative feedback, despite their serious concerns about body image. Even more important, interest in negative feedback served as a risk factor for the later development of bulimic symptoms. Hence, negative feedback-seeking not only occurred simultaneously with bulimic symptoms but also predicted later increases in symptoms. The final piece of this puzzle was that body dissatisfaction mediated the predictive relationships of feedback-seeking on bulimic symptom development. That is, an interest in negative feedback led to the development of a poorer body image, that in turn led to increased bulimic symptoms.

This study was short in duration, and requires replication before firm conclusions are drawn. Nonetheless, the results suggest that self-verification theory may provide insight as to why bulimic symptoms often persist for years, sometimes even despite intervention. In an effort to meet basic needs for self-confirmation, bulimic women may invite the very responses they fear (e.g., negative feedback about appearance) and thus propagate their symptoms. An example of this might be a bulimic woman, holding the belief that she is "fat," being drawn to places such as health clubs and fitness centers because workers and patrons there confirm her belief that she should reduce her body fat. Such places not only provide the opportunity to exercise (and therefore achieve the goal of being thinner) but also may provide a source of negative feedback to the extent that they emphasize the need for her to lose weight. That feedback, although consistent with her body image, further draws attention to her belief that she is fat and likely promotes feelings of distress and low self-worth.

Sociotropy

As we discussed in chapter 9, sociotropy represents a stable set of cognitions characterized by concerns over interpersonal intimacy, social neediness, and dependency. We presented the idea that sociotropy may exacerbate the chronicity of depression through interpersonal mechanisms. That is, sociotropic cognitions are played out in the interpersonal arena, with behaviors such as reassurance-seeking and neediness engendering environments that maintain depression. In this section, we discuss how sociotropy and its corresponding interpersonal sequelae may also occur among bulimic persons.

Evidence suggests that sociotropy and bulimia are indeed connected. In particular, Friedman , Whisman, and colleagues (Friedman & Whisman, 1998; Hayaki, Friedman, Whisman, Delinsky, & Brownell, 2003) delineated the relation of sociotropy and bulimic symptoms in two studies. In the first, Friedman and Whisman demonstrated that sociotropy was significantly associated with bulimic symptoms among a nonclinical sample of undergraduate women, even controlling for depressed mood. This finding suggests that the presence of maladaptive, interpersonally oriented cognitions and behaviors among bulimic women is not simply a function of their level of depression. Expanding on that study, Hayaki et al. replicated the earlier finding among undergraduate women, and also found the same process at work among a clinical sample of bulimic women. Once again, the relation between sociotropy and bulimia was independent of the shared relation with depression, which is noteworthy given the high association between these three variables. The conclusion drawn from these two studies, therefore, is that bulimia appears to be specifically related to the construct of sociotropy.

How might sociotropy manifest in the context of bulimia? Just as depressed persons tend to engage in a pattern of excessive reassurance-seeking to allay fears about their self-worth, so may bulimic persons. An interesting notion that has yet to be investigated is whether those with bulimia are more likely to seek assurances within the specific domains of appearance, body size, and the like. If they are more likely to engage in such behaviors, then excessive reassurance-seeking about appearance may have the unintended consequence of actually pushing others away, which may then be interpreted by the bulimic individual as a rejection because of his or her "unattractiveness." It is important to note that this sequence of events has not yet been put to the empirical test—rather, we propose a possible cycle based on knowledge of reassurance-seeking among depressed persons.

Another pathway through which sociotropic cognitions may affect the development and maintenance of bulimia is interpersonal dependence and conflict avoidance. We discuss this pathway in the next section.

Dependence and Conflict Avoidance

We have already discussed how interpersonal dependence, and the key component of interpersonal conflict avoidance, propagates depression. Might these same factors promote bulimia chronicity? Two issues are relevant to answering this question. First, do bulimic persons display dependency in general, and interpersonal conflict avoidance in particular? Second, what is the impact of such behaviors on subsequent bulimic symptomatology?

With regard to the issue of the presence of interpersonal dependence and conflict avoidance, a number of characteristics are consistent with the notion that bulimic persons do indeed display such behaviors. Empirical data indicate that bulimic persons often have low self-esteem and exhibit a strong desire to please others (Thelen, Farmer, Mann, & Pruitt, 1990), both of which are common among persons with excessive interpersonal dependence. Further bolstering the notion of dependence among bulimic persons, Bornstein (2001) conducted a meta-analysis of studies that examined the association of eating disorders and interpersonal dependency. Results from his meta-analysis indicate that bulimia is significantly associated with symptoms of dependence and with dependent personality disorder. In addition, bulimic persons display high sensitivity to rejection (Duemm, Adams, & Keating, 2003), which is a core feature of sociotropy and a variable associated with the avoidance of interpersonal conflict. Especially germane to the notion of conflict avoidance, persons with eating disorders (including bulimia) display low assertiveness, even as compared with persons with other psychiatric disorders (Williams, Chamove, & Miller, 1990). Thus, the answer to the question of whether bulimic individuals display interpersonal dependence and conflict avoidance is a resounding "yes."

What about the second question, namely, the impact of dependence and conflict avoidance on bulimia? To begin with, poor social adjustment may be linked to the onset and the maintenance of bulimia. Moreover, social maladjustment may represent a relatively stable risk factor for bulimia, as it appears to persist for up to several years, even after remission of bulimic symptoms (Keel, Mitchell, Miller, Davis, & Crow, 2000). Likewise, social adaptation prior to the treatment of bulimia is predictive of later treatment response, such that those with poorer social functioning at the beginning of treatment are more likely to display incomplete recovery at the end of treatment (Steiger, Leung, & Thibaudeau, 1993). Consistent with findings of the long-term risk of poor social adaptation, daily fluctuations in social functioning have also been associated with bulimic symptoms (Steiger, Gauvin, Jabalpurwala, Seguin, & Stotland, 1999). More specifically, currently and formerly bulimic women displayed a hypersensitivity to negative social interactions as compared with never-bulimic women, such that they become more self-critical and endorse a more negative mood following such interactions. An even more remarkable finding was that negative social interactions and bulimic women's perceptions thereof preceded binge-eating episodes. Although the long-term impact of dependence and conflict avoidance on bulimia has not been sufficiently examined, related characteristics of social maladjustment do appear to be both immediate and long-term risk factors for disordered eating among persons with bulimia.

DEVELOPMENT OF INTERPERSONAL PROBLEMS: CHILDHOOD ABUSE

Clearly, persons with bulimia display maladaptive interpersonal behaviors that maintain the disorder, and it appears as though some of these behaviors are risk factors for the initial development of the disorder. How do these interpersonal styles develop, and what is their unique relation to bulimia?

It is likely that multiple pathways lead to the interpersonal dependency, sensitivity to rejection, and negative feedback-seeking shown among persons with bulimia, but one pathway that has received substantial attention from researchers has been abuse during childhood, particularly sexual abuse. Estimated rates of childhood sexual abuse among bulimic persons vary widely (e.g., 7%–70%) depending on samples studied and criteria for abuse. At this point, the conclusion most consistent with empirical data is that childhood sexual abuse places individuals at risk for psychopathology in general but is not necessarily specific to bulimia.

Interpersonal behaviors may play a key role in the relation between childhood sexual abuse and the development of later psychopathology, including bulimia. In general, the notion is that childhood abuse impedes the development of the social skills that are necessary for healthy relationships; this in turn leads to social isolation or impaired social interactions. Impaired social functioning is then viewed as a proximal risk factor for the development of psychopathology, with this often occurring in adolescence or early adulthood. In this model, then, impaired social abilities mediate the association of childhood abuse and psychopathology. Mallinckrodt, McCreary, and Robertson (1995) extended a version of this model to eating disorders and found evidence in support of the model. In their sample, childhood incest survivors displayed elevated rates of eating disorders (39%) and poor social competencies. Moreover, among incest survivors, those with the poorest social competencies and poorest relationships with their mothers were most likely to display eating disorders. Hence, these data provide evidence that the negative impact of childhood sexual abuse (in terms of later eating pathology) occurs at least partly through the detrimental influence it has on interpersonal relations.

TREATMENT OF BULIMIA FROM AN INTERPERSONAL PERSPECTIVE

In chapter 12, we discuss treatment of depression from an interpersonal perspective in depth. Many of the treatment components for bulimia are similar to depression, yet we highlight some specific therapeutic goals and techniques for bulimia in this section.

To the degree that bulimic persons engage their interpersonal environment in ways that maintain or exacerbate symptoms, therapies focusing on the interpersonal may be indicated. Consistent with this notion, short-term psychotherapies that focus on modifying current interpersonal problems do lead to reductions in bulimic symptoms, with interpersonal therapy (IPT–BN) representing an empirically validated treatment for bulimia (Fairburn, 1998).

Within the context of IPT–BN or other treatments for bulimia (e.g., cognitive–behavioral therapy [CBT]), the presence of specific interpersonal behaviors that perpetuate bulimia may represent fruitful targets for intervention. For example, negative self-verification strivings among bulimic persons represent a risk factor for continued bulimic symptoms. Why is it that bulimic persons do not sacrifice self-confirmation and escape bulimia? According to Swann, Stein-Seroussi, and Giesler (1992), the self-confirmation motive is extremely difficult to overcome because it serves fundamental human needs for predictability, certainty, and a consistent identity. Perhaps the goal, then, should not be to vanquish bulimic persons' self-confirmation needs but, rather, to simultaneously meet them and reduce bulimic symptoms. Emphasizing other, more positive aspects of patients' esteem (e.g., academic abilities) while working on bulimic symptoms might be one approach, or gently validating body image concerns while targeting more adaptive coping behaviors (e.g., regular diet and exercise vs. binge–purge) may be another.

From a self-verification perspective, the specific emphasis of IPT–BN on facilitating role change (i.e., role transitions–disputes) is ideal. Without techniques specifically developed to ease role and identity change, bulimic women may resist intervention because it threatens the fulfillment of self-verification needs. For this reason, noninterpersonal therapies such as antidepressant medications and CBT, although empirically validated themselves, may benefit from an added interpersonal focus. Second, insofar as low self-esteem underlies negative feedback-seeking (Pettit & Joiner, 2001b), self-esteem change seems an important psychotherapeutic focus. Swann (1996) showed that self-esteem change is a very difficult matter, consistent with the view that people will protect self-esteem (even if negative) to preserve a sense of consistency and stability. Mere assurances or affirmations do not significantly affect self-esteem. Instead, self-esteem may be improved by repeated emphasis of a specific aspect of self-esteem that the person deems positive (e.g., athletic ability). Also, Swann (1996) argued that self-verifying information, even if negative, comforts people to the point that they become ready for self-esteem change. Accordingly, clinicians may be advised to delicately verify negative self-views in the service of readying the person for positive change (cf. Finn & Tonsager, 1992).

IPT–BN is also well poised to exploring discrepancies and setbacks that might exist in the interpersonal domain. The early phases of IPT–BN involve investigation of the circumstances preceding bulimic episodes and specific behaviors (e.g., binges). Because binge episodes are often precipitated by aversive interpersonal events, the episodes may be viewed as markers of interpersonal problems that are worthy of investigation. In particular, IPT–BN recognizes several standard problem areas including interpersonal disputes, role transitions, and interpersonal–social skills. In the case of interpersonal disputes, the goal is to clarify the nature of the dispute (e.g., partner is too demanding, client does not feel cared for by parent), consider the possibilities for change on both sides, and then actively explore such possibilities, resulting in a renegotiation of the relationship or dissolution. In the case of role transitions, the goal is to help the client abandon the old role and adopt the new one (e.g., establishing independence from parents) by exploring what the new role involves and how it can be mastered. In these ways, interpersonal discrepancies from standards are addressed with changes actively sought. With regard to social skills, IPT–BN's emphasis on interpersonal and social skills as a possible target for intervention may be of value when working with bulimic patients who display deficits in this area.

As alluded to earlier, CBT is also an empirically validated treatment for bulimia. This approach justifiably focuses on a number of maladaptive intrapsychic cognitions, such as perfectionism, unrealistic drive for thinness, and so on. In addition to those, targeting the interpersonally oriented cognitions and behaviors we have discussed in this chapter may increase the effectiveness of treatment. For example, treatment may encourage the exploration and restructuring of bulimic patients' beliefs about the need for approval and reassurance from others (cf. sociotropy) or may also include assertiveness training components with the goal of reducing interpersonal dependence and conflict avoidance.

Consider the following interaction with a bulimic patient in which I (Pettit) use a "paradoxical questioning" technique (Swann, Pelham, & Chidester, 1988) to modify the patient's self-views and thereby decrease negative feedback-seeking. We caution that this particular technique is most appropriate for patients who are very certain of their beliefs, and only after a solid patient-therapist rapport has been established. The goal here is not to offend patients but to catch them off guard and force them to take a less extreme position.

Patient: I just feel so bad every time I look in the mirror.

Me: So, what you're telling me is that you find yourself so disgustingly fat that you can't even look at yourself in the mirror.

Patient: Well, I didn't say that—I'm not that fat, you know.

In this example, I "forced" the patient to adopt a more conservative and realistic view of her body. Research suggests that using such techniques may lead to changes in beliefs (Swann et al., 1988) that in turn serve as the driving force behind feedback-seeking behaviors (Pettit & Joiner, 2001b). In this sense, the patient may be somewhat less self-critical and therefore less likely to seek confirming negative feedback from others.

Helping patients to explicitly connect their interpersonal behaviors to their feelings and bulimic symptoms may be another fruitful therapeutic approach. The following dialogue illustrates how I (Pettit) have used that approach:

> Me: After monitoring your desires to binge over the past week, it seems as though the desires are strongest after conversations with Victoria about how you look.
>
> Patient: Yes, it seems that way.
>
> Me: What's even more puzzling is that this seems to be the case *even when* Victoria tells you that you look nice.
>
> Patient: It doesn't make much sense, does it?
>
> Me: The issue isn't really whether it makes sense. The key issue is identifying whether this behavior—asking Victoria how you look—helps you get better or makes you feel worse.
>
> Patient: It seems to be the latter.

In this brief dialogue, an approach similar to the cognitive–behavioral analysis system of psychotherapy (McCullough, 2000) allowed the patient to see that her requests for reassurances had the unintended effect of increasing her bulimic symptoms. As such, she may be less likely to excessively seek reassurances about her appearance, and her bulimic symptoms may decrease. In sum, by highlighting the interpersonal in treatment for bulimia, patients will likely experience immediate symptom relief and establish patterns of interpersonal behavior that will reduce the likelihood of relapse and recurrence of the disorder.

SUMMARY

In this chapter, we examined the high overlap between bulimia and depression and further discussed maladaptive interpersonal behaviors that occur in the context of bulimia. We highlighted how certain interpersonal patterns, namely negative feedback-seeking, sociotropy, and dependence and conflict avoidance, may contribute to the development and maintenance of bulimic symptoms. Moreover, we discussed how one distal vulnerability factor for bulimia, childhood sexual abuse, may increase risk for bulimia through its deleterious impact on social behaviors. We concluded with a brief discussion of how treatments for bulimia may incorporate interventions geared toward these interpersonal targets with the goal of producing lasting reductions in bulimic symptoms. In the next chapter, we return our focus to depression and devote attention to a complex, yet necessary, procedure: clinical assessment of depression.

12

CLINICAL ASSESSMENT

In this chapter on clinical assessment, we first address general issues important to the diagnosis and assessment of depressive disorders. We transition to methods of assessing depression, then conclude the chapter with suggestions for how clinicians may incorporate the interpersonal processes described in chapters 3 through 8 into the assessment procedure.

GENERAL ISSUES IN THE ASSESSMENT OF DEPRESSION

We began this book with a discussion of "what is depression?" As we near the end of the book and consider the assessment of depression, we return to the same issue. It is clear that a prior question to "how do we measure something?" is "what exactly *is* this something?" What exactly *is* depression? As discussed in chapter 2, there are some things we know, and some things we do not know, and both sets of things inform assessment of depression.

On the basis of what is and is not currently known about depression, Joiner, Walker, Pettit, Perez, and Cukrowicz (in press) proposed that an evidence-based assessment of depression include or account for the following: (a) adequate coverage of the symptoms that cohere to form the valid and distinct syndrome of major depression; (b) adequate coverage of depressed mood, anhedonia, and suicidality, which appear to be of particular importance; (c) regarding suicidality, an approach that distinguishes between Resolved Plans and Preparations and Suicidal Desire and Ideation, and includes past history of attempts; (d) assessment of the atypical subtype and, less definitively, the melancholic subtype as well; (e) parameters of course and chronicity; (f) comorbidity and bipolarity; (g) ambiguity regarding the categorical versus dimensional nature of depression; and (h) ambiguity regarding whether and when clinician ratings outperform self-report. In addition to these, an interpersonal focus on depression will include the assessment of the specific behaviors described in chapters 3 through 8. We briefly discuss each of the foregoing in the remainder of this chapter.

Symptoms of Major Depression

Depressive symptoms—sadness, anhedonia, suicidality, slowing, low self-esteem, guilt, and problems with energy, concentration, sleep, and appetite—cohere to form a valid and distinct syndrome, with several well-characterized parameters including course, comorbidity patterns, and treatment response. The construct of major depression has been well validated, and it is clear that the disorder represents more than just distress or demoralization. In particular, clinical manifestations of depression are more often evidenced by the presence of three symptoms, even controlling for severity of symptoms: depressed mood, anhedonia, and suicidality (Santor & Coyne, 2001). Consistent with this, Lewinsohn, Pettit, Joiner, and Seeley (2003) found depressed mood to be the most common feature of major depressive episodes, occurring among 90% to 95% of depressed people. This was considerably higher than anhedonia, which occurred in two thirds to three fourths of depressed people, and suicidality, which occurred in just under half of the depressed persons in the sample. The results therefore suggested depressed mood is the most common symptom of a major depressive episode, more so than anhedonia and other symptoms. Depressed mood, though very commonly experienced by those with major depression, is not very specific to the syndrome; anhedonia, by contrast, is more unique to major depression (i.e., discriminates major depression from other overlapping disorders like anxiety). Assessment of major depression should include all depressive symptoms, and the findings of Santor and Coyne (2001) and Lewinsohn et al. (2003) indicate that the three symptoms (i.e., depressed mood, anhedonia, and suicidality) are of particular import in the assessment of depression.

Suicidality

Suicidality is both a clear indicator of the depressive syndrome and a topic that understandably causes a great deal of preoccupation among clinicians. Epidemiological studies suggest that suicidality is surprisingly common. For example, Lewinsohn et al. (2003) conducted a study among depressed adolescents and young adults and found that between 38% and 48% experienced suicidal ideation during any given depressive episode (Lewinsohn et al., 2003). Moreover, Grunbaum et al. (2002) found that 20% of high school students—not just those who are depressed—reported suicidal ideation during the course of 1 year. As such, assessment of suicide risk represents a crucial component of working with depressed persons, and treatment providers should be prepared for the possibility that their patients will experience suicidal episodes. We do not have sufficient space to thoroughly discuss suicide risk assessment here (see Joiner, Walker, Rudd, & Jobes, 1999), but we highlight two factors that are of primary importance in suicide assessment: facets of suicidality and past history of suicidal behaviors.

Suicidality is a complex construct. Joiner, Rudd, and Rajab (1997) found that it can be adequately reduced to two primary and distinguishable facets. They labeled the first facet *Resolved Plans and Preparations* and it is represented by phenomena such as the absence of fear about making an attempt, a sense of competence to make an attempt, availability of means to and opportunity for attempt, specificity of plan for attempt, preparations for attempt, duration of suicidal ideation, and intensity of suicidal ideation. Those who endorse the items on this factor may experience more intense and acute forms of suicidality, and the foreboding tone of the items highlights the possibility that they may be at substantial risk for impending suicide attempt, a possibility supported by other studies (e.g., Joiner et al., 2003).

Joiner, Rudd, and Rajab (1997) labeled the second facet of suicidality *Suicidal Desire and Ideation*, and it comprises the following symptoms: (a) reasons for living (reversed), (b) wish to die, (c) frequency of ideation, (d) wish not to live, (e) passive attempt, (f) desire for attempt, (g) expectancy of attempt, (h) lack of deterrents to attempt, and (i) talk of death or suicide. The factor is made up of items that assess ongoing thoughts, ideas, and desires regarding suicide (perhaps chronic, less acute suicidal ideation) but not of items reflecting intense ideation or readiness to commit suicide.

A main implication of the distinction between the two facets of suicidality is that Resolved Plans and Preparation is an extremely important indicator of dangerousness, whereas Suicidal Desire and Ideation represents less of a risk for suicide attempt or completion. To be clear, both facets should be routinely and systematically assessed among depressed persons, and the presence of suicidal symptoms corresponding to either facet is of clinical concern. However, the symptoms of Resolved Plans and Preparation indicate a greater vulnerability to both nonfatal suicide attempt and eventual death by suicide (Joiner et al., 2003).

In addition to Resolved Plans and Preparation and Suicidal Desire and Ideation, past history of suicidal behavior must be assessed among depressed persons. Research has consistently demonstrated that the best predictor of future suicidal behavior is past suicidal behavior and that persons who have made multiple previous suicide attempts represent a distinct group from those who have made just one previous attempt or have never made an attempt. Individuals with a past history of multiple suicide attempts who also endorse symptoms of Resolved Plans and Preparation are at greatest risk for suicidal behavior. Again, we refer readers to Joiner, Walker, et al. (1999) for a more in-depth discussion of suicide risk assessment and attendant courses of action.

A final point with regard to the importance of assessing for suicidality is in order. Adequate assessment not only reduces the immediate risk for self-harm but also may identify those at risk for a more chronic course of depression. Among a large sample of depressed adolescents and young adults, Pettit, Lewinsohn, and Joiner (2004) found that girls who experienced symptoms related to suicidality in their first depressive episode (regardless of whether they acted on those symptoms) were at a significantly greater risk for recurrent episodes than those who did not endorse suicidality. A possible clinical implication of this is that, at least among young women, those who endorse suicidality may be candidates for treatments that emphasize the prevention of recurrence (see also chap. 13 on therapeutics).

Subtypes

Numerous subtypes of depression have been proposed, with most not receiving consistent empirical backing. A couple of subtypes have received mixed empirical support (melancholic–endogenous, hopelessness), although their relevance to treatment is less substantiated. Support for the atypical subtype of major depression appears to be more uniformly positive. The atypical subtype includes symptoms such as the presence of mood reactivity to positive events, significant weight gain, hypersomnia, leaden paralysis (i.e., arms or legs feeling like they are weighted down), and interpersonal rejection sensitivity. Several studies have shown atypical depression to be discernible from other depressive symptoms factorially (e.g., Kendler et al., 1996) and neurophysiologically (see Klein, 1993). Perhaps the most persuasive line of validity evidence comes from studies on differential treatment response—people with atypical depression have been shown to be particularly responsive to monoamine oxidase inhibitors such as phenelzine (e.g., Klein, 1993). Hence, the presence of atypical depression should be assessed, as it is associated with a somewhat unique symptom profile and may be relevant for treatment consideration if medications are used.

Course and Chronicity

Several aspects of depression course and chronicity can be distinguished, each of which is a negative prognostic indicator and thus deserves attention in assessment: (a) early age of first onset (e.g., before age 13); (b) severity of past episode(s); (c) past episode(s) characterized by psychotic or severe suicidal symptoms; (d) an episode superimposed on a preexisting dysthymia (i.e., double depression); (e) long duration of an individual episode; (f) the resumption of symptoms shortly following the remission of an episode (i.e., relapse); (g) long-standing, residual, subclinical depressive symptoms that persist following an episode; and (h) the reestablishment of major depression following a diagnosis-free period (i.e., recurrence).

Depressions that first occur in later life, as compared with those that first occur in childhood, adolescence, and early adulthood, may be less severe, less associated with suicidal and anxious symptoms, and less related to personality problems, such as excessive dependency and avoidance. It is interesting to note that they also may be about equally common in men and women (whereas earlier onset depressions are more common in women), less associated with first-degree relatives' depression risk, and more related to neurological or medical disease.

Comorbidity

Critical to the assessment and treatment of depression is distinguishing it from related conditions, as well as identifying comorbid disorders. According to an analysis by Newman, Moffit, Caspi, and Silva, (1998), individuals with comorbid mental disorders experience more inauspicious conditions than those with a single disorder. Their disorders typically display a more chronic course, have a poorer prognosis of recovery, and are less responsive to treatment. The presence of multiple disorders is also linked to a number of lifestyle factors such as job stress, physical illness, frequent moving, lack of social support, weak ties to family, unemployment, and dependence on welfare. Such individuals are more likely to have used mental health services, including hospitalization and psychotropic medications. Consequently, the per capita medical expenditure for individuals with comorbid diagnoses is 1.5 times higher than for those with a single illness and 5 times higher than those without an illness.

As discussed elsewhere, major depression has high rates of comorbidity with anxiety, eating, substance use, and personality disorders. Perhaps the highest rates of comorbidity are with the various anxiety disorders, and the reasons for this overlap are interesting to consider, because they likely differ per the different anxiety disorders. The reasons for the overlap of major depression and generalized anxiety disorder (GAD) are likely shared etiology; the genetic risks for major depression and for GAD overlap considerably or perhaps even entirely (Kendler, Neale, Kessler, & Heath, 1992). Accordingly, a person with major depression should be screened for GAD and vice versa, because if a person meets criteria for one, he or she is therefore at high genetic risk for the other. The reasons for the association of major depression and obsessive–compulsive disorder (OCD), for example, are likely different.

Shared etiology is unlikely (e.g., the basal ganglia are implicated in OCD but not in major depression; e.g., Rapoport, 1990); rather, those who have OCD experience distress and life impairment to the degree that a major depressive episode is likely. In other words, depression is a common consequence of OCD (but OCD is not a common consequence of depression). Therefore, those with OCD should be screened for depression, but those with depression are not particularly likely to have OCD.

Although the reason for overlap of depression and anxiety disorders likely differs by each anxiety disorder, a relatively simple method of assessing for the presence of depressive and anxious symptoms is the Postive and Negative Affect Scale (PANAS; Watson, Clark, & Tellegen, 1988). The PANAS derives from the tripartite model of depression and anxiety, which asserts that depression is characterized by high negative affect and low positive affect. In contrast, anxiety disorders are characterized by high negative affect, relatively normal levels of positive affect, and another component specific to each disorder (e.g., physiological hyperarousal is the specific component of panic disorder). Thus, the absence of positive affect, as measured by the PANAS, suggests the presence of depression. Although general anxious symptoms may be assessed with the PANAS, more detailed assessment is required to determine which particular anxiety disorder may be present.

In addition to assessing for comorbid anxiety disorders, eating disorders (see chap. 11), substance use disorders, and personality disorders should be assessed. In the case of substance use, depression often precedes the development of the substance use disorders by several years (Abraham & Fava, 1999). This highlights the importance of regularly reassessing for substance abuse among those with chronic depression. In contrast, eating disorders often precede the development of depression (e.g., Zaider, Johnson, & Cockell, 2002).

Bipolarity

The usually obvious difference between bipolar spectrum disorders and major depression should be emphasized. It is not unusual for chronically depressed people who do not have bipolar disorder (but may have heard of it through friends or the media) to describe their non-ill times as *manic episodes*. But careful questioning reveals that these episodes are periods of normal functioning (e.g., good, stable mood; ideas more or less in tune with reality and with loved ones; sleeping between 6 and 9 hours per night). These times may seem manic to a formerly depressed person because they contrast so starkly with the symptoms of major depression. A useful rule of thumb, applicable in the majority of cases (but not all), is that people with bipolar spectrum disorders will be able to identify three phases—a manic phase, a depressed phase, and a euthymic, essentially symptom-free phase (one exception to this rule is people who are so ill that they are virtually always depressed or manic, but their severity of illness makes differential diagnosis from major depression a moot point). By contrast, people with major depression can identify two major phases—depressed versus not depressed (again, this is not a perfect rule because, to take one example, people sometimes experience long-standing, residual, subclinical depressive symptoms that persist following a major depressive episode).

Another point of differentiation involves sleep. People with major depression very much desire to sleep well and often point to insomnia as among the most troubling of their symptoms. By contrast, people with bipolar disorder experience reduced need and desire for sleep and are often engaged in goal-directed activity when they would otherwise be asleep.

The foregoing components of depression assessment are all based on what empirical data have shown us about the nature of depression and its relation to other psychological phenomena. In addition to these, a couple of important areas in depression assessment represent "unknowns" in the sense that research has not yet produced reliable answers. We discuss each of them throughout the following sections.

Categorical or Dimensional?

Is depression a category, an all-or-none, "either-you-have-it-or-you-don't" phenomenon, similar to heart attack, or, a clearer example, biological gender? Or is depression a continuum, distributed along a graded dimension, similar to temperature or mass, in which a thing can have very little of it or a little more of it, and so on, up to having very much of it? There are staunch advocates of both positions, as we discussed in chapter 2 (e.g., Coyne, 1994; Vredenburg, Flett, & Krames, 1993).

This question has not been definitively answered and is in essence a taxometric question. Despite the value of taxometric analysis for addressing these types of nosologic questions, the application of taxometrics to psychopathology is still in its relatively early stages. This is particularly true with regard to mood disorder nosology—major depression has not been well studied using taxometric methods.

The taxometric analyses of major depression that have been conducted to date have produced mixed results, with some supporting a dimensional view (e.g., Ruscio & Ruscio, 2000) and others supporting a taxonic view (e.g., Beach & Amir, 2003). Investigations that support the dimensionality of depression have typically focused on self-reported depressive symptoms. It is interesting to note that initial evidence suggests that distinguishing between symptoms of mere distress versus hallmark symptoms of major depression leads to the following breakdown: hallmark symptoms (e.g., depressed mood, anhedonia, suicidality) are taxonic, whereas general distress symptoms are dimensional. This raises the possibility that depression is taxonic but that most studies to date have not used rigorous enough indicators to detect depression taxa.

What is needed is a study with rigorous analytic sophistication and general assessment that also focuses on a large sample of people ("enriched" to ensure substantial subsets of people with mood disorders) and that uses multimodal assessment indicators (i.e., clinician ratings as well as depression self-report scales) focusing on hallmark symptoms of major depression. We eagerly await the results of such a study; until then, the jury is out regarding whether depression is best viewed categorically or dimensionally.

Self-Report Versus Clinician Ratings

The second unknown (i.e., method of assessment) has actually received substantial empirical attention. Although a consensus appears to have emerged that clinician-rated, structured clinical interviews represent a kind of gold standard in psychopathology assessment, it is worth noting that the empirical basis for this consensus is not beyond question. A problem with this literature is the lack of studies in which both self-rating and clinician rating of symptoms are referenced to a third data source that is relatively impervious to various biases associated with both self-rating and clinician rating (e.g., neuroendocrine response to biological challenge). Moreover, there are instances in which patients' self-ratings may outperform clinicians' ratings. For example, among depressed inpatients, self-reported depression severity at admission was significantly associated with severity at discharge (Pettit, Averill, Wassef, Gruber, & Schneider, 2005), which is consistent with findings that initial severity of a depressive episode is one of the best predictors of later severity within that same episode. In contrast, psychiatrists' ratings of depression severity at admission displayed no association (almost zero!) to severity at discharge. Supporting the notion that patients may have more accurately judged symptom severity, nurses' ratings were consistent with the patients'.

The superiority of self-ratings over clinicians' ratings may be most dramatic in the area of suicidality. For example, Jobes, Jacoby, Cimbolic, and Hustead (1997) tracked patients who had initially presented with suicidal symptoms and, on the basis of the later course of the suicidal symptoms, classified patients into "acute resolver" and "chronic nonresolver" outcome categories. Patients' initial self-ratings were better than clinicians' ratings at predicting eventual group membership. Similarly, among a large group of suicidal young adults, Joiner, Rudd, and Rajab (1999) found that patients' self-ratings were more telling than clinicians' ratings regarding recurrence of suicidal symptoms at 6-, 12-, and 18-month follow-up sessions. The well-known biases and distortions associated with symptom self-report scales, taken together with instances in which self-report may have outperformed clinicians' ratings, suggest two things: (a) conclusions regarding this topic must be specific and nuanced (the view that one or the other approach is always categorically best does not withstand empirical scrutiny) and (b) to produce nuanced conclusions, more work with very powerful designs is needed.

Which Method to Use?

Up to this point, we have presented the following criteria as necessary components of a science-based assessment of depression: (a) adequate coverage of symptoms; (b) in-depth assessment of suicidality; (c) assessment of the atypical subtype and, less definitively, the melancholic subtype as well; (d) parameters of course and chronicity; (e) comorbidity and bipolarity; (f) ambiguity regarding the categorical versus dimensional nature of depression; and (g) ambiguity regarding whether and when clinician ratings outperform self-report. Of course, it goes without saying that any particular measure needs to meet accepted standards of psychometric reliability and validity. On the basis of those criteria, how should clinicians assess for depression?

As we alluded to earlier, structured clinical interviews appear to be the gold standard of depression assessment. Certain structured clinical interviews meet all or nearly all of the criteria presented above. The Structured Clinical Interview (SCID–I; Spitzer, Williams, Gibbon, & First, 1992) for the *Diagnostic and Statistical Manual of Mental Disorders* (4th ed., *DSM–IV*; American Psychiatric Association, 1994) is perhaps the most commonly used structured clinical interview. It is a comprehensive interview used to make Axis I diagnoses for the *DSM–IV* (e.g., major depressive episode), and as such, it closely conforms to the *DSM–IV* diagnostic decision trees. Regarding the criteria outlined above for (a), the SCID–I's coverage of depressed mood, anhedonia, suicidality, and other symptoms is good, and interrater reliability per each of the syndrome's symptoms is adequate (e.g., Lewinsohn et al., 2003); for (b), regarding suicidality, the SCID–I differentiates between a specific plan or attempt, on the one hand (cf. Resolved Plans and Preparations), and thoughts of death and suicidal ideation, on the other hand (cf. Suicidal Desire and Ideation), albeit in abbreviated form; for (c), the SCID–I specifically assesses for the atypical subtype, and, although many of the symptoms of the melancholic subtype are evaluated as well, some are not; for (d), parameters of course and chronicity, such as age of onset, number of past episodes, and preexisting dysthymia, are noted; for (e), comorbidity and bipolarity are very well assessed; for (f), regarding the categorical versus dimensional nature of depression, the SCID–I is designed to produce categorical diagnoses, but counts of specific symptoms can add rough dimensional information; and for (g), regarding clinician ratings versus self-report, the SCID–I's format requires some degree of clinical judgment but also includes a number of open-ended queries; the combination of open-ended queries and clinical judgment may incorporate the advantages of both self-report and clinician ratings. The general reliability and validity of the SCID–I is now well established. Other structured interviews perform similarly to the SCID–I, such as the Mini International Neuropsychiatric Interview (hereinafter *Mini*; Sheehan et al., 1997) and the Longitudinal Interval Follow-up Evaluation (LIFE; Keller et al., 1987).

The Mini does not have as extensive a track record of general reliability and validity as the SCID–I but shows good agreement with other standardized structured clinical interviews for Axis I disorders (Sheehan et al., 1997). Regarding the criteria outlined above for (a) and (b), the Mini's coverage of depressed mood, anhedonia, suicidality, and other symptoms is good; regarding suicidality, the Mini differentiates between a specific plan or attempt, on the one hand (cf. Resolved Plans and Preparations), and thoughts of death and suicidal ideation, on the other hand (cf. Suicidal Desire and Ideation), albeit in abbreviated form; for (c), the Mini specifically assesses for the melancholic subtype but not the atypical subtype; for (d), parameters of course and chronicity are not well evaluated, although whether past episodes occurred is noted; for (e), comorbidity and bipolarity are well assessed by the Mini; for (f), regarding the categorical versus dimensional nature of depression, the Mini is designed to produce categorical diagnoses, but counts of specific symptoms can add rough dimensional information; and for (g), regarding clinician ratings versus self-report, the Mini's format requires clinical judgment and does not include many open-ended queries; the Mini, therefore, may incorporate the advantages of clinician ratings but not self-report.

Overall, the SCID–I has the advantage over the Mini of detailed coverage of disorders, a more extensive track record, coverage of the atypical subtype, more comprehensive coverage of course and chronicity parameters, and incorporation of the advantages of clinician rating and self-report; however, the Mini is briefer and easier to learn and use and provides good coverage of the melancholic subtype. Combination of the Mini's melancholic subtype module with the SCID–I would meet all the criteria outlined above, except for assessment of seasonality, use in mass screening, and the tracking of changes in symptom severity over time.

The LIFE (Keller et al., 1987) also deserves mention. Its format is similar to the SCID–I, but it is geared toward detailed information about the course of psychiatric symptoms and disorders since an initial diagnosis, with rigorous criteria for recovery from a disorder (i.e., symptom-free for 8 or more weeks). It is thus particularly strong on the parameters of course and chronicity, especially as they are affected by treatment. However, for the short-term tracking of symptom changes, including in response to treatment, as well as mass screening, self-report scales, which are mentioned next, may be preferable.

In contrast to the structured clinical interviews, self-report symptom scales struggle to meet some of the criteria outlined above. Though their reliability and validity characteristics are good, scales like the Beck Depression Inventory (BDI; Beck & Steer, 1987), the Center for Epidemiologic Studies Depression Scale (CES–D; Radloff, 1977), and the Inventory to Diagnose Depression (IDD; Zimmerman & Coryell, 1987) rarely have adequate coverage of the different factors of suicidality, atypical and melancholic subtypes, and parameters of course and chronicity; they of course cannot incorporate the advantages of clinician ratings. Their primary role in evidence-based assessment appears to involve documentation of severity of depressive symptoms and periodic use as a quick and convenient index of treatment response.

The BDI–II is a self-report inventory of depressive symptoms, with 21 items. Each item is rated on a 0 to 3 scale; total scores thus range from 0 to 63. The BDI–II is a revision of earlier versions of the BDI (Beck & Steer, 1987) that conforms to changes made in the *DSM–IV* (American Psychiatric Association, 1994). The internal consistency and factor structure of the BDI–II has received ample support among outpatient samples of adults and adolescents (coefficient αs typically at or above .90; e.g., Beck, Steer, & Brown, 1996; Steer, Ball, Ranieri, & Beck, 1997; Steer, Ball, Ranieri, & Beck, 1999; Steer, Kumar, Ranieri, & Beck, 1998; Steer, Rissmiller, & Beck, 2000), indicating that the BDI–II is very reliable and well-validated as an index of depressive symptom severity. Regarding the criteria outlined above for (a) and (b), the BDI–II includes items to assess sadness, anhedonia, and suicidal ideation but fails to assess symptoms of Resolved Plans and Preparations; for (c), the BDI–II (in contrast to the earlier BDI) assesses certain symptoms of the atypical subtype of major depression, such as hypersomnia and weight gain, but is not appropriate alone for diagnosing subtypes; for (d), parameters of course and chronicity are not evaluated; for (e), comorbidity and bipolarity are not assessed by the BDI–II. Because the BDI–II is brief and because its metric is well-known, we view it as the premier instrument for the assessment of depressive symptom severity and the tracking of short-term changes in severity in outpatient settings (e.g., in response to treatment). It was designed for this purpose and was specifically not designed to establish formal depressive diagnoses. Regarding (f), the categorical versus dimensional nature of depression, the BDI–II is designed primarily as a dimensional measure of symptom severity, and cut scores for categorical placement are relatively arbitrary; and regarding (g), clinician ratings versus self-report, its format incorporates the advantages of self-report ratings, but does not allow for clinical judgment.

The CES–D is a self-report index of the frequency of occurrence of 20 depressive symptoms, each rated on a 0 to 3 scale, yielding total scores with a possible range from 0 to 60. The CES–D has been demonstrated to be a reliable and valid assessment instrument in a variety of samples (Joiner, Pfaff, & Acres, 2002; Roberts, Lewinsohn, & Seeley, 1991). Regarding the criteria outlined above, the CES–D for (a) and (b) assesses depressed mood and anhedonia but fails to evaluate suicidality; for (c), the CES–D does not assess subtypes of major depression; for (d), parameters of course and chronicity are not evaluated; and for (e), comorbidity and bipolarity are not assessed. It has received less empirical attention than the BDI–II as an instrument to monitor symptom changes and was not designed to establish formal depressive diagnoses. Regarding (f), the categorical versus dimensional nature of depression, the CES–D is designed primarily as a dimensional measure of symptom severity, and cut scores for categorical placement are relatively arbitrary; and regarding (g), clinician ratings versus self-report, the CES–D's format incorporates the advantages of self-report ratings but does not allow for clinical judgment. Because it was designed for use with general community samples, the CES–D is perhaps the best instrument for mass screening situations.

The IDD (Zimmerman & Coryell, 1987) performs similarly to the BDI–II and CES–D with regard to most criteria. Reliability and validity data for the scales are not as extensive as those for the BDI and CES–D but appear to be adequate (Uehara, Sato, Sakado, & Kameda, 1997; Zimmerman & Coryell, 1987). The primary distinguishing feature of the IDD is its performance with regard to (d), parameter and course. In particular, the IDD includes questions on chronicity and past history. One version of the scale is geared toward current symptoms, and for each item, respondents are asked not only to rate its severity but also to indicate whether it has lasted more or less than 2 weeks. A second version of the scale assesses the most depressed week in one's life; here again, respondents are asked not only to rate its severity but also to indicate whether it has lasted more or less than 2 weeks. Moreover, respondents are asked about total length of any depressive episode, impairment resulting from the episode, and total number of past episodes. Both versions include 22 items, each rated on a 0 to 4 scale, each yielding total score ranges from 0 to 88. Given the emphasis on parameters, like chronicity and impairment, the IDD is clearly the instrument of choice for attempts to formally diagnose people through self-report; nevertheless, even supportive studies of the IDD in this regard sound a note of caution about diagnosing through self-report (e.g., Uehara et al., 1997), a caution with which we agree.

A final assessment device that merits discussion is the Hamilton Rating Scale for Depression (HRSD; Hamilton, 1967). The HRSD is neither a structured interview nor a self-report inventory; rather, it was developed primarily as a clinician rating scale of depression severity for patients already diagnosed with a depressive disorder (Rehm & O'Hara, 1985). HRSD versions of different item length are available (e.g., 17, 21, 24), although only 17 are typically used for assessing depression severity. The interrater reliability, internal consistency, and construct validity of the HRSD have received ample support (e.g., Bech, 1987; Rehm & O'Hara, 1985). Regarding the criteria outlined above for (a) and (b), the HRSD includes items to assess sadness, anhedonia, and suicidality; for (b), regarding suicidality, the HRSD fails to assess symptoms of Resolved Plans and Preparations; for (c), the HRSD includes a subscale for assessing the melancholic subtype but does not assess the atypical or seasonal subtypes; for (d), parameters of course and chronicity are not evaluated; for (e), comorbidity and bipolarity are not assessed by the HRSD; for (f), regarding the categorical versus dimensional nature of depression, the HRSD is designed primarily as a dimensional measure of symptom severity, and cut scores for categorical placement are relatively arbitrary; and for (g), regarding clinician ratings versus self-report, the HRSD relies heavily on clinical judgment, and therefore may incorporate the advantages of clinician ratings but not self-report. Similar to the BDI–II, the HRSD is most appropriate for assessment of depressive symptom severity and the tracking of the short-term changes in severity, particularly in inpatient settings.

SPECIFIC INTERPERSONAL BEHAVIORS

Throughout this book, we have emphasized the interpersonal nature of depression. We have also detailed how specific interpersonal behaviors play a role in the development and the maintenance of depression. Inclusion of such behaviors into an assessment framework is not necessary for the purposes of diagnosis. In cases of chronic depression, however, assessing for their presence may provide insight as to what factors are at work in prolonging the depressive experience. Furthermore, identification of these behaviors opens the door for interventions focused on reducing maladaptive interpersonal patterns and promoting constructive interpersonal behaviors, as we discuss in the next chapter.

For some of the behaviors we have described, validated self-report measures already exist. For example, the Reassurance-Seeking Scale (Joiner & Metalsky, 2001) is a brief scale (4-item) that reliably assesses people's tendency to excessively seek reassurance from others. Likewise, the Feedback-Seeking Questionnaire (Swann, Wenzlaff, Krull, & Pelham, 1992) assesses people's interest in feedback from others within five self-relevant domains: intellectual, social, musical–artistic, athletic abilities, and physical attractiveness. A composite score indicates the general degree to which they are interested in positively or negatively valenced feedback. The Self-Handicapping Scale (Rhodewalt, 1990) is a 25-item scale that assesses individuals' tendencies to self-handicap. With respect to a couple of other self-propagatory processes, specific measures have not been developed, but existing measures likely tap into the constructs of interest. For example, measures of shyness (e.g., Buss, 1986) present one means by which to assess interpersonal conflict avoidance. Similarly, measures of dyadic adjustment (e.g., Spanier, 1976) can be used to assess blame maintenance. Of course, assessment of blame maintenance requires assessment of relationship partners. Validated self-report measures for other processes discussed in this book (e. g., stress generation) are not available and are more difficult to develop. However, most of these behaviors may be assessed through thorough questioning about interpersonal relationships. For example, interpersonal psychotherapy, discussed in chapter 13, routinely involves a thorough review of interpersonal histories. Connie Hammen (1991) has also extensively used an approach of collecting detailed histories and rating the degree to which person contributed to the occurrence of stressors. For example, a general assessment of stress generation could be widely used in clinical settings and would only involve collecting detailed histories about salient negative life events. In our experiences, the collection of such histories often reveals the extent to which depressed persons engaged in certain behaviors that contributed to the occurrence of that event. Moreover, by going through a detailed recollection of the event, depressed persons often recognize by themselves how they contributed to its occurrence.

We recommend just such a detailed assessment of interpersonal behaviors and relationships among those with chronic forms of depression. As alluded to in chapter 3, we also think that a thorough exploration of depressed patients' significant interpersonal relationships at the outset of therapy is useful in helping patients to understand the role of interpersonal behaviors in depression, as well as to identify potential targets for intervention. This stage of assessment, although not necessary for diagnostic purposes, could entail something as simple as asking patients to list the significant relationships in their lives, along with what they have gotten out of those relationships.

SUMMARY

From diverse perspectives, there is little doubt that depressive symptoms cohere to form a valid and distinct syndrome, with several well-characterized parameters. Consideration of these parameters, such as the prominence of depressed mood, anhedonia, and suicidality as symptoms, factors of suicidality, subtyping, course and chronicity, and so forth, shows that thorough, evidence-based assessment of depression requires intensive and somewhat complex procedures. No one extant procedure is ideal, but structured clinical interviews (e.g., SCID–I, the Mini, and LIFE) approach the ideal, especially when their respective advantages are incorporated into an overall assessment scheme. These interviews deserve their favored place over self-report instruments, not because of the rote (and sometimes questionable) superiority of clinician ratings over self-report but, rather, because these interviews adequately capture the many aspects of assessment necessary for state of the art evidence-based assessment of depression. Beyond diagnosis, assessing the extent to which depressed persons engage in the maladaptive interpersonal behaviors described in chapters 3 through 8 may provide useful targets for intervention among those with chronic depression.

13

THERAPEUTICS

As we discussed in chapter 2, depression mars the lives of millions of individuals, leaving pernicious health consequences and astounding economic repercussions in its wake. Given the magnitude and intensity of the impact of major depressive disorder, it is no surprise that a significant amount of research during the past few decades has focused on the development of more effective treatments. Fortunately, the development and systematic research of treatments has been followed by an increase in the percentage of depressed persons in treatment in recent years. A recent examination of nationwide trends in treatment of depression suggests that the rate of people seeking any form of outpatient treatment for depression increased 300% from 1987 to 1997 (Olfson et al., 2002). It is interesting to note that the proportion of treated individuals who used antidepressant medications doubled from 37.3% to 74.5%, whereas the proportion who received psychotherapy declined (71.1% vs. 60.2%).

Despite the overall increase in the rate of people seeking treatment for depression, estimates suggest that only one half of depressed persons receive any form of treatment, and less than half of those who seek help receive adequate treatment (Kessler et al., 2003). Thus, there exists a need not only to promote treatment of depression but also to more routinely and effectively implement treatments that we know to be effective.

In previous chapters, we provided specific examples of how each of the six interpersonal processes plays out in patients' lives. In this chapter, we present a more general overview of current treatment approaches to depression and how these relate to the theory, research, and practice presented throughout this book.

CHRONIC CONDITION VERSUS RAPID CHANGE

Habit is habit and not to be flung out of the window by any man, but coaxed downstairs a step at a time.

—Mark Twain

Depression, as we have demonstrated, can be a chronic condition. Contrary to the chronic nature of depression, however, is the demand for interventions that produce rapid symptom relief. This demand is felt from numerous sources. On the one hand, mental health professionals feel internal pressure from their own desire to provide the help that will lead to the largest and fastest amelioration of depression among their patients. On the other hand, pressure for faster acting treatments also comes from the outside. Patients often get frustrated if they do not believe that they are improving quickly and may discontinue treatment. In addition, practitioners feel pressure from insurance companies (i.e., managed care) to produce significant symptom reductions in what often seem like unreasonably short periods of time. Indeed, the expectation that a severely depressed person who has had the disorder for years will evidence substantial treatment gains in 12 sessions or less, for example, poses a daunting challenge! It is not surprising that a survey of the American Psychological Association's licensed practitioner members revealed that 4 out of 5 viewed managed care as having a negative impact on their professional work (Phelps, Eisman, & Kohut, 1998).

Although we do not wish to devote space to a discussion of the relative benefits and drawbacks of managed care, we do propose that a mild sense of pressure—regardless of the source—may be a good thing when it comes to treating chronic depression. Why? Simply stated, because results are needed quickly. Chronically depressed persons are at risk for all sorts of negative outcomes, both in the short- and long-term. As such, clinicians need to feel a motivating pressure to produce substantial symptom reduction in a relatively short period of time. Currently, only a handful of approaches are available to produce rapid change among this difficult-to-treat group.

PHARMACOLOGICAL TREATMENT OPTIONS

One proven effective treatment of depression, chronic or otherwise, is the implementation of pharmacological mood-altering agents. Pharmacological treatments have gained popularity during the past 50 years as a method of treatment intervention for depression. They have been proven to be effective in ameliorating the symptoms of a large percentage of depressed individuals and are the most common form of treatment for depression (Narrow, Regier, Rae, Manderscheid, & Locke, 1993). Moreover, and consistent with the call for faster acting treatments, antidepressant outcome studies suggest that symptom change—not complete remission, but change—can be identified during the first 1 to 2 weeks of treatment (Stahl, Nierenberg, & Gorman, 2001).

Antidepressant medications are classified depending on their chemical structure and how they work, and all categories of antidepressants tend to be comparably efficacious. They can be categorized into four basic groups: heterocyclics (HCAs), monoamine oxidase inhibitors (MAOIs), serotonin reuptake inhibitors (SRIs), and atypical drugs. Medications in the current antidepressant pharmacopoeia are in general hypothesized to work by altering the activity of biogenic amine neurotransmitters (e.g., acetylcholine, norepinephrine, serotonin, and dopamine). This view is oversimplified, as antidepressants also affect presynaptic receptors, postsynaptic second-messengers, and neurophysiologic response systems (Barden, Reul, & Holsboer, 1995; Manji, 1992; Thase & Kupfer, 1996; Wachtel, 1990). Because of the varying nature of antidepressants, and the lack of a thorough understanding of their mechanisms of action, it is impossible to completely explain the therapeutic properties of antidepressant medications.

Most antidepressant medications have a fairly high success rate of ameliorating acute depressive symptoms, and treatment outcome studies indicated that HCAs, MAOIs, and SRIs significantly reduce depressive symptoms for approximately 50% of patients who initiate treatment, and for approximately 65% of those who complete treatment (Anderson & Tomenson, 1994; Depression Guideline Panel, 1993; Song et al., 1993). Beneficial treatment effects of antidepressant medications cannot be explained entirely by "placebo effects," as the average treatment response difference between medication and placebo ranges from 20% to 40% (Depression Guideline Panel, 1993).

Despite the relatively high rates of positive treatment response during acute phase depression, the picture becomes more bleak when considering depression chronicity. Antidepressants are much less successful at preventing the relapse or recurrence of depression if they are discontinued shortly after the remission of symptoms (Hollon, Shelton, & Loosen, 1991; Thase, 1990). Thase (1999) reported that up to 50% of patients relapse unless treated 4 to 6 months after the initial acute phase therapy (see also Simons, Murphy, Levine, & Wetzel, 1986; Thase & Sullivan, 1995). Nevertheless, administration of the drugs can be continued for long periods of time, in which case they more effectively prevent relapse or recurrence.

We elaborate on this notion—and relevant research findings—in our discussion of preventing depression chronicity in chapter 14.

Empirical evidence addressing the response of chronically depressed persons to specific medications is just beginning to accumulate. Provocative findings from Kornstein et al. (2000) suggest that chronically depressed, premenopausal women may respond better to sertraline (a commonly prescribed SRI), whereas chronically depressed men may respond more favorably to imipramine (a commonly prescribed HCA). Furthermore, men responded more quickly to medication treatment than did women. Although these results are preliminary, they provide hope for future matching of pharmacological treatment matching to patient characteristics.

On the surface, it appears as though pharmacological treatment is inconsistent with the interpersonal nature of chronic depression we have presented thus far. We would like to address this with a few points. First, although interpersonal factors serve as a vulnerability to and maintaining factor for depression, effective treatment does not necessarily have to directly address these factors. The notion that treatments must reflect causes is referred to as *homeopathy*. Homeopathy leads to efficacious treatment in certain cases, but it is a quite common misconception that treatments must incorporate or address the cause of a disorder.

Second, interpersonal factors are not the only cause of chronic depression. Although we have argued that they often play an important role in developing and maintaining depression, several other factors (e.g., neuroendocrine functioning) are clearly related to the disorder. Finally, it may be the case that antidepressants' beneficial effects result in part from improved interpersonal functioning. Antidepressant agents frequently have a relatively rapid activating effect on depressed persons, such that they begin to feel more energized. This increased level of activity is likely viewed by others as effort and improvement in the depressed person, which may lead to decreased levels of rejection and hostility. Indeed, this minor change in activity level may be acknowledged with increased levels of support, encouragement, and positive social interactions. In addition, the depressed person may seek out more positive social interactions simply as a by-product of increased energy levels.

PSYCHOSOCIAL TREATMENT OPTIONS

Similar to pharmacological treatment interventions, psychosocial treatments typically produce significant reductions in acute depressive symptoms among approximately 50% to 70% of individuals receiving these forms of treatment (Miller, Norman, & Keitner, 1990). Accordingly, reviews of psychotherapeutic and pharmacological treatments reveal similar levels of efficacy when applied to mild to moderate depressive episodes (Depression Guideline Panel, 1993; Dobson, 1989). A long-standing belief among mental health professionals holds that pharmacological treatments outperform psychosocial treatments in cases of severe depression (although in actual practice, many people receive both forms of treatment). Recent evidence, however, has challenged that notion. For example, depression treatment outcome researchers at the University of Pennsylvania reported that cognitive–behavioral therapy (CBT) and antidepressant medications were equally effective in treating severe cases of depression (DeRubeis, Gelfand, Tang, & Simons, 1999). A large amount of research suggests that psychotherapy typically yields lower relapse rates relative to the relapse rates following medication trials. Nevertheless, maintenance treatment with pharmacotherapy does appear to be comparably effective in the prevention of relapse. (Again, we elaborate on treatment geared toward prevention of relapse and recurrence in chap. 14).

Several different forms of psychotherapy have demonstrated efficacy in the treatment of chronic depression. Particularly germane to interpersonal problems in chronic depression, interpersonal psychotherapy (IPT; Klerman, Weissman, Rounsaville, & Chevron, 1984) is a brief treatment (usually 12–16 weeks) with demonstrated efficacy (i.e., superior to placebo; Elkin et al., 1989). As the name implies, IPT focuses on patients' interpersonal functioning as it relates to current depression and the onset of depression. In IPT, patients work toward developing appropriate interpersonal skills for dealing with problems such as grief, role issues, and interpersonal deficits. As Markowitz (2003) explained, IPT must be modified somewhat for use with chronically depressed persons. That is, IPT usually focuses on the link between current life events and the onset of a depressive disorder. With chronic cases of depression, which may last for years, connecting the disorder to recent and specific life events becomes more difficult and loses meaning for patients who often view depression as "the way they are" rather than a response to environmental circumstances.

The focus in these cases must shift from recent life events to interpersonal deficits. In fact, when salient life events are not identifiable, treatment itself may be used as a role transition from chronic illness to a healthy person (Markowitz, 1998). IPT works toward remedying a number of interpersonal deficits or maladaptive interpersonal behaviors. Among chronically depressed persons, there is a particular emphasis on self-assertion. This fits quite well with the common finding of interpersonal conflict avoidance seen among chronically depressed persons (chap. 6). In fact, with its emphasis on role disputes and transitions, as well as social skills, IPT is well positioned to remedy the role changes inherent in becoming less avoidant, less self-derogatory, and less blameworthy in others' eyes. Further, a focus on social skills training may facilitate wide-ranging behavioral and attitudinal change of avoidance, negative feedback-seeking, and excessive reassurance-seeking.

For example, specific components on these topics could be integrated into the general IPT framework, wherein the concepts of negative feedback-seeking, excessive reassurance-seeking, or others relevant to the patient are presented as part of a treatable illness (i.e., depression). Therapists may also wish to emphasize that the chronic nature of patients' depression likely compromised their behaviors in these areas (e.g., self-handicapping has become a default approach to social evaluation over many years of being depressed; Markowitz, 2003) but should likewise convey hope to patients that a change in these behaviors will improve the way they feel. Validation and normalization of the bases of these interpersonal behaviors may reduce feelings of guilt or self-blame while simultaneously opening the door for change. For instance, therapists may tell patients that everyone desires comfort and assurances from loved ones, that it is not bad to feel that way, and then examine various ways of responding to those feelings.

The cognitive–behavioral analysis system of psychotherapy (CBASP; McCullough, 2000; see also Driscoll, Cukrowicz, Reardon, & Joiner, 2003) is a CBT approach to treating chronic depression. Like IPT, CBASP emphasizes depressed persons' interpersonal encounters but addresses problems in this domain through cognitive and behavioral exercises. More specifically, CBASP emerged out of the idea that chronically depressed patients do not learn from problematic interpersonal interactions and modify their behavior accordingly (McCullough, 2000). To redress this problem, CBASP combines behavioral, cognitive, and interpersonal techniques to teach the patient to focus on the consequences of behavior and to use a problem-solving approach to resolve interpersonal difficulties. Ongoing investigations of the treatment take place at 12 academic centers, and results thus far support its efficacy when administered alone or in combination with the atypical antidepressant nefazodone (e.g., Keller et al., 2000).

COMBINED TREATMENT OPTIONS

Recent years have seen an increase in the administration of pharmacotherapy and psychotherapy combined for treating depressed persons. Although research has not typically demonstrated large discrepancies in the magnitude of effects for combined versus single treatment modalities, combined treatment generally appears to be slightly more effective than either psychotherapy alone or pharmacotherapy alone (see Pettit, Voelz, & Joiner, 2001, for a review of combined treatment). A dearth of information exists with regard to using combined treatment modalities for individuals with chronic depression. Nevertheless, strong support for the superiority of combined treatment for chronic depression was obtained recently by Keller et al. (2000). In a study of over 500 chronically depressed patients, they compared 12 weeks of treatment with nefazodone, CBT, and a combination of the two. Just over 50% of patients in both single modality conditions significantly improved over the course of treatment, whereas 85% of patients receiving the combination of nefazadone and CBT demonstrated significant improvement. Not only did depressive symptoms improve most among patients who received combined treatment; these patients also displayed significantly greater social, work, and overall functioning than did patients in the other two conditions, even when controlling for the level of depressive symptom improvement (Hirschfeld et al., 2002). Consistent with this finding, research from another group indicates that the addition of cognitive therapy among depressed persons with only a partial response to antidepressant treatment leads to an improvement in interpersonal functioning and depressive symptoms (Scott et al., 2000).

Results of empirical studies on treatment for depression vary somewhat but tend to converge on a single theme: Combined psychotherapy and pharmacotherapy may be more effective than psychotherapy alone or pharmacotherapy alone in the treatment of depressive episodes (Hollon, Thase, & Markowitz, 2002; Pettit et al., 2001). Throughout the literature on combined therapy versus pharmacotherapy or psychotherapy alone, a modest effect exists indicating that combined therapy is the treatment of choice. This effect is not large and is generally not great enough to be of importance when referring only to the acute treatment phase. When considering acute treatment, relapse prevention, and recurrence prevention, however, this finding is large enough to merit attention. As Hollon et al. (2002) appropriately noted, the principal goal of depression treatment should be full remission and long-term recovery, not simply acute phase symptom remission. Combined treatment appears to be an effective way to attain both the short-term benefits of medication and the enduring effects of psychotherapy (Hollon et al., 2002).

There are still no specific findings indicating that certain antidepressant medications are superior to others in treating depression, although the general category of SRIs are often favored, largely because they lead to fewer negative side effects. In reference to psychotherapies, cognitive, cognitive–behavioral, and interpersonal therapies have received the most support and have been the focus of the most empirical research conducted with depression.

If a single modality treatment is selected, psychotherapy appears to be preferable to pharmacotherapy in the treatment of chronic depression because evidence suggests that it leads to lower relapse rates than pharmacotherapy after discontinuation of treatment (e.g., Evans et al., 1992; Fava, Rafanelli, Grandi, Conti, & Belluardo, 1998). Despite the advantage of psychotherapy in preventing relapse, as compared with previous pharmacotherapy, continued medication seems to be equally effective at preventing relapse.

FOCUS ON THE INTERPERSONAL

The treatments described in the previous sections produce substantial improvement among chronically depressed persons. It is likely that part of this change occurs through interpersonal mechanisms. That is, changes in methods of interacting with and responding to others probably produce direct effects on depressive symptomatology, and indirect effects through increased frequency, quality, and reciprocal nature of the interactions. Furthermore, changes in patterns of interpersonal behaviors likely play an even greater role in staving off recurrent bouts of depression. Not only have formerly depressed persons become more active, effective agents on their environments; over time, others' perceptions of the person change to reflect their new interpersonal repertoire (in contrast to blame maintenance [chap. 8]). We discuss how this may happen—and how to promote its occurrence in therapy—later in this chapter.

The psychosocial treatments previously mentioned do not explicitly focus on concepts such as self-handicapping, negative feedback-seeking, reassurance-seeking, and the like, but they likely target such behaviors indirectly during the process of examining social interactions. Indeed, insofar as many self-propagatory processes may depend on the existence of at least subclinical depressive symptoms, any empirically validated depression treatment may, in itself, mute self-propagatory processes. However, even successful treatment may not always drastically reduce chronicity rates (Pettit et al., 2001). Accordingly, direct treatment of self-propagatory processes deserves consideration as a supplement to standard therapeutics. This is particularly the case among depressed persons who are especially vulnerable to depression chronicity (e.g., those with early age at first depression; those with previous episodes lasting a year or more; Kovacs, Obrosky, Gatsonis, & Richards, 1997; Maier, 1996; Shapiro & Keller, 1981).

Explicit inclusion of these processes into existing treatment protocols has not yet been put to the empirical test, although it is interesting to note that other well-developed and validated therapies may target specific features of self-propagatory processes. For example, there are treatment protocols to redress social reticence (cf. conflict avoidance; e.g., Barlow, Esler, & Vitali, 1998; Heimberg, Salzman, Holt, & Blendell, 1993) and couples' problems (cf. blame maintenance; e.g., Baucom, Sayers, & Sher, 1990; Jacobson, Dobson, Fruzetti, & Schmaling, 1991). Nevertheless, although well-developed and investigated therapies may target self-propagatory processes and thus reduce depression chronicity, rote reliance on these therapies may not adequately address self-propagatory processes. For instance, if an unorganized mosaic of negative expectancies is addressed by a cognitive–behavioral therapist, without reference to how such expectancies encourage negative feedback-seeking, excessive reassurance-seeking, or avoidance, these latter processes may remain intact to induce depression chronicity. Similarly, if negative self-views—which, in varying degrees, underlie many of the self-propagatory processes—are merely challenged and confronted, there is danger that they will be reflexively protected by the patient because according to self-verification theory, they sustain fundamental needs for control, predictability, and familiarity. Swann (1996) has recommended that clinicians delicately verify negative self-views (cf. client-centered technique of "reflection," Rogers, 1951; or self psychological technique of "empathic attunement," Kohut, 1984), so that the person experiences enough of a sense of control and familiarity that gradual positive change is possible. In tangential empirical support of this view, Finn and Tonsager (1992) found that accurate psychological assessment feedback, even if negative, proved therapeutic.

It seems plausible that within the context of existing therapies for chronic depression, directly identifying, naming, and developing exercises to modify the phenomena presented in chapters 3 through 8 would lead to positive therapeutic outcomes. Consider the following hypothetical example of a discussion between patient and therapist:

Patient: [describing an interaction with his girlfriend] I was staining her coffee table, but the stain didn't spread evenly in one area, so it was darker in that area. She said the table looked nice, but then I showed her the darker part and said it didn't look good.

Therapist: What happened then?

Patient: She said it looked natural and that nobody would notice, so I opened the blinds and showed her the contrast in direct sunlight.

Therapist: How did she respond?

Patient: She said it looked okay, and that I shouldn't worry about it. But I pointed it out again and asked her how she couldn't see that it looked bad, and then she said, "Fine—if you want me to say it looks bad, then it looks bad." I wanted honest feedback about it, but she didn't have to be so harsh.

On the basis of that exchange, a therapist using the CBASP approach might say something to this effect in the remediation phase:

Therapist: How did your comments hurt you or prevent you from getting what you wanted in that situation? How could they be altered to help you get what you want the next time such a situation comes up?

We think that is a good approach and tentatively propose that it might have an even greater impact if the therapist followed up on these questions by labeling the patient's behavior as negative feedback-seeking, explaining that it is common among depressed persons, and that it can have untoward interpersonal consequences, just as the patient experienced. Adding these brief comments would only modify treatment to a small extent but may increase the salience of the example to the patient and thereby increase the likelihood that the he does not engage in these behaviors in the future.

Similar approaches could be used for the other interpersonal behaviors presented in chapters 3 through 8. For example, existing treatments could incorporate modules on excessive reassurance-seeking with relative ease. This would likely be easy for both clinicians and patients—anecdotally, people who engage in excessive reassurance-seeking, as well as their relationship partners, have very little trouble understanding what is meant by excessive reassurance-seeking and its interpersonal effects. Often, discussion of the topic is met with knowing nods from patients and their partners—it is not a mysterious or abstract process. Accordingly, it seems feasible to develop a psychoeducational module on reassurance-seeking, that can be integrated into broader, empirically validated treatments for depression, such as cognitive–behavioral therapy, interpersonal therapy, problem-solving therapies, time-limited supportive-expressive dynamic psychotherapy, and marital therapy. Insofar as each of these therapies, either directly or implicitly, attempts to alter interpersonal style, discussion of excessive reassurance-seeking seems an easy fit. A similar psychoeducational prevention program also seems workable, perhaps targeted at people particularly at risk for depression (e.g., those with a past history of depression).

Likewise, treatment modules could be constructed to address the persistent problem of blame maintenance. As we pointed out in chapter 8, negative views of chronically depressed persons gain an autonomous quality in that they selectively guide memory, attention, and expectancies and thus confirm and perpetuate themselves (Sacco, 1999). This social–cognitive process may even occur outside the awareness of the perceiver. Therefore, the depressed, excessive reassurance-seeking person, even when recovered from depression, may face continued negative views from others, which have been shown to be predictors of depression relapse (Hooley & Teasdale, 1989) and to intensify the deleterious effects of the depressed person's own negative self-view (Katz & Beach, 1997b). What to do?

Rote reliance on individual therapy, and potentially even on couples therapy, may not be adequate to address blame maintenance. The literature on category-based versus individuated person perception, however, may provide an answer. Research in this field has shown that when people believe that their own personally meaningful outcomes depend on interaction with a target person, their impressions of the target person are individuated (i.e., based on his or her present attributes, not on labels or on general schematics; e.g., Neuberg & Fiske, 1987). Similar research shows that enhanced motivation to attend to all available information about a person decreases category-based, stereotypic impressions (Johnston & Macrae, 1994). In summary, *motivated attention* (e.g., by dependency on another for meaningful outcomes) encourages individuated views of another person. As applied to depressed people and their relationship partners, motivated attention to the depressed person's positive features may disconfirm the negative person schemata of the depressed person's relationship partners. How can a therapist achieve motivated attention? Motivated attention can be achieved simply by articulating it as a goal (e.g., in couples' therapy, the spouse of a depressed person may be assigned the homework of logging his or her spouse's positive behaviors; e.g., Johnston & Macrae, 1994). In addition, as demonstrated by Neuberg and Fiske (1987), motivated attention may be enhanced by increasing others' outcome dependence on the depressed person (e.g., contracting that a couple have a relatively active social life and that the depressed person and only the depressed person be responsible for arranging the couple's social schedule). In so doing, significant others are likely to incorporate these proactive behaviors into their schemata of the depressed partner and so chip away at well-engrained negative views that hinder their partner's recovery. Hence, just as social–cognitive mechanisms conspire to consolidate and sustain negative person schemata, so may they be used as guides to change such schemata.

In the context of couples' treatment, for example, a very simple intervention is to ask spouses with critical views of their formerly depressed partners to list the qualities that originally attracted them to their partners (e.g., "she was funny," "he was cute," "we shared similar religious beliefs"). This can be done either in session or as homework and generally has the effect of shifting spouses' focus from their partners' negative qualities to their positive qualities. This exercise can also be extended to the present time by asking spouses to list qualities of their partners that still attract them. In addition to shifting spouses' attention to the positive, the formerly depressed patient will gain a clearer understanding of behaviors that promote harmony with their spouses.

In the context of specifically targeting blame maintenance (or any of the other processes), simultaneous attention to the other processes is warranted, lest resolution of one exacerbate another (cf. compensatory processes as discussed in chap. 10). As an example, blame may serve as a source of self-verification for depressed people. If blame is reduced, negative self-verification strivings may be thwarted, which, in turn, may lead to attempts to restore blame or to meet self-verification needs in other ways (e.g., by reducing performance in a previously adaptive domain) or in other relationships (e.g., with friends).

We have provided examples of how minor adjustments to existing, empirically supported treatments for chronic depression may enhance recovery and reduce the likelihood of relapse and recurrence into depression. Similar modules could be developed with the goal of targeting other interpersonal phenomena that propagate depression. On the basis of substantial research on interpersonal processes, we expect that the incorporation of such interventions would likely improve on existing treatments, and we eagerly await data that speak to the validity of our expectation.

ADJUNCTS TO PRIMARY TREATMENT METHODS

A number of other issues may be considered as adjuncts to or points of focus in the context of existing treatments. We will not review them all here (they deserve an entire book on their own) but highlight two: exercise as an adjunct to treatment and positive emotions as a focus of treatment.

Exercise

A relatively simple supplement to existing treatments is exercise (suggestions for ways in which to incorporate exercise into treatment are available; e.g., Hays, 1999). Extensive data indicate that exercise promotes positive mood and leads to modest reductions in depressive symptoms and may be most effective when used as an adjunct to other treatments, such as antidepressant medication (Manber, Allen, & Morris, 2002). For example, Mather et al. (2002) randomly assigned depressed older adults receiving antidepressant medications to attend either exercise classes or health education talks. After 10 weeks, over half (55%) of the exercise group experienced a greater than 30% decline in depression, compared with only one third (33%) of the health education group. A separate group of researchers found comparable rates of improvement in response to the SRI sertraline (Zoloft), aerobic exercise, and the combination of the two (Babyak et al., 2000). It is interesting to note, however, that those in the exercise group were less likely to relapse during a 10-month follow-up than those in the medication group. What is more, the authors found that patients who continued to exercise on their own after the conclusion of treatment had a reduced probability of relapse. That is, the protective effect of exercise therapy with regard to relapse may be due to the fact that some people continue to exercise after treatment. Joiner and Tickle (1998) found similar results in support of the "antidepressant" of exercise among women and also found that one of the mechanisms of change was enhanced self-esteem. Namely, exercise predicted positive changes in self-esteem, which in turn partly accounted for decreases in depressive symptoms. However, self-esteem changes did not entirely account for depressive symptom changes, which suggests that other mechanisms may also mediate the exercise—depressive symptoms link. For example, exercise can increase the circulation of beta-endorphins, which are thought to have mood-enhancing effects; exercise may improve mood by elevating body temperature (i.e., the *pyrogen hypothesis*); or exercise may improve mood by increasing self-efficacy or providing a means of distraction (Martinsen, 1987; Tkachuk & Martin, 1999).

Capitalizing on Positive Emotions

In addition to considering exercise as an augment to treatment, we recommend that clinicians pay special attention to brief periods of positive emotions when working with chronically depressed persons. Research by Fredrickson (1998), as well as by Joiner, Pettit, et al. (2001), suggests that capitalizing on such periods in treatment may enhance outcomes. The basic idea, as set forth in Fredrickson's "broaden-and-build" model of positive emotions, is that emotions such as joy, interest, and contentment have the momentary effect of broadening cognition and behavior so that exploration, experimentation, and play are more likely. Furthermore, because positive emotions subserve exploration and experimentation, they have the long-term effect of resource building. Through exploration and experimentation, new ideas and actions are discovered, building up an individual's repertoire of physical, intellectual, and social resources.

The clinical implications of the broaden-and-build model are potentially numerous. For example, according to the logic of the model, skill-related interventions (e.g., CBT) timed to correspond with relatively positive moods may enhance outcomes. Similarly, patients who, despite their disorder, are relatively more prone than other patients to experience positive moods may more firmly and quickly acquire therapy-based skills and therefore achieve better outcomes. Patients who are relatively more prone than others to experience negative moods may need more time to acquire therapy-based skills.

Joiner, Pettit, et al. (2001) found support for this notion among suicidal young adults in a problem-solving treatment. In particular, they found that suicidal patients who were prone to positive moods, as compared with those less prone to such moods, displayed more positive problem-solving attitudes following treatment for suicidal symptoms and, partly as a function thereof, displayed enhanced treatment response. Similarly, Fredrickson, Tugade, Wauh, and Larkin (2003) found that experiencing positive emotions such as interest and love in the aftermath of a crisis served as a buffer against depression among resilient people.

At this point, readers may be questioning the applicability of this approach to chronically depressed patients because positive moods rarely occur in this group. Granted, chronically depressed people often spend the bulk of their time feeling sad, disinterested, and so on, but short periods of more positive feelings do occur. Clinicians may induce positive emotions among depressed patients prior to engaging in skill-building components of treatment. Such moods may be induced through a variety of straightforward therapeutic exercises and techniques, some of which are well-known. For example, Zeiss, Lewinsohn, and Munoz (1979) documented that a cognitive and behavioral focus on scheduling and engaging in pleasant activities (e.g., listening to favorite music, reading favorite books, talking with supportive friends, going to favorite restaurants, taking walks, playing with pets, engaging in favorite hobbies and pastimes, etc.) has clear mood-enhancement effects. Another straightforward example is to ask patients to dwell on their "best of times" (i.e., times in their lives when they were delighted, joyful, proud, etc.) or engaging them in other similar visualization activities (Rudd, Joiner, & Rajab, 2000). In so doing, clinicians may increase the likelihood that patients will benefit from the existing psychosocial treatments for depression.

SUMMARY

Chronic depression, by nature, can be difficult to treat. Juxtaposed to its chronic nature is the pressure for faster treatment effects. A handful of treatments have demonstrated efficacy for ameliorating chronic cases of depression in relatively brief periods (e.g., 20 weeks or less). These treatments include antidepressant medications, certain psychosocial interventions, and the combination of antidepressants and psychosocial treatments. All classes of antidepressant medications appear to be equally effective, although certain newer medications may have a more rapid onset of effect. Among psychosocial interventions, IPT and CBASP stand out as empirically validated treatments for chronic depression. The combination of IPT or CBASP with antidepressant medications appears to have the greatest impact on depressive symptoms and other areas of functioning. In this chapter, we proposed that the beneficial effects of treatment may work in part through their influence on the interpersonal environments of depressed persons. Moreover, we suggested ways in which more explicitly addressing certain interpersonal phenomena (e.g., negative feedback-seeking, excessive reassurance-seeking, and blame maintenance) in the context of existing psychosocial treatments may amplify the salutary effects of treatment. Finally, we highlighted the potentially beneficial effects of capitalizing on periods of positive emotions and using exercise as an adjunct to treatment.

14

PREVENTION:
THE POTENTIAL TO SAVE LIVES

As we discussed in chapter 2, depression is prevalent, costly, painful, and potentially lethal (World Health Organization, 2002). Depression's chronicity only augments its pernicious nature. Effectively treating depression (see chap. 13) is of high importance for depressed persons, their families and friends, employers, insurance companies, and many other organizations. In spite of the effectiveness of treatments in the acute phase (i.e., until remission of symptoms), most people experience recurring forms of depression. Given that fact, as well as our focus on self-propagatory processes in depression, it makes more sense to focus on the prevention of relapse and recurrence, as opposed to prevention of the disorder entirely (although that would certainly be ideal!). An interesting idea for future research, however, is whether interventions designed to reduce the processes described in chapters 3 through 8 would be effective at preventing depression among people who display them but have not yet experienced a depressive episode.

Prior to discussing potential strategies for relapse and recurrence prevention, we emphasize, as we did at the outset, that parts of this book are speculative and extend beyond currently available data. Although we attempt to offer suggestions for prevention based on existing empirical findings, preventive issues should be considered only with this caveat firmly in mind.

EXISTING PREVENTIVE STRATEGIES

As we discussed in chapter 13, the prevention of relapse and recurrence is no easy matter, with the majority of depressed persons experiencing at least two depressive episodes. For example, recurrence rates for major depressive disorder over extended periods of time range from 60% to 85% (e.g., Mueller et al., 1999; Solomon et al., 2000). Over a period of 15 years, Mueller et al. found the cumulative proportion of recurrence to be 63% at 5 years, 80% at 10 years, and 83% at 15 years. Even more problematic, the risk of recurrence for depression appears to increase with each subsequent episode (e.g., Kessing, Andersen, & Andersen, 2000). Numerical estimates of this "snowball effect" suggest that the risk of recurrence increases by approximately 15% with each successive recurrence (Kessing & Andersen, 1999; Solomon et al., 2000). Consistent with the notion of self-propagation, this phenomenon appears to result from the experience of episodes themselves rather than from the initial severity of the disorder (Kessing, Anderson, Mortensen, & Bolwig, 1998). Worse yet, evidence suggests that the time interval between episodes decreases with each additional episode (Taschev, 1974).

Unfortunately, high rates of relapse and recurrence are seen even after depressed patients have received different forms of psychotherapy or drug treatments (Frank et al., 1990; Thase & Sullivan, 1995). As mentioned in chapter 13, up to 50% of patients relapse unless treated 4 to 6 months after the initial acute phase therapy (Thase, 1999). Even more startling estimates come from Fava, Rafanelli, Grandi, Conti, and Belluardo (1998), who found that after discontinuation of drug therapy, formerly depressed patients who had received pharmacotherapy alone had a relapse or recurrence rate of 80% over a 2-year period (those who received pharmacotherapy combined with cognitive–behavioral therapy had a relapse or recurrence rate of 25%—a point we return to later in this chapter). Given the high rate of relapse after discontinuation of treatment, much attention has focused on the continuation phase of treatment (i.e., the weeks and months following successful response to antidepressant treatment). This appears to be a crucial component to treatment for at least three reasons. First, continuation of antidepressant medications during this phase reduces the risk of relapse by 20% to 50% (Prien & Kupfer, 1986). Second, depressed persons who have received treatment are roughly 3 times as likely to experience a relapse than a recurrence (Hollon, Thase, & Markowitz, 2002), emphasizing the high likelihood of relapse following a discontinuation of medication. Third, the presence of residual, or lingering, symptoms following recovery from depression predicts recurrence of full syndrome depression (e.g., Judd et al., 1998). On the basis of this evidence, the American Psychiatric Association (2000) set forth a recommendation that successful treatment of depression should be followed by a minimum of 6 months of continuation treatment.

Given the high rate of recurrence, even after successful treatment of acute depression and prevention of relapse, some have argued that maintenance treatment with antidepressants is warranted, particularly for at-risk persons such as those with multiple previous depressive episodes or other forms of chronic depression (Kupfer, 1991). For instance, Hochstrasser et al. (2001) found that maintenance treatment for a year or longer with the SRI citalopram significantly lengthened time to recurrence among patients with a history of multiple depressive episodes. Similarly, Flint and Rifat (1999) found that older adult patients experiencing their first episode of depression had a cumulative 61% recurrence rate after discontinuation of 2-year maintenance antidepressant therapy. After reinstatement of treatment, however, almost all patients improved. Hence, the argument could be made that long-term treatment (i.e., years, perhaps the remainder of their lives) is necessary to treat acute episodes and prevent relapse and recurrence, at least among older adults. Also supportive of maintenance pharmacotherapy, Gelenberg et al. (2003) reported that patients with chronic major depression, double-depression (i.e., major depression superimposed on dysthymia), or recurrent major depression with incomplete interepisode recovery were significantly less likely to recur over a 1-year period if they were maintained on the maximum dose of the atypical antidepressant nefazodone (Serzone), as compared with those who received a placebo. Therefore, the claim can be made that individuals with chronic forms of depression likely require chronic forms of treatment, at least within the treatment modality of pharmacotherapy.

This is not always advisable (or feasible) over long periods of time, however, as long-term antidepressant use is costly, often has unpleasant side effects, may present the means for suicide (especially for the heterocyclics), and may lead to an increased risk of adverse medical outcomes. Furthermore, the preventive effects of maintenance pharmacotherapy end upon discontinuation of the medication (Hollon et al., 2002), and a small body of evidence even suggests that recurrence occurs very rapidly and at a high rate after discontinuation of maintenance therapy (e.g., Belsher & Costello, 1988; Frank et al., 1990; Kupfer et al., 1992; Prien et al., 1984).

In summary, continuation of pharmacotherapy in the initial weeks and months following recovery from depression is one available strategy to reduce the risk of relapse, and maintenance pharmacotherapy (i.e., at least 6 months, but often longer) is an available strategy to reduce the likelihood of recurrence.

As made reference to in chapter 13, certain forms of psychotherapy have traditionally fared better than (discontinued) pharmacotherapy when applied to the prevention of relapse and recurrence. This greater relapse prevention possibly arises from lasting changes in behavioral and cognitive patterns resulting from psychotherapy. In contrast, pharmacotherapy, if administered over a brief period of time, temporarily alters biological processes in the brain and may not protect an individual from depressive episodes after the drug treatment is discontinued. When administered over longer periods of time, however, drugs may result in more permanent (and presumably beneficial) alterations in brain chemistry.

With regard to specific psychosocial treatment approaches, interpersonal psychotherapy (IPT) has modest support in the prevention of relapse and recurrence. For example, over an 18-month follow-up, relapse rates for patients who showed full remission by the end of the acute treatment phase were 33% for IPT, 36% for cognitive–behavioral therapy (CBT), and 50% for pharmacotherapy (which was discontinued at the end of acute treatment; Shea et al., 1992). Unfortunately, a sizeable proportion of patients in each treatment condition continued to display subthreshold depressive symptoms (a risk factor for full syndrome recurrence), leading to the conclusion that acute phase IPT, CBT, or pharmacotherapy may not be sufficient by themselves to prevent relapse. It is interesting to note that evidence suggests that IPT, if continued beyond initial symptom remission, may lead to long-term improvements in general social adjustment (Paykel & Weissman, 1973; Weissman, Klerman, Paykel, Prusoff, & Hanson, 1974; Weissman, Klerman, Prusoff, Sholomskas, & Padian, 1981). Consistent with our view of self-propagatory processes in depression, two areas of social functioning showing the greatest improvement were submissive dependency (cf. interpersonal conflict avoidance, chap. 6) and family attachment (cf. blame maintenance, chap. 8). With regard to recurrence, evidence suggests that the implementation of 4 monthly IPT sessions in the continuation phase is superior to placebo in preventing recurrence over periods up to 3 years, although not as effective as maintenance pharmacotherapy (Frank et al., 1990; Frank, Kupfer, Wagner, McEachran, & Cornes, 1991). Research has yet to investigate whether more frequent (e.g., biweekly) IPT sessions in the continuation phase would produce relapse rates comparable to that of maintenance pharmacotherapy.

Evidence similarly supports the efficacy of cognitive therapy (CT) and CBT to prevent relapse and recurrence. For example, Evans et al. (1992) found that depressed patients had a 64% reduction in risk for relapse if they received CT as opposed to discontinued pharmacotherapy. Moreover, several empirical studies indicate that even after discontinuation of CT, its ability to prevent relapse and recurrence is as great as continued pharmacotherapy (e.g., Evans et al., 1992). Continuation of CT after remission of symptoms also appears to be an effective way to reduce relapse. For example, Jarrett et al. (2001) added a continuation component to CT that focused on teaching patients relapse prevention skills. Among patients with a history of recurrent depression who responded to acute phase CT, the addition of the 10-session continuation phase significantly reduced relapse rates over an 8-month follow-up. Similarly, the Fava et al. (1998) study mentioned in this chapter found that the addition of a 20-week CBT course as patients were tapered off medications reduced the risk of recurrence more than three-fold over a 2-year follow-up.

As is evident from this brief review, psychosocial treatment options such as IPT and CT are effective at preventing relapse and recurrence, and this may particularly be the case when treatment is continued during the weeks and months immediately following symptom remission. Consistent with the material presented in chapter 13, the combination of pharmacotherapy and psychotherapy appears to produce a modest beneficial effect in relapse–recurrence prevention (see Pettit, Voelz, & Joiner, 2001, for a review). For example, Reynolds et al. (1999) found that among older adults, maintenance treatment with combined IPT and nortriptyline was effective in preventing recurrence. To wit, the combination of IPT and nortriptyline led to a 3-year relapse rate of 20%, compared with 43% for nortriptyline alone, 64% for IPT alone, and 90% for placebo. In spite of these favorable estimates, a sizeable proportion of patients continue to experience chronic forms of depression. What else can be done to prevent this from happening?

Improving pharmacological therapies is one approach, and ongoing research seeks to do just that (although no evidence exists to suggest that newer antidepressant medications are more efficacious than older ones). Alternatively, existing psychotherapies could be improved on to prevent relapse and recurrence. Some therapies already incorporate components on relapse prevention (e.g., continuation CT), but the addition of material regarding the interpersonal processes described in chapters 3 through 8 may further promote the preventive effects of such treatments. How can this be done?

EDUCATION ABOUT SELF-PROPAGATORY PROCESSES: PREVENTING RELAPSE AND RECURRENCE

People in remission from depression, as well as their relationship partners, may benefit from education regarding self-propagatory processes. Development of written or videotaped materials discussing, for example, excessive reassurance-seeking, negative feedback-seeking, their motivations, and their consequences, seems quite feasible. Indeed we are currently undertaking that endeavor. Such education should draw the motivated attention of formerly depressed people and their close others; motivated attention, in turn, may alter the social–cognitive representations responsible for depression chronicity, as was discussed in chapter 13 (cf. Fiske, 1993). One possible approach would be to add such materials to the continuation phase of therapy. This seems like an especially promising strategy, given that existing continuation therapies often reduce the risk for relapse and recurrence. By integrating segments on interpersonal processes such as conflict avoidance, self-handicapping, and the like, as well as involving significant others in treatment sessions, it may be possible to magnify the beneficial effects of continuation therapies.

Among depressed persons who achieve remission through the treatment approaches presented in chapter 13 (or even spontaneously), the extent that they can reduce or at least keep in check the interpersonal propagatory processes may determine whether they experience future depressive episodes. This would entail the reduction of interpersonal stress generation through improved problem-solving capacities, reduction of excessive reassurance-seeking and negative feedback-seeking through improved self-esteem, greater interpersonal agency and less self-handicapping through self-assertion, and reductions in blame maintenance through others' motivated attention to formerly depressed persons' new and improved behavioral repertoire. This is a lot to attend to, especially among people who may possess deficits in each of these areas! Nonetheless, we propose that it is attainable through careful attention and diligent work on the part of treatment providers, patients, and those close to them.

SUMMARY

Depression is marked by chronicity, with the frequently occurring phenomena of relapse and recurrence providing evidence of its persistence. Although 60% to 85% of depressed persons will experience at least two depressive episodes, current treatment strategies are somewhat effective in preventing relapse and recurrence. Possible therapeutic approaches to prevent relapse and recurrence include continuation phase pharmacotherapy, psychotherapy, or both. Maintenance pharmacotherapy may also be indicated for preventing recurrence among older adults and those with particularly chronic cases of depression. Evidence suggests that certain forms of psychotherapy, like CT, may be as effective in preventing relapse and recurrence as continued pharmacotherapy. Moreover, limited evidence indicates that combined treatment likely maximizes depressed people's chances of remaining free from depression after initial symptom remission. We propose that educating formerly depressed people and those close to them about the self-propagatory processes described in chapters 3 through 8 may lead to even lower rates of relapse and recurrence. Such education could be done fairly easily within the context of existing continuation therapies.

REFERENCES

Abraham, H. D., & Fava, M. (1999). Order of onset of substance abuse and depression in a sample of depressed outpatients. *Comprehensive Psychiatry, 40*(1), 44–50.

Abrams, R. C., Rosendhal, E., Card, C., & Alexopoulos, G. S. (1994). Personality disorder correlates of late and early onset depression. *Journal of the American Geriatrics Society, 42,* 727–731.

Abramson, L. Y., Metalsky, G. I., & Alloy, L. B. (1989). Hopelessness depression: A theory-based subtype of depression. *Psychological Review, 96,* 358–372.

Abramson, L. Y., Seligman, M. E. P., & Teasedale, J. D. (1978). Learned helplessness in humans: Critique and reformulation. *Journal of Abnormal Psychology, 87,* 49–74.

Adrian, C., & Hammen, C. (1993). Stress exposure and stress generation in children of depressed mothers. *Journal of Consulting and Clinical Psychology, 61,* 354–359.

Alexopoulos, G. S., Young, R. C., Meyers, B. S., Abrams, R. C., & Shamoian, C. A. (1988). Late-onset depression. *Psychiatric Clinics of North America, 11*(1), 101–115.

Alfano, M. S., Joiner, Jr., T. E., Perry, M., & Metalsky, G. I. (1994). Attributional style: A mediator of the shyness-depression relationship? *Journal of Research in Personality, 28,* 287–300.

Alloy, L. B., & Abramson, L. Y. (1982). Learned helplessness, depression, and the illusion of control. *Journal of Personality and Social Psychology, 42,* 1114–1126.

Alloy, L. B., & Abramson, L. Y. (1988). Depressive realism: four theoretical perspectives. In L. B. Alloy (Ed.), *Cognitive processes in depression* (pp. 223–265). New York: Guilford Press.

Alloy, L. B., & Abramson, L. Y. (1999). The Temple–Wisconsin cognitive vulnerability to depression project: Conceptual background, design, and methods. *Journal of Cognitive Psychotherapy, 13,* 227–262.

Alloy, L. B., Abramson, L. Y., Tashman, N. A., Berrebbi, D. S., Hogan, M. E., Whitehouse, W. G., et al. (2001). Developmental origins of cognitive vulnerability to depression: Parenting, cognitive, and inferential feedback styles of the parents of individuals at high and low cognitive risk for depression. *Cognitive Therapy and Research, 25,* 397–423.

Alpert, J. E., Uebelacker, L. A., McLean, N. E., & Nierenberg, A. A. (1997). Social phobia, avoidant personality disorder and atypical depression: Co-occurrence and clinical implications. *Psychological Medicine, 27,* 627–633.

Ambrosini, P., Bennett, D. S., Cleland, C. M., & Haslam, N. (2002). Taxonicity of adolescent melancholia: A categorical or dimensional construct? *Journal of Psychiatric Research, 36,* 247–256.

American Psychiatric Association. (1980). *Diagnostic and statistical manual of mental disorders* (3rd ed.). Washington, DC: Author.

American Psychiatric Association. (1987). *Diagnostic and statistical manual of mental disorders* (3rd ed., rev.). Washington, DC: Author.

American Psychiatric Association. (1994). *Diagnostic and statistical manual of mental disorders* (4th ed.). Washington, DC: Author.

American Psychiatric Association. (2000). Practice guidelines for the treatment of patients with major depressive disorder (rev.). *American Journal of Psychiatry, 157*(Suppl. 4).

Anderson, C. A., & Harvey, R. J. (1988). Discriminating between problems in living: An examination of measures of depression, loneliness, shyness, and social anxiety. *Journal of Social and Clinical Psychology, 6,* 482–491.

Anderson, I. M., & Tomenson, B. M. (1994). The efficacy of selective serotonin reuptake inhibitors in depression: A meta-analysis of studies against tricyclic antidepressants. *Journal of Psychopharmacology, 8,* 238–249.

Angst, J. (1996). Comorbidity of mood disorders: A longitudinal prospective study. *British Journal of Psychiatry, 168*(Suppl. 30), 31–37.

Arkin, R. M., & Baumgardner, A. H. (1985). Self-handicapping. In J. H. Harvey and G. Weary (Eds.), *Attribution: Basic issues and applications* (pp. 169–202). New York: Academic Press.

Asendorpf, J. B., & Ostendorf, F. (1998). Is self-enhancement healthy? Conceptual, psychometric, and empirical analysis. *Journal of Personality and Social Psychology, 74,* 955–966.

Asnis, G. M. (1981). Cortisol secretion and dexamethasone response in depression. *American Journal of Psychiatry, 138,* 1218–1221.

Babyak, M., Blumenthal, J. A., Herman, S., Khatri, P., Doraiswamy, M., Moore, K., et al. (2000). Exercise treatment for major depression: Maintenance of therapeutic benefit at 10 months. *Psychosomatic Medicine, 62,* 633–638.

Ball, S. G., Otto, M. W., Pollack, M. H., & Rosenbaum, J. F. (1994). Predicting prospective episodes of depression in patients with panic disorder: A longitudinal study. *Journal of Consulting and Clinical Psychology, 62,* 359–365.

Bansal, A., Monnier, J., Hobfoll, S. E., & Stone, B. (2000). Comparing men's and women's loss of perceived social and work resources following psychological distress. *Journal of Social and Personal Relationships, 17,* 265–281.

Barden, N., Reul, J. M., & Holsboer, F. (1995). Do antidepressants stabilize mood through actions on the hypothalamic–pituitary–adrenocortical system? *Trends in Neuroscience, 18*(1), 6–11.

Barlow, D. H., Esler, J. L., & Vitali, A. E. (1998). Psychosocial treatments for panic disorders, phobias, and generalized anxiety disorder. In P. E. Nathan & J. M. Gorman (Eds.), *A guide to treatments that work* (pp. 288–318). New York: Oxford University Press.

Baucom, D. H., Sayers, S. L., & Sher, T. G. (1990). Supplementing behavioral marital therapy with cognitive restructuring and emotional expressiveness training: An outcome investigation. *Journal of Consulting and Clinical Psychology, 58,* 636–645.

Baumeister, R. F., & Leary, M. R. (1995). The need to belong: Desire for interpersonal attachments as a fundamental human motivation. *Psychological Bulletin, 117*, 497–529.

Baumeister, R. F., Tice, D. M., & Hutton, D. G. (1989). Self-presentational motives and personality differences in self-esteem. *Journal of Personality, 57*, 547–579.

Baumgardner, A. H. (1991). Claiming depressive symptoms as a self-handicap: A protective self-presentation strategy. *Basic and Applied Social Psychology, 12*(1), 97–113.

Beach, S. R. H., & Amir, N. (2003). Is depression taxonic, dimensional, or both? *Journal of Abnormal Psychology, 112*, 228–236.

Beardslee, W. R., Keller, M. B., Lavori, P. W., Staley, J. E., & Sacks, N. R. (1993). The impact of parental affective disorder on depression in offspring: A longitudinal follow-up in a nonreferred sample. *Journal of the American Academy of Child and Adolescent Psychiatry, 32*, 723–730.

Bech, P. (1987). Observer rating scales of anxiety and depression with reference to DSM–III for clinical studies in psychosomatic medicine. *Advances of Psychosomatic Medicine, 17*, 55–70.

Beck, A. T. (1976). *Cognitive therapy and the emotional disorders.* Oxford, England: International Universities Press.

Beck, A. T. (1996). Beyond belief: A theory of modes, personality, and psychopathology. In P. M. Salkovskis (Ed.), *Frontiers of cognitive therapy* (pp. 1–25). New York: Guilford Press.

Beck, A. T., Epstein, N., & Harrison, R. (1983). Cognitions, attitudes and personality dimensions in depression. *British Journal of Cognitive Psychotherapy, 1*(1), 1–16.

Beck, A. T., Rush, A. J., Shaw, B. F., & Emery, G. (1979). *Cognitive therapy of depression.* New York: Guilford.

Beck, A. T., & Steer, R. A. (1987). *Manual for the revised Beck Depression Inventory.* San Antonio, TX: Psychological Corporation.

Beck, A. T., Steer, R. A., & Brown, G. K. (1996). *Manual for the Beck Depression Inventory—II.* San Antonio, TX: The Psychological Corporation.

Beck, R., Robbins, M., Taylor, C., & Baker, L. (2001). An examination of sociotrophy and excessive reassurance seeking in the prediction of depression. *Cognitive Therapy and Research, 23*(2), 101–105.

Belle, D. (1987). Gender differences in the social moderators of stress. In R. S. Barnett, L. Biener, & G. K. Baruch (Eds.), *Gender and stress* (pp. 257–277). New York: Free Press.

Belsher, G., & Costello, C. G. (1988). Relapse after recovery from unipolar depression: A critical review. *Psychopharmacology Bulletin, 104*, 84–96.

Benazon, N. R. (2000). Predicting negative spousal attributions toward depressed persons: A test of Coyne's interpersonal model. *Journal of Abnormal Psychology, 109*, 550–554.

Bergeman, C. S., Plomin, R., Pederson, N. L., McClearn, G. E., & Nesselroade, J. R. (1990). Genetic and environmental influences on social support: The Swedish Adoption/Twin Study of Aging. *Journals of Gerontology, 45*(3), 101–106.

Berman, A. L., & Jobes, D. A. (1991). *Adolescent suicide: Assessment and intervention.* Washington, DC: American Psychological Association.

Bibring, E. (1953). The mechanism of depression. In P. Greenacre (Ed.), *Affective disorders* (pp. 13–48). London: International University Press.

Blackburn, I. M., Eunson, K. M., & Bishop, S. (1986). A two-year naturalistic follow-up of depressed patients treated with cognitive therapy, pharmacotherapy, and a combination of both. *Journal of Affective Disorders, 10,* 67–75.

Bland, R. C., Newman, S. C., & Orn, H. (1986). Schizophrenia: Lifetime comorbidity in a community sample. *Acta Psychiatrica Scandinavica, 75,* 383–391.

Blazer, D. G. (1983). The assessment of social support in an elderly community population. *American Journal of Social Psychiatry, 3*(1), 29–36.

Bornstein, R. F. (2001). A meta-analysis of the dependency eating-disorders relationship: Strength, specificity, and temporal stability. *Journal of Psychopathology and Behavioral Assessment, 23*(3), 151–162.

Bothwell, R., & Scott, J. (1997). The influence of cognitive variables on recovery in depressed inpatients. *Journal of Affective Disorders, 43,* 207–212.

Bradbury, T. N., & Fincham, F. D. (1990). Attributions in marriage: Review and critique. *Psychological Bulletin, 107,* 3–33.

Brent, D. A., Kerr, M. M., Goldstein, C., & Bozigar, J. (1989). An outbreak of suicide and suicidal behavior in a high school. *Journal of the American Academy of Child & Adolescent Psychiatry, 28,* 918–924.

Brewin, C. R., McCarthy, B., Duda, K., & Vaughn, C. E. (1991). Attribution and expressed emotion in the relatives of patients with schizophrenia. *Journal of Abnormal Psychology, 100,* 546–554.

Brown, G. W., & Harris, T. (1978). *Social origins of depression.* London: Free Press.

Brugha, T. S., Bebbington, P. E., MacCarthy, B., & Stuart, E. (1990). Gender, social support, and recovery from depressive disorders: A prospective clinical study. *Psychological Medicine, 20,* 147–156.

Buchwald, A. M., & Rudick-Davis, D. (1993). The symptoms of major depression. *Journal of Abnormal Psychology, 102,* 197–205.

Burvill, P. W., Hall, W. D., Stampfer, H. G., & Emerson, J. P. (1989). A comparison of early-onset and late-onset depressive illness in the elderly. *British Journal of Psychiatry, 155,* 673–679.

Buss, A. H. (1986). *Social behavior and personality.* Hillsdale, NJ: Erlbaum.

Buss, A. H. (1991). The EAS theory of temperament. In J. Strelau & A. Angleitner (Eds.), *Explorations in temperament: International perspectives on theory and measurement* (pp. 43–60). New York: Plenum Press.

Butler, A. C., Hokanson, J. E., & Flynn, H. A. (1994). A comparison of self-esteem lability and low trait self-esteem as vulnerability factors for depression. *Journal of Personality and Social Psychology, 66,* 166–177.

Carver, C. S., & Scheier, M. F. (1981). *Attention and self-regulations: A control theory approach to human behavior*. New York: Springer-Verlag.

Cassano, G. B., Akiskal, H. S., Savino, M., Soriani, A., Musetti, L., & Perugi, G. (1993). Single episode of major depressive disorder: First episode of recurrent mood disorder or distinct subtype of late-onset depression? *European Archives of Psychiatry and Clinical Neuroscience, 242*, 373–380.

Catalano, R., Aldrete, E., Vega, W., Kolody, B., & Aguilar-Gaxiola, S. (2000). Job loss and major depression among Mexican-Americans. *Social Science Quarterly, 81*, 477–487.

Chambless, D. L., & Steketee, G. (1999). Expressed emotion and behavior therapy outcome: A prospective study with obsessive–compulsive and agoraphobic outpatients. *Journal of Consulting and Clinical Psychology, 67*, 658–665.

Cheek, J. M., & Busch, C. M. (1981). The influence of shyness on loneliness in a new situation. *Personality and Social Psychology Bulletin, 7*, 572–577.

Cheek, J. M., & Buss, A. H. (1981). Shyness and sociability. *Journal of Personality and Social Psychology, 41*, 330–339.

Clark, D. A., Steer, R. A., & Beck, A. T. (1994). Common and specific dimensions of self-reported anxiety and depression: Implications for the cognitive and tripartite models. *Journal of Abnormal Psychology, 103*, 645–654.

Clark, L. A., & Watson, D. (1991). Tripartite model of anxiety and depression: Psychometric evidence and taxonomic implications. *Journal of Abnormal Psychology, 100*, 316–336.

Collins, N. L., Dunkel-Schetter, C., Lobel, M., & Scrimshaw, S. C. (1993). Social support in pregnancy: Psychosocial correlates of birth outcomes and postpartum depression. *Journal of Personality and Social Psychology, 65*, 1243–1258.

Colvin, C. R., Block, J., & Funder, D. C. (1995). Overly positive self-evaluations and personality: Negative implications for mental health. *Journal of Personality and Social Psychology, 68*, 1152–1162.

Costello, C. G. (1982). Social factors associated with depression: A retrospective community study. *Psychological Medicine, 12*, 329–339.

Counts, D. A. (1980). Fighting back is not the way: Suicide and the women of Kaliai. *American Ethnologist, 7*, 332–351.

Coryell, W., Endicott, J., Winokur, G., Akiskal, H., Solomon, D., Leon, A., et al. (1995). Characteristics and significance of untreated major depressive disorder. *American Journal of Psychiatry, 152*, 1124–1129.

Coryell, W., & Winokur, G. (1992). Course and outcome. In E. Paykel (Ed.), *Handbook of affective disorders* (pp. 89–108). New York: Guilford Press.

Coyne, J. C. (1976a). Depression and the response of others. *Journal of Abnormal Psychology, 85*, 186–193.

Coyne, J. C. (1976b). Toward an interactional description of depression. *Psychiatry, 39*, 28–40.

Coyne, J. C. (1994). Self-reported distress: Analog or ersatz depression? *Psychological Bulletin, 116*, 29–45.

Coyne, J. C., & Whiffen, V. E. (1995). Issues in personality as a diathesis for depression: The case of sociotropy/dependency and autonomy/self-criticism. *Psychological Bulletin, 118*, 358–378.

Cross-National Collaborative Group. (1992). The changing rate of major depression: Cross-national comparisons. *Journal of the American Medical Association, 268*, 3098–3105.

Cruz, J., Joiner, T. E., Jr., Johnson, J. G., Heisler, L. K., Spitzer, R. L., & Pettit, J. W. (2000). Self-defeating personality disorder reconsidered. *Journal of Personality Disorders, 14*(1), 64–71.

Cuijpers, P., & Smit, F. (2002). Excess mortality in depression: A meta-analysis of community studies. *Journal of Affective Disorders, 72*, 227–236.

Cummings, E. M. (1994). Marital conflict and children's functioning. *Social Development, 3*(1), 16–36.

Cummings, E. M., & Davies, P. T. (1999). Depressed parents and family functioning: Interpersonal effects and children's functioning and development. In T. E. Joiner Jr. & J. C. Coyne (Eds.), *The interactional nature of depression: Advances in interpersonal approaches* (pp. 299–327). Washington, DC: American Psychological Association.

Daley, S. E., Hammen, C., Burge, D., & Davila, J. (1997). Predictors of the generation of episodic stress: A longitudinal study of late adolescent women. *Journal of Abnormal Psychology, 106*, 251–259.

Davies, P. T., & Cummings, E. M. (1998). Exploring children's emotional security as a mediator of the link between marital relations and child adjustment. *Child Development, 60*, 124–139.

Davila, J., Bradbury, T. N., Cohan, C. L., & Tochluk, S. (1997). Marital functioning and depressive symptoms: Evidence for a stress generation model. *Journal of Personality and Social Psychology, 73*, 849–861.

Davila, J., Hammen, C., Burge, D., Daley, S. E., & Paley, B. (1996). Cognitive/interpersonal correlates of adult interpersonal problem-solving strategies. *Cognitive Therapy and Research, 20*, 465–480.

Davila, J., Hammen, C., Burge, D., & Paley, B. (1995). Poor interpersonal problem solving as a mechanism of stress generation in depression among adolescent women. *Journal of Abnormal Psychology, 104*, 592–600.

DeCatanzaro, D. (1995). Reproductive status, family interactions, and suicidal ideation: Surveys of the general public and high-risk groups. *Ethology and Sociobiology, 16*, 385–394.

De Leeuw, J. R. J., De Graeff, A., Ros, W. J. G., Hordijk, G. J., Blijham, G. H., & Winnubst, J. A. M. (2000). Negative and positive influences of social support on depression in patients with head and neck cancer: A prospective study. *Psycho-Oncology, 9*(1), 20–28.

Depression Guideline Panel. (1993, April). *Depression in primary care: Vol. 1. Detection and diagnosis* (Clinical Practice Guideline, No. 5; AHCPR Publication No. 93-0550). Rockville, MD: U.S. Department of Health and Human Services, Public Health Service, Agency for Health Care Policy and Research.

DeRubeis, R. J., Gelfand, L. A., Tang, T. Z., & Simons, A. D. (1999). Medications versus cognitive behavior therapy for severely depressed outpatients: Mega-analysis of four randomized comparisons. *American Journal of Psychiatry, 156,* 1007–1013.

DiMascio, A., Weissman, M. M., Prusoff, B. A., Neu, C., Zwilling, M., & Klerman, G. L. (1979). Differential symptom reduction by drugs and psychotherapy in acute depression. *Archives of General Psychiatry, 36,* 1450–1456.

Dobson, K. S. (1989). A meta-analysis of the efficacy of cognitive therapy of depression. *Journal of Consulting and Clinical Psychology, 57,* 414–419.

Dobson, K. S. (2000). Chronic processes in depression: differentiating self and other influences in onset, maintenance, and relapse/recurrence. *Clinical Psychology: Science and Practice, 7,* 236–239.

Domino, G., Fragoso, A., & Moreno, H. (1991). Cross-cultural investigations of the imagery of cancer in Mexican nationals. *Hispanic Journal of Behavioral Sciences, 13,* 422–435.

Drigotas, S. M., Rusbult, C. E., Wieselquist, J., & Whitton, S. W. (1999). Close partner as sculptor of the ideal self: Behavioral affirmation and the Michelangelo phenomenon. *Journal of Personality and Social Psychology, 77,* 293–323.

Driscoll, K. A., Cukrowicz, K. C., Reardon, M. L., & Joiner, T. E., Jr. (2003). *Simple treatments for complex problems.* Mahwah, NJ: Erlbaum.

Duemm, I., Adams, G. R., & Keating, L. (2003). The addition of sociotropy to the dual pathway model of bulimia. *Canadian Journal of Behavioral Science, 35,* 281–291.

Durkheim, E. (1897). *Le suicide: Etude de socologie* [Suicide: Study of sociology]. Paris: F. Alcan.

Duval, S., & Wicklund, R. (1972). *A theory of objective self-awareness.* San Diego, CA: Academic Press.

Ebata, A. T., & Moos, R. H. (1994). Personal, situational, and contextual determinants of coping in adolescents. *Journal of Research on Adolescence, 4,* 99–122.

Edelstein, B., Kalish, K. D., Drozdick, L. W., & McKee, D. R. (1999). Assessment of depression and bereavement in older adults. In P. Lichtenberg (Ed.), *Handbook of assessment in clinical gerontology. Wiley series on adulthood and aging* (pp. 11–58). New York: Wiley.

Egeland, J. A., & Hostetter, A. M. (1983). Amish study: I. Affective disorders among the Amish, 1976–1980. *American Journal of Psychiatry, 140,* 56–61.

Elkin, I., Shea, M. T., Watkins, J. T., Imber, S. D., Sotsky, S. M., Collins, J. F., et al. (1989). National Institute of Mental Health Treatment of Depression Collaborative Program: General effectiveness of treatments. *Archives of General Psychiatry, 46,* 971–982.

Emslie, G., Rush, A. J., Weinberg, W. A., & Guillon, C. M. (1997). Recurrence of major depressive disorder in hospitalized children and adolescents. *Journal of the American Academy of Child & Adolescent Psychiatry, 36,* 785–792.

Ennis, N. E., Hobfoll, S. E., & Schroeder, K. E. E. (2000). Money doesn't talk, it swears: How economic stress and resistance resources impact inner-city women's depressive mood. *American Journal of Community Psychology, 28*(2), 149–173.

Evans, M. D., Hollon, S. D., DeRubeis, R. J., Piasecki, J. M., Grove, W. M., Garvey, M. J., & Tuason, V. B. (1992). Differential relapse following cognitive therapy and pharmacotherapy for depression. *Archives of General Psychiatry, 49,* 802–808.

Fairburn, C. (1998). Interpersonal psychotherapy for bulimia nervosa. In J. C. Markowitz (Ed.), *Interpersonal psychotherapy* (pp. 99–128). Washington, DC: American Psychiatric Association.

Fallon, B. A., Walsh, T. B., Sadik, C., Saoud, J. B., & Lukasik, V. (1991). Outcome and clinical course in inpatient bulimic women: A 2- to 9-year follow-up study. *Journal of Clinical Psychiatry, 52*(6), 272–278.

Faulkner, W. (1932). *Light in August.* New York: Smith & Haas.

Fava, G. A., Rafanelli, C., Grandi, S., Conti, S., & Belluardo, P. (1998). Prevention of recurrent depression with cognitive behavioral therapy: Preliminary findings. *Archives of General Psychiatry, 55,* 816–820.

Fava, M., Alpert, J. E., Borus, J. S., & Nierenberg, A. A. (1996). Patterns of personality disorder comorbidity in early-onset versus late-onset major depression. *American Journal of Psychiatry, 153,* 1308–1312.

Fehrenbach, T. R. (1995). *Fire and blood: A history of Mexico.* New York: Da Capo Press.

Fenichel, O. (1945). *The psychoanalytic theory of neurosis.* New York: Norton.

Ferrari, J. R., & Tice, D. M. (2000). Procrastination as a self-handicap for men and women: A task-avoidance strategy in a laboratory setting. *Journal of Research in Personality, 34*(1), 73–83.

Finn, S. E., & Tonsager, M. E. (1992). Therapeutic impact of providing MMPI–2 feedback to college students awaiting therapy. *Psychological Assessment, 4,* 278–287.

Fiske, S. T. (1993). Social cognition and social perception. *Annual Review of Psychology 44,* 155–194.

Flint, A. J., & Rifat, S. L. (1999). Recurrence of first-episode geriatric depression after discontinuation of maintenance antidepressants. *American Journal of Psychiatry, 156,* 943–945.

Frank, E., Kupfer, D. J., Perel, J. M., Cornes, C., Jarret, D. B., Mallinger, A. G., et al. (1990). Three-year outcomes for maintenance therapies in recurrent depression. *Archives of General Psychiatry, 47,* 1093–1099.

Frank, E., Kupfer, D. J., Wagner, E. F., McEachran, A. B., & Cornes, C. (1991). Efficacy of interpersonal psychotherapy as a maintenance treatment of recurrent depression: Contributing factors. *Archives of General Psychiatry, 48,* 1053–1059.

Franklin, L., Strong, D., & Greene, R. (2002). A taxometric analysis of the MMPI–2 depression scales. *Journal of Personality Assessment, 79,* 110–121.

Franks, P., Shields, C., Campbell, T., & McDaniel, S. (1992). Association of social relationships with depressive symptoms: Testing an alternative to social support. *Journal of Family Psychology, 6,* 49–59.

Fredrickson, B. L. (1998). What good are positive emotions? *Review of General Psychology, 2,* 300–319.

Fredrickson, B. L., Tugade, M. M., Waugh, C. E., & Larkin, G. R. (2003). What good are positive emotions in crisis? A prospective study of resilience and emotions following the terrorist attacks on the United States on September 11th, 2001. *Journal of Personality and Social Psychology, 84,* 365–376.

Freud, S. (1951). Mourning and melancholia. In J. Strachey (Ed. & Trans.), *Standard edition of the complete psychological works of Sigmond Freud* (Vol. 14, pp. 237–258). London: Hogarth Press. (Original work published 1917)

Friedman, M. A., & Whisman, M. A. (1998). Sociotropy, autonomy, and bulimic symptomatology. *International Journal of Eating Disorders, 23,* 439–442.

Garber, J., & Hollon, S. D. (1991). What can specificity designs say about causality in psychopathology research? *Psychological Bulletin, 110,* 129–136.

Garcia, M., & Marks, G. (1989). Depressive symptomatology among Mexican-American adults: An examination with the CES-D scale. *Psychiatry Research, 27,* 137–148.

Ge, X., & Conger, R. D. (1999). Adjustment problems and emerging personality characteristics from early to late adolescence. *American Journal of Community Psychology, 27,* 429–459.

Gelenberg, A. J., Trivedi, M. H., Rush, A. J., Thase, M. E., Howland, R. E., Klein, D. N., et al. (2003). Randomized, placebo-controlled trial of nefazodone maintenance treatment in preventing recurrence in chronic depression. *Biological Psychiatry, 54,* 806–817.

Gibb, B. E., Alloy, L. B., Abramson, L. Y., Rose, D. T., Whitehouse, W. G., Donovan, P., et al. (2001). History of childhood maltreatment, negative cognitive styles, and episodes of depression in adulthood. *Cognitive Therapy and Research, 25,* 425–446.

Giesler, R. B., Josephs, R. A., & Swann, W. B., Jr. (1996). Self-verification in clinical depression: The desire for negative evaluation. *Journal of Abnormal Psychology, 105,* 358–368.

Gilbert, P. (1997). The evolution of social attractiveness and its role in shame, humilation, guilt, and therapy. *British Journal of Medical Psychology, 70,* 113–147.

Golding, J., Karno, M., & Rutter, C. M. (1990). Symptoms of major depression among Mexican-American and non-Hispanic Whites. *American Journal of Psychiatry, 147,* 861–866.

Gotlib, I. H., & Asarnow, R. F. (1979). Interpersonal and impersonal problem-solving skills in mildly and clinically depressed university students. *Journal of Consulting and Clinical Psychology, 47,* 86–95.

Gray, J. A. (1987). The neuropsychology of emotion and personality. In S. M. Stahl & S. D. Iverson (Eds.), *Cognitive neurochemistry* (pp. 171–190). London: Oxford University Press.

Greaven, S. H., Santor, D. A., Thompson, R., & Zuroff, D. C. (2000). Adolescent self-handicapping, depressive affect, and maternal parenting style. *Journal of Youth and Adolescence, 29,* 631–646.

Gross, C. P., Anderson, G. F., & Powe, N. R. (1999). The relation between funding by the National Institutes of Health and the burden of disease. *New England Journal of Medicine, 340,* 1881–1887.

Grove, W. M., Andreasen, N. C., Young, M., & Endicott, J. (1987). Isolation and characterization of a nuclear depressive syndrome. *Psychological Medicine, 17,* 471–484.

Grunbaum, J. A., Kann, L., Kinchen, S. A., Williams, B., Ross, J. G., Lowry, R., & Kolbe, L. (2002). Youth risk behavior surveillance—United States, 2001. *MMWR. Surveillance Summaries: Morbidity and Mortality Weekly Report, 51,* 1–62.

Gudykunst, W. B. (1998). Individualistic and collectivistic perspectives on communication: An introduction. *International Journal of Intercultural Relations, 22,* 107–134.

Gurtman, M. B., Martin, K. M., & Hintzman, N. M. (1990). Interpersonal reactions to displays of depression and anxiety. *Journal of Social and Clinical Psychology, 9,* 256–267.

Hale, W. W., Jansen, J. H. C., Bouhuys, A. L., Jenner, J. A., & van den Hoffdakker, H. (1997). Non-verbal behavioral interactions of depressed patients with partners and strangers: The role of behavioral social support and involvement in depression persistence. *Journal of Affective Disorders, 44,* 111–122.

Hamilton, E. W., & Abramson, L. Y. (1983). Cognitive patterns and major depressive disorders: A longitudinal study in a hospital setting. *Journal of Abnormal Psychology, 92,* 173–184.

Hamilton, M. (1967). Development of a rating scale for primary depressive illness. *British Journal of Social and Clinical Psychology, 6,* 278–296.

Hammen, C. (1991). Generation of stress in the course of unipolar depression. *Journal of Abnormal Psychology, 100,* 555–561.

Hammen, C. (1999). The emergence of an interpersonal approach to depession. In T. E. Joiner Jr. & J. C. Coyne (Eds.), *The interactional nature of depression* (pp. 21–36). Washington, DC: American Psychological Association.

Hammen, C., Davila, J., Brown, G., Ellicott, A., & Gitlin, M. (1992). Psychiatric history and stress: Predictors of severity of unipolar depression. *Journal of Abnormal Psychology, 101,* 45–52.

Hankin, B. L., & Abramson, L. Y. (2001). Development of gender differences in depression: An elaborated cognitive vulnerability-transactional stress theory. *Psychological Bulletin, 127,* 773–796.

Hankin, B. L., Abramson, L. Y., Miller, N., & Haeffel, G. J. (2004). Cognitive vulnerability-stress theories of depression: Examining affective specificity in the prediction of depression versus anxiety in three prospective studies. *Cognitive Therapy and Research, 28,* 309–345.

Hankin, B. L., Abramson, L. Y., Moffit, T. E., Silva, P. A., McGee, R., & Angell, K. E. (1998). Development of depression from preadolescence to young adulthood: Emerging gender differences in a 10-year longitudinal study. *Journal of Abnormal Psychology, 107,* 128–140.

Hankin, B. L., Abramson, L. Y., & Siler, M. (2001). A prospective test of the hopelessness theory of depression in adolescence. *Cognitive Therapy and Research*, *25*, 607–632.

Hankin, B. L., Fraley, R. C., Lahey, B. B., & Waldman, I. D. (2005). Is depression best viewed as a continuum or a discrete category? A taxometric analysis of childhood and adolescent depression in a population-based sample. *Journal of Abnormal Psychology*, *114*, 96–110.

Haslam, N., & Beck, A. T. (1994). Subtyping major depression: A taxometric analysis. *Journal of Abnormal Psychology*, *103*, 686–692.

Hatfield, E., Cacioppo, J. T., & Rapson, R. L. (1993). Emotional contagion. *Current Directions in Psychological Science*, *2*, 96–99.

Haw, C. M. (1994). A cluster of suicides at a London psychiatric unit. *Suicide and Life-Threatening Behavior*, *24*, 256–266.

Hawton, K. (1992). Suicide and attempted suicide. In E. Paykel (Ed.), *Handbook of affective disorders* (pp. 635–650). New York: Guilford Press.

Hay, P. (2003). Quality of life and bulimic eating disorder behaviors: Findings from a community-based sample. *International Journal of Eating Disorders*, *33*, 434–442.

Hayaki, J., Friedman, M. A., Whisman, M. A., Delinsky, S. S., & Brownell, K. D. (2003). Sociotropy and bulimic symptoms in clinical and nonclinical samples. *International Journal of Eating Disorders*, *34*, 172–176.

Hays, K. F. (1999). *Working it out: Using exercise in psychotherapy*. Washington, DC: American Psychological Association.

Hays, R. D., Wells, K. B., Sherbourne, C. D., Rogers, W., & Spritzer, K. (1995). Functioning and well-being outcomes of patients with depression compared with chronic general medical illnesses. *Archives of General Psychiatry*, *52*, 11–19.

Heimberg, R. G., Salzman, D. G., Holt, C. S., & Blendell, K. A. (1993). Cognitive-behavioral group treatment for social phobia: Effectiveness at five-year follow-up. *Cognitive Therapy and Research*, *17*, 325–339.

Henderson, A. S., Korten, A. E., Jacomb, P. A., MacKinnon, A. J., Jorm, A. F., Christensen, H., & Rodgers, B. (1997). The course of depression in the elderly: A longitudinal community-based study in Australia. *Psychological Medicine*, *27*(1), 119–129.

Hersen, M., Bellack, A. S., Himmelhoch, J. M., & Thase, M. E. (1984). Effects of social skill training, amitriptyline, and psychotherapy in unipolar depressed women. *Behavior Therapy*, *15*, 21–40.

Higgins, E. T. (1987). Self-discrepancy: A theory relating self and affect. *Psychological Review*, *94*, 319–340.

Hildebrand-Saints, L., & Weary, G. (1989). Depression and social information gathering. *Personality and Social Psychology Bulletin*, *15*(2), 150–160.

Hirschfeld, R. A., Dunner, D. L., Keitner, G., Klein, D. N., Koran, L. M., Kornstein, S., et al. (2002). Does psychosocial functioning improve independent of depressive symptoms? A comparison of nefazodone, psychotherapy, and their combination. *Biological Psychiatry*, *51*, 123–133.

Hochstrasser, B., Isaksen, P. M., Koponen, H., Lauritzen, L., Mahnert, F. A., Rouillon, F., et al. (2001). Prophylactic effect of citalopram in unipolar, recurrent depression: Placebo-controlled study of maintenance therapy. *British Journal of Psychiatry*, *178*, 304–310.

Holahan, C. J., & Moos, R. H. (1987). Personal and contextual determinants of coping strategies. *Journal of Personality and Social Psychology*, *52*, 946–955.

Hollon, S. D., & Beck, A. T. (1994). Cognitive and cognitive–behavioral therapies. In A. E. Bergin & S. L. Garfield (Eds.), *Handbook of psychotherapy and behavior change* (pp. 428–466). New York: Wiley.

Hollon, S. D., Kendall, P. C., & Lumry, A. (1986). Specificity of depressotypic cognitions in clinical depression. *Journal of Abnormal Psychology*, *95*, 52–59.

Hollon, S. D., Shelton, R. C., & Davis, D. D. (1993). Cognitive therapy for depression: Conceptual issues and clinical efficacy. *Journal of Consulting and Clinical Psychology*, *61*, 270–275.

Hollon, S. D., Shelton, R. C., & Loosen, P. T. (1991). Cognitive therapy and pharmacotherapy for depression. *Journal of Consulting and Clinical Psychology*, *59*, 88–99.

Hollon, S. D., Thase, M. E., & Markowitz, J. C. (2002). Treatment of prevention of depression. *Psychological Science*, *3*(2), 39–77.

Hooley, J. M. (1987). The nature and origins of expressed emotion. In K. Hahlweg & M. J. Goldstein (Eds.), *Understanding major mental disorder: The contribution of family interaction research* (pp. 176–194). New York: Family Process Press.

Hooley, J. M., & Licht, D. M. (1997). Expressed emotions and causal attributions in the spouses of depressed patients. *Journal of Abnormal Psychology*, *106*, 298–306.

Hooley, J. M., & Teasdale, J. D. (1989). Predictors of relapse in unipolar depressives: Expressed emotion, marital distress, and perceived criticism. *Journal of Abnormal Psychology*, *98*, 229–235.

Hovey, J. D., & King, C. A. (1996). Acculturative stress, depression, and suicidal ideation among immigrant and second-generation Latino adolescents. *Journal of the Academy of Child & Adolescent Psychiatry*, *35*, 1183–1192.

Huprich, S. K. (2003). Depressive personality and its relationship to depressed mood, interpersonal loss, negative parental perceptions, and perfectionism. *Journal of Nervous and Mental Disease*, *191*(2), 73–79.

Hur, Y., & Bouchard, T. J. (1995). Genetic influences on perceptions of childhood family environment: A reared apart twin study. *Child Development*, *66*, 330–345.

Jack, D. C. (1991). *Silencing the self: Women and depression*. Cambridge, MA: Harvard University Press.

Jacobson, N. S., Dobson, K., Fruzetti, A. E., & Schmaling, K. B. (1991). Marital therapy as a treatment for depression. *Journal of Consulting and Clinical Psychology*, *59*, 547–557.

Jarrett, R. B., Kraft, D., Doyle, J., Foster, B. M., Eaves, G. G., & Silver, P. C. (2001). Preventing recurrent depression using cognitive therapy with and without a continuation phase. *Archives of General Psychiatry*, *58*, 381–388.

Jobes, D. A., Jacoby, A. M., Cimbolic, P., & Hustead, L. A. T. (1997). Assessment and treatment of suicidal clients in a university counseling center. *Journal of Consulting and Clinical Psychology, 44*, 368–377.

Johnston, L. C., & Macrae, C. N. (1994). Changing social stereotypes: The case of the information seeker. *European Journal of Social Psychology, 24*, 581–592.

Joiner, T. E., Jr. (1994). Contagious depression: Existence, specificity to depressed symptoms, and the role of reassurance seeking. *Journal of Personality and Social Psychology, 67*, 287–296.

Joiner, T. E., Jr. (1995). The price of soliciting and receiving negative feedback: Self-verification theory as a vulnerability to depression theory. *Journal of Abnormal Psychology, 104*, 364–372.

Joiner, T. E., Jr. (1997). Shyness and low social support as interactive diatheses, and loneliness as mediator: Testing an interpersonal-personality view of depression. *Journal of Abnormal Psychology, 106*, 386–394.

Joiner, T. E., Jr. (1998). *Correlation between excessive reassurance-seeking and traits of shyness and sociability*. Unpublished raw data.

Joiner, T. E., Jr. (1999a). The clustering and contagion of suicide. *Current Directions in Psychological Science, 8*, 89–92.

Joiner, T. E., Jr. (1999b). Self-verification and bulimic symptoms: Do bulimic women play a role in perpetuating their own dissatisfaction and symptoms? *International Journal of Eating Disorders, 26*, 145–151.

Joiner, T. E., Jr. (1999c). A test of interpersonal theory of depression in youth psychiatric inpatients. *Journal of Abnormal Child Psychology, 27*(1), 77–85.

Joiner, T. E., Jr. (2003). Contagion of suicidal symptoms as a function of assortative relating and shared relationship stress in college roommates. *Journal of Adolescence, 26*, 495–504.

Joiner, Jr., T. E., Alfano, M. S., & Metalsky, G. I. (1992). When depression breeds contempt: Reassurance-seeking, self-esteem, and rejection of depressed college students by their roommates. *Journal of Abnormal Psychology, 101*, 165–173.

Joiner, T. E., Jr., Alfano, M. S., & Metalsky, G. I. (1993). Caught in the crossfire: Depression, self-consistency, self-enhancement, and the response of others. *Journal of Social and Clinical Psychology, 12*, 113–134.

Joiner, T. E., Jr., Catanzaro, S., & Laurent, J. L. (1996). The tripartite structure of positive and negative affect, depression, and anxiety in child and adolescent psychiatric inpatients. *Journal of Abnormal Psychology, 105*, 401–409.

Joiner, T. E., Jr., Heatherton, T. F., & Keel, P. (1997). Ten-year stability and predictive validity of five bulimotypic indicators. *American Journal of Psychiatry, 154*, 1133–1138.

Joiner, T. E., Jr., & Katz, J. (1999). Contagion of depressive symptoms and mood: Meta-analytic review and explanations from cognitive, behavioral, and interpersonal viewpoints. *Clinical Psychology and Science Practice, 6*, 149–164.

Joiner, T. E., Jr., Katz, J., & Lew, A. (1997). Self-verification and depression in youth psychiatric inpatients. *Journal of Abnormal Psychology, 106*, 608–618.

Joiner, T. E., Jr., Katz, J., & Lew, A. (1999). Harbingers of depressotypic reassurance seeking: Negative life events, increased anxiety, and decreased self-esteem. *Journal of Personality and Social Psychology Bulletin, 25,* 630–637.

Joiner, T. E., Jr., & Kistner, J. (2005). *On seeing clearly and thriving: Interpersonal perspicacity as adaptive (not depressive) realism (or where three theories meet).* Manuscript under review.

Joiner, T. E., Jr., & Metalsky, G. I. (1995). A prospective test of an integrative interpersonal theory of depression: A naturalistic study of college roommates. *Journal of Social and Clinical Psychology, 69,* 778–788.

Joiner, T. E., Jr., & Metalsky, G. I. (2001). Excessive reassurance seeking: Delineating a risk factor involved in the development of depressive symptoms. *Psychological Science, 12,* 371–378.

Joiner, T. E., Jr., Metalsky, G. I., Katz, J., & Beach, S. R. H. (1999). Depression and excessive reassurance-seeking. *Psychological Inquiry, 10,* 269–278.

Joiner, T. E., Jr., Metalsky, G. I., & Wonderlich, S. A. (1995). Bulimic symptoms and the development of depressive symptoms: The moderating role of attributional style. *Cognitive Therapy and Research, 19,* 651–666.

Joiner, T. E., Jr., Perez, M., Wagner, K. D., Berenson, A., & Marquina, G. (2001). On fatalism, pessimism, and depressive symptoms among Mexican-American and other adolescents attending an obstetrics-gynecology clinic. *Behaviour Research and Therapy, 39,* 887–896.

Joiner, T. E., Jr., Pettit, J. W., Perez, M., Burns, A. B., Gencoz, T., Gencoz, F., & Rudd, M. D. (2001). Can positive emotion influence problem-solving attitudes among suicidal adults? *Professional Psychology: Research and Practice, 32,* 507–512.

Joiner, T. E., Jr., Pettit, J. W., Walker, R. L., Voelz, Z. R., Cruz, J., Rudd, M. D., & Lester, D. (2002). Perceived burdensomeness and suicidality: Two studies on the suicide notes of those attempting and those completing suicide. *Journal of Social and Clinical Psychology, 21,* 531–545.

Joiner, T. E., Jr., Pfaff, J., & Acres, J. (2002). A brief screening tool for suicidal symptoms in adolescents and young adults in general health settings: Reliability and validity data from the Australian National General Practice Youth Suicide Prevention Project. *Behaviour Research & Therapy, 40,* 471–481.

Joiner, T. E., Jr., & Rudd, M. D. (2000). Intensity and duration of suicidal crises vary as a function of previous suicide attempts and negative life events. *Journal of Consulting and Clinical Psychology, 68,* 909–916.

Joiner, T. E., Jr., Rudd, M. D., & Rajab, M. H. (1997). The Modified Scale for Suicidal Ideation among suicidal adults: Factors of suicidality and their relation to clinical and diagnostic indicators. *Journal of Abnormal Psychology, 106,* 260–265.

Joiner, T. E., Jr., Rudd, M. D., & Rajab, M. H. (1999). Agreement between self- and clinician-rated suicidal symptoms in a clinical sample of young adults: Explaining discrepancies. *Journal of Consulting and Clinical Psychology, 67,* 171–176.

Joiner, T. E., Jr., & Schmidt, N. B. (1998). Excessive reassurance-seeking predicts depressive but not anxious reactions to acute stress. *Journal of Abnormal Psychology, 107,* 533–537.

Joiner, T. E., Jr., Steer, R., Brown, G., Beck, A. T., Pettit, J. W., & Rudd, M. D. (2003). Worst-point suicidal plans: A dimension of suicidality predictive of past suicide attempts and eventual death by suicide. *Behaviour Research and Therapy*, *41*, 1469–1480.

Joiner, T. E., Jr., & Tickle, J. J. (1998). Exercise and depressive and anxious symptoms: What is the nature of their interrelations? *Journal of Occupational Rehabilitation*, *8*(3), 191–198.

Joiner, T. E., Jr., Vohs, K. D., & Schmidt, N. B. (2000). Social appraisal as correlate, antecedent, and consequence of mental and physical health outcomes. *Journal of Social and Clinical Psychology*, *19*, 336–331.

Joiner, T. E., Jr., Walker, R. L., Pettit, J. W., Perez, M., & Cukrowicz, K. (in press). Evidence-based assessment of depression in adults. *Psychological Assessment*.

Joiner, T. E., Jr., Walker, R. L., Rudd, M. D., & Jobes, D. (1999). Scientizing and routinizing the outpatient assessment of suicidality. *Professional Psychology: Research and Practice*, *30*, 447–453.

Joiner, T. E., Jr., Wingate, L., Gencoz, T., & Gencoz, F. (2005). Stress generation in depression: Three studies on resilience, possible mechanism, and symptom specificity. *Journal of Social and Clinical Psychology*, *24*, 236–253.

Joiner, T. E., Jr., Wonderlich, S. A., Metalsky, G. I., & Schmidt, N. B. (1995). Body dissatisfaction: A feature of bulimia, depression, or both? *Journal of Social and Clinical Psychology*, *14*, 339–355.

Jones, E. E., & Berglas, S. (1978). Control of attributions about the self through self-handicapping strategies: The appeal of alcohol and the role of underachievement. *Personality and Social Psychology Bulletin*, *4*, 200–206.

Jones, I. H., Stoddart, D. M., & Mallick, J. (1995). Towards a sociobiological model of depression: A marsupial model (*Petaurus breviceps*). *British Journal of Psychiatry*, *166*, 475–479.

Jones, W. H., Briggs, S. R., & Smith, T. G. (1986). Shyness: Conceptualization and measurement. *Journal of Personality and Social Psychology*, *51*, 629–639.

Judd, L. L., Akiskal, H. S., Maser, J. D., Zeller, P. J., Endicott, J., Coryell, W., et al. (1998). Major depressive disorder: A prospective study of residual subthreshold depressive symptoms as predictor of rapid relapse. *Journal of Affective Disorders*, *50*(2–3), 97–108.

Kagan, J., Reznick, J. S., & Snidman, N. (1987). The physiology and psychology of behavioral inhibition in children. *Child Development*, *58*, 1459-1473.

Kagan, J., & Snidman, N. (1991). Temperamental factors in human development. *American Psychologist*, *46*, 856–862.

Katz, J., & Beach, S. R. H. (1997a). Romance in the crossfire: When do women's depressive symptoms predict partner relationship dissatisfaction? *Journal of Social and Clinical Psychology*, *16*, 243–258.

Katz, J., & Beach, S. R. H. (1997b). Self-verifcation and depressive symptoms in marriage and courtship: A multiple pathway model. *Journal of Marriage and the Family*, *59*, 903–914.

Katz, J., Beach, S. R. H., & Joiner, T. E., Jr. (1999). Contagious depression in dating couples. *Journal of Social and Clinical Psychology, 18*, 1–13.

Katz, J., & Joiner, T. E., Jr. (2002). Being known, intimate, and valued: Global self-verification and dyadic adjustment in couples and roommates. *Journal of Personality, 70*(1), 33–58.

Keel, P. K., Mitchell, J. E., Miller, K. B., Davis, T. L., & Crow, S. J. (2000). Social adjustment over 10 years following diagnosis with bulimia. *International Journal of Eating Disorders, 27*, 21–28.

Keller, M. B., Lavori, P. W., Friedman, B., Nielsen, E., Endicott, J., & McDonald-Scott, P. A. (1987). The Longitudinal Interval Follow-up Examination: A comprehensive method for assessing outcome in retrospective longitudinal studies. *Archives of General Psychiatry, 44*, 540–548.

Keller, M. B., McCullough, J. P., Klein, D. N., Arnow, B., Dunner, D. L., Gelenberg, A., et al. (2000). A comparison of nefazodone, the cognitive behavioral-analysis system of psychotherapy, and their combination for the treatment of chronic depression. *New England Journal of Medicine, 342*, 1462–1470.

Kelly, B., Burnett, P., Pelusi, D., Badger, S., Varghese, F., & Robertson, M. (2003). Factors associated with the wish to hasten death: A study of patients with terminal illness. *Psychological Medicine, 33*, 75–81.

Kendler, K. S., Eaves, L. J., Walters, E. E., Neale, M. C., Heath, A. C., & Kessler, R. C. (1996). The identification and validation of distinct depressive syndromes in a population-based sample of female twins. *Archives of General Psychiatry, 53*, 391–399.

Kendler, K. S., Neale, M. C., Kessler, R. C., & Heath, A. C. (1992). Major depression and generalized anxiety disorder: Same genes, (partly) different environments? *Archives of General Psychiatry, 49*, 716–722.

Kessing, L. V., Andersen, E. W., & Andersen, P. K. (2000). Predictors of recurrence in affective disorder: Analyses accounting for individual heterogeneity. *Journal of Affective Disorders, 57*(1–3), 139–145.

Kessing, L. V., & Andersen, P. K. (1999). The effect of episodes on recurrence in affective disorder: A case register study. *Journal of Affective Disorders, 53*, 225–231.

Kessing, L. V., Anderson, P. K., Mortensen, P. B., & Bolwig, T. G. (1998). Recurrence in affective disorder: I. Case register study. *British Journal of Psychiatry, 172*, 23–28.

Kessler, R. C., Berglund, P., Demler, O., Jin, R., Koretz, D., Merikangas, K. R., et al. (2003). The epidemiology of major depressive disorder: results from the National Comorbidity Survey Replication (NCS-R). *Journal of the American Medical Association, 289*, 3095–3105.

Kessler, R. C., Downey, G., Milavsky, J. R., & Stipp, H. (1988). Clustering of teenage suicides after television news stories about suicides: A reconsideration. *American Journal of Psychiatry, 145*, 1379–1383.

Kessler, R. C., McGonagle, K. A., Zhao, S., Nelson, C. R., Highes, M., Eshleman, S., et al. (1994). Lifetime and 12-month prevalence of DSM–III–R psychiatric disorders in the United States: Results from the National Comorbidity Survey. *Archives of General Psychiatry, 51*, 8–19.

Kim, M. S., Sharkey, W. F., & Singelis, T. M. (1994). The relationship between individuals' self-construals and perceived importance of interactive constraints. *International Journal of Intercultural Relations, 18*, 117–140.

King, D., & Heller, K. (1984). Depression and the response of others: A re-evaluation. *Journal of Abnormal Psychology, 93*, 477–480.

Klein, D. F. (1993). The treatment of atypical depression. *European Psychiatry, 8*, 251–255.

Klein, D. N., & Shih, J. H. (1998). Depressive personality: Associations with DSM–III–R mood and personality disorders and negative and positive affectivity, 30-month stability, and prediction of course of axis I depressive disorders. *Journal of Abnormal Psychology, 107*, 319–327.

Klerman, G. L., & Weissman, M. M. (1989). Increasing rates of depression. *Journal of the American Medical Association, 261*, 2229–2235.

Klerman, G. L., Weissman, M. M., Rounsaville, B. J., & Chevron, E. S. (1984). *Interpersonal therapy for depression*. New York: Basic Books.

Klier, C. M., Geller, P. A., & Neugebauer, R. (2000). Minor depressive disorder in the context of miscarriage. *Journal of Affective Disorders, 59*(1), 13–21.

Kohut, H. (1984). *How does psychoanalysis cure?* Chicago: University of Chicago Press.

Kornstein, S. G., Schatzberg, A. F., Thase, M. E., Yonkers, K. A., McCullough, J. P., Keitner, G. I., et al. (2000). Gender differences in treatment response to sertraline versus imipramine in chronic depression. *American Journal of Psychiatry, 157*, 1445–1452.

Kovacs, M., Gastonis, C., Paulauskas, S., & Richards, C. (1989). Depressive disorders in childhood: IV. A longitudinal study of comorbidity with and risk for anxiety disorders. *Archives of General Psychiatry, 46*, 776–782.

Kovacs, M., Obrosky, S., Gatsonis, C., & Richards, C. (1997). First-episode major depressive and dysthymic disorder in childhood: Clinical and sociodemographic factors in recovery. *Journal of the American Academy of Child & Adolescent Psychiatry, 36*, 777–784.

Kovacs, M., Rush, A. J., Beck, A. T., & Hollon, S. D. (1981). Depressed outpatients treated with cognitive therapy or pharmacotherapy: A one-year follow-up. *Archives of General Psychiatry, 38*, 33–39.

Krishnan, K. R. R., Hays, J. C., Tupler, L. A., & George, L. K. (1995). Clinical and phenomenological comparisons of late-onset and early-onset depression. *American Journal of Psychiatry, 152*, 785–788.

Krupnick, J. L., Sotsky, S. M., Simmens, S., Moyer, J., Watkins, J., Elkin, I., & Pilkonis, P. A. (1996). The role of the therapeutic alliance in psychotherapy and pharmacotherapy outcome: Findings in the National Institute of Mental Health Treatment of Depression Collaborative Research Program. *Journal of Consulting and Clinical Psychology, 64*, 532–539.

Kupfer, D. J. (1991). Long-term treatment of depression. *Journal of Clinical Psychiatry, 52*, 28–42.

Kupfer, D. J., Frank, E., Perel, J. M., Cornes, C., Mallinger, A. G., Thase, M. E., et al. (1992). Five-year outcome for maintenance therapies in recurrent depression. *Archives of General Psychiatry, 49*, 769–773.

Lara, M. E., Leader, J., & Klein, D. N. (1997). The association between social support and course of depression: Is it confounded with personality? *Journal of Abnormal Psychology, 106*, 478–482.

Leary, M. R., & Shepperd, J. A. (1986). Behavioral self-handicaps versus reported self-handicaps: A conceptual note. *Journal of Personality and Social Psychology, 51*, 1265–1268.

Lee, A. S., & Murray, R. M. (1988). The long-term outcome of Maudsley depressives. *British Journal of Psychiatry, 153*, 741–751.

Lewicki, T., Hill, T., & Czyzewska, M. (1992). Nonconscious acquisition of information. *American Psychologist, 47*, 796–801.

Lewinsohn, P. M. (1974). A behavioral approach to depression. In R. J. Friedman & M. M. Katz (Eds.), *The psychology of depression: Contemporary theory and research* (pp. 157–185). Washington, DC: Wiley.

Lewinsohn, P. M., Hoberman, H. M., & Rosenbaum, M. (1988). A prospective study of risk factors for unipolar depression. *Journal of Abnormal Psychology, 97*, 251–264.

Lewinsohn, P. M., & Libet, J. (1972). Pleasant events, activity schedules, and depressions. *Journal of Abnormal Psychology, 79*, 291–295.

Lewinsohn, P. M., Pettit, J. W., Joiner, T. E., Jr., & Seeley, J. R. (2003). The phenomenology of major depressive disorder in adolescents and young adults. *Journal of Abnormal Psychology, 112*, 244–252.

Lewinsohn, P. M., Roberts, R. E., Seeley, J. R., Rohde, P., Gotlib, I. H., & Hops, H. (1994). Adolescent psychopathology: II. Psychosocial risk factors for depression. *Journal of Abnormal Psychology, 103*, 302–315.

Lewinsohn, P. M., Steinmetz, J. L., Larson, D. W., & Franklin, J. (1981). Depression-related cognitions: Antecedent or consequence? *Journal of Abnormal Psychology, 90*, 213–219.

Linehan, M. M., Camper, P., Chiles, J., Strosahl, K., & Shearin, E. (1987). Interpersonal problem-solving and parasuicide. *Cognitive Therapy and Research, 11*, 1–12.

Lloyd, G. E. R. (Ed.). (1978). *Hippocratic writings*. Harmondsworth, England: Penguin.

Lopez, S. R., Nelson, K. A., Snyder, K. S., & Mintz, J. (1999). Attributions and affective reactions of family members and course of schizophrenia. *Journal of Abnormal Psychology, 108*, 307–314.

Lyubomirsky, S., Caldwell, N. D., & Nolen-Hoeksema, S. (1998). Effects of ruminative and distracting responses to depressed mood on retrieval of autobiographical memories. *Journal of Personality and Social Psychology, 75*, 166–177.

Maier, W. (1996). Onset and course of affective disorders in subjects at risk: A prospective family study. *Psychiatric Annals, 26,* 315–319.

Mallinckrodt, B., McCreary, B. A., & Robertson, A. K. (1995). Co-occurrence of eating disorders and incest: The role of attachment, family environment, and social competencies. *Journal of Counseling Psychology, 42,* 178–186.

Manber, R., Allen, J. J. B., & Morris, M. M. (2002). Alternate treatments for depression: Empirical support and relevance to women. *Journal of Clinical Psychiatry, 63,* 628–640.

Manji, H. K. (1992). G Proteins: Implications for psychiatry. *American Journal of Psychiatry, 149,* 746–760.

Markowitz, J. C. (1998). *Interpersonal psychotherapy for dysthymic disorder.* Washington, DC: American Psychiatric Press.

Markowitz, J. C. (2003). Interpersonal psychotherapy for chronic depression. *Journal of Clinical Psychiatry, 59,* 847–858.

Martinsen, E. W. (1987). The role of aerobic exercise in the treatment of depression. *Stress Medicine, 3,* 93–100.

Mather, A. S., Rodriguez, C., Guthrie, M. F., McHarg, A. M., Reid, I. C., & McMurdo, M. E. T. (2002). Effects of exercise on depressive symptoms in older adults with poorly responsive depressive disorder: Randomised controlled trial. *British Journal of Clinical Psychiatry, 180,* 411–415.

McCullough, J. P., Jr. (2000). *Treatment for chronic depression: Cognitive Behavioral Analysis System of Psychotherapy (CBASP).* New York: Guilford Press.

McCullough, J. P., Jr., Arnow, B., Blalock, J., Eaves, G., Manber, R., Rothbaum, B., & Vivian, D. (1997, November). *Cognitive behavior therapy for chronic depression.* Workshop presented at the annual convention of the Association for Advancement of Behavior Therapy, Miami, FL.

McGrath, E., Keita, G. P., Strickland, B. R., & Russo, N. F. (1990). *Women and depression: Risk factors and treatment issues: Final report of the American Psychological Association's National Task Force on Women and Depression.* Washington, DC: American Psychological Association.

McLean, P. D., & Hakistian, A. R. (1990). Relative endurance of unipolar depression treatment effects: Longitudinal follow-up. *Journal of Consulting and Clinical Psychology, 58,* 482–488.

McLeod, J. D., Kessler, R. C., & Landis, K. R. (1992). Speed of recovery from major depressive episodes in a community sample of married men and women. *Journal of Abnormal Psychology, 101,* 277–286.

McNiel, D., Arkowitz, H., & Pritchard, B. (1987). The response of others to face-to-face interaction with depressed patients. *Journal of Abnormal Psychology, 96,* 341–344.

Mehlman, P. T., Higley, J. D., Faucher, I., Lilly, A. A., Taub, D. M., Vickers, J., et al. (1995). Correlation of CSF 5-HIAA concentration with sociality and the timing of emigration in free-ranging primates. *American Journal of Psychiatry, 152,* 907–913.

Metalsky, G. I., & Joiner, T. E., Jr. (1992). Vulnerability to depressive symptomatology: A prospective test of the diathesis-stress and causal mediation components of the hopelessness theory of depression. *Journal of Personality and Social Psychology, 63*, 667–675.

Metalsky, G. I., Joiner, T. E., Jr., Hardin, T. S., & Abramson, L. Y. (1993). Depressive reactions to failure in a naturalistic setting: A test of the hopelessness and self-esteem theories of depression. *Journal of Abnormal Psychology, 102*, 101–109.

Miklowitz, D. J., Simoneau, T. L., Sachs-Ericsson, N., & Warner, R. (1996). Family risk indicators in the course of bipolar affective disorder. In C. Mundt & M. J. Goldstein (Eds.), *Interpersonal factors in the origin and course of affective disorders* (pp. 204–217). London: Gaskell/Royal College of Psychiatrists.

Miller, I. W., Norman, W. H., & Keitner, G. I. (1990). Treatment response of high cognitive dysfunction depressed inpatients. *Comprehensive Psychiatry, 30*, 61–72.

Miller, P. M., Ingham, J. G., Kreitman, N. B., & Surtees, P. G. (1987). Life events and other factors implicated in onset and in remission of psychiatric illness in women. *Journal of Affective Disorders, 12*, 73–88.

Mineka, S., Watson, D., & Clark, L. A. (1998). Comorbidity of anxiety and unipolar mood disorders. *Annual Review of Psychology, 49*, 377–412.

Monroe, S. M., & Simmons, A. D. (1991). Diathesis-stress theories in the context of life stress research: Implications for the depressive disorders. *Psychological Bulletin, 110*, 406–425.

Moore, R. G., & Blackburn, I. (1996). The stability of sociotropy and autonomy in depressed patients undergoing treatment. *Cognitive Therapy and Research, 20*(1), 69–80.

Mueller, T. I., Leon, A. C., Keller, M. B., Solomon, D. A., Endicott, J., Coryell, W., et al. (1999). Recurrence after recovery from major depressive disorder during 15 years of observational follow-up. *American Journal of Psychiatry, 156*, 1000–1006.

Mufson, L., Weissman, M. M., Moreau, D., & Garfinkel, R. (1999). Efficacy of interpersonal psychotherapy for depressed adolescents. *Archives of General Psychiatry, 56*, 573–579.

Nacht, S., & Racamier, P.-C. (1961). The depressive states. *Psyche, 14*, 417–574.

Narrow, W. E., Regier, D. A., Rae, D. S., Manderscheid, R. W., & Locke, B. Z. (1993). Use of services by persons with mental and addictive disorders: Findings from the National Institute of Mental Health Epidemiological Catchment Area Program. *Archives of General Psychiatry, 50*, 95–107.

Needles, D. J., & Abramson, L. Y. (1990). Positive life events, attributional style, and hopelessness: Testing a model of recovery from depression. *Journal of Abnormal Psychology, 99*, 156–165.

Neuberg, S. L., & Fiske, S. T. (1987). Motivational influences on impression formation: Outcome dependency, accuracy-driven attention, and individuating processes. *Journal of Personality and Social Psychology, 53*, 431–444.

Newcomb, T. M. (1961). *The acquaintance process*. Oxford: Holt, Rinehart & Winston.

Newman, D. L., Moffit, T. E., Caspi, A., & Silva, P. A. (1998). Comorbid mental disorders: Implications for treatment and sample selection. *Journal of Abnormal Psychology, 107,* 305–311.

Nezlek, J. B., & Gable, S. L. (2001). Depression as a moderator of relationships between positive daily events and day-to-day psychological adjustment. *Personality and Social Psychology Bulletin, 27,* 1692–1704.

Nolen-Hoeksema, S. (1987). Sex differences in unipolar depression: Evidence and theory. *Psychological Bulletin, 101,* 259–282.

Nolen-Hoeksema, S. (1990). *Sex differences in depression*. Stanford, CA: Stanford University Press.

Nolen-Hoeksema, S. (2000a). Further evidence for the role of psychosocial factors in depression chronicity. *Clinical Psychology: Science and Practice, 7,* 224–227.

Nolen-Hoeksema, S. (2000b). The role of rumination in depressive disorders and mixed anxiety/depressive symptoms. *Journal of Abnormal Psychology, 109,* 504–511.

Nolen-Hoeksema, S., & Girgus, J. S. (1994). The emergence of gender differences in depression during adolescence. *Psychological Bulletin, 115,* 424–443.

Nolen-Hoeksema, S., Girgus, J. S., & Seligman, M. E. P. (1986). Learned helplessness in children: A longitudinal study of depression, achievement, and explanatory style. *Journal of Personality and Social Psychology, 51,* 435–442.

Nolen-Hoeksema, S., Girgus, J. S., & Seligman, M. E. P. (1992). Predictors and consequences of childhood depressive symptoms: A 5-year longitudinal study. *Journal of Abnormal Psychology, 101,* 405–422.

Nolen-Hoeksema, S., Morrow, J., & Fredrickson, B. L. (1993). Response styles and the duration of episodes of depressed mood. *Journal of Abnormal Psychology, 102,* 20–28.

Nystrom, S., & Lindegard, B. (1975). Depression: Predisposing factors. *Acta Psychiatrica Scandinavica, 51,* 77–87.

O'Connor, B. P., & Vallerand, R. J. (1998). Psychological adjustment variables as predictors of mortality among nursing home residents. *Psychology and Aging, 13,* 368–374.

Olfson, M., Marcus, S. C., Druss, B., Elinson, L., Tanielian, T., & Pincus, H. A. (2002). National trends in the outpatient treatment of depression. *Journal of the American Medical Association, 287,* 203–209.

Otto, M. W., Pava, J. A., & Sprich-Buckminster, S. (1996). Treatment of major depression: Applications and efficacy of cognitive-behavioral therapy. In M. H. Pollack, M. W. Otto, & J. F. Rosenbaum (Eds.), *Challenges in clinical practice* (pp. 31–52). New York: Guilford Press.

Pacini, R., Muir, F., & Epstein, S. (1998). Depressive-realism from the perspective of cognitive-experiential self-theory. *Journal of Personality and Social Psychology, 74,* 1056–1068.

Paris, T. S., & Baker, B. L. (2000). Applications of the expressed emotion construct to young children with externalizing behavior: Stability and prediction over time. *Journal of Child Psychology and Psychiatry and Applied Disciplines, 41,* 457–462.

Parker, G., Hadzi-Pavlovic, D., Brodaty, H., & Boyce, P. (1992). Predicting the course of melancholic and nonmelancholic depression: A naturalistic comparison study. *Journal of Nervous and Mental Disease, 180,* 693–702.

Paykel, E. S., & Weissman, M. M. (1973). Social adjustment and depression: A longitudinal study. *Archives of General Psychiatry, 28,* 659–663.

Peeters, F., Nicolson, N. A., Berkhof, J., Delespaul, J., & deVries, M. (2003). Effects of daily events on mood states in major depressive disorder. *Journal of Abnormal Psychology, 112,* 203–211.

Pettit, J. W., Averill, P. M., Wassef, A. A., Gruber, N. P., & Schneider, L. (2005). Ratings of early major depressive disorder symptom change during a brief psychiatric hospitalization. *Psychiatric Quarterly, 76,* 33–48.

Pettit, J. W., & Joiner, T. E., Jr. (2001a). Negative feedback leads to an increase in depressed symptoms: Further support for self-verification theory as a vulnerability to depression theory. *Journal of Psychopathology and Behavioral Assessment, 23*(1), 69–74.

Pettit, J. W., & Joiner, T. E., Jr. (2001b). Negative life events predict negative feedback seeking as a function of impact on self-esteem. *Cognitive Therapy and Research, 25,* 733–741.

Pettit, J. W., Lam, A. G., Voelz, Z. R., Walker, R. L., Joiner, T. E., Jr., Lester, D., & He, Z. X. (2002). Perceived burdensomeness and lethality of suicide method among suicide completers in the People's Republic of China. *Omega: Journal of Death and Dying, 45*(1), 57–67.

Pettit, J. W., Lewinsohn, P. M., & Joiner, T. E., Jr. (2004). *Capturing chronicity: Identifying markers for recurrence of major depressive disorder.* Manuscript submitted for publication.

Pettit, J. W., Voelz, Z. R., & Joiner, T. E., Jr. (2001). Combined treatments for depression. In M. T. Sammons & N. B. Schmidt (Eds.), *Combined treatments for mental disorders: A guide to psychological and pharmacological interventions* (pp. 131–159). Washington, DC: American Psychological Association.

Phelps, R., Eisman, E. J., & Kohout, J. (1998). Psychological practice and managed care results of the CAPP practitioner survey. *Professional Psychology: Research and Practice, 29,* 31–36.

Phillips, D. P., & Carstensen, L. L. (1986). Clustering of teenage suicides after television news stories about suicide. *New England Journal of Medicine, 315,* 685–689.

Pini, S., Cassano, G. B., Simonini, E., & Savino, M. (1997). Prevalence of anxiety disorders comorbidity in bipolar depression, unipolar depression, and dysthymia. *Journal of Affective Disorders, 42,* 145–153.

Post, R. M. (1994). Mechanisms underlying the evolution of affective disorders: Implications for long-term treatment. In L. Grunhaus & J. F. Greden (Eds.), *Progress in Psychiatry: 44. Severe depressive disorders* (pp. 23–65). Washington, DC: American Psychiatric Association.

Post, R. M., Weiss, S. R. B., Leverich, G. S., George, M. S., Frye, M., & Ketter, T. A. (1996). Developmental psychobiology of cyclic affective illness: Implications for early therapeutic intervention. *Development and Psychopathology, 8*, 273–305.

Potthoff, J. G., Holahan, C. J., & Joiner, T. E., Jr. (1995). Reassurance-seeking, stress generation, and depressive symptoms: An integrative model. *Journal of Personality and Social Psychology, 68*, 664–670.

Pratto, R., & John, O. P. (1991). Automatic vigilance: The attention-grabbing power of negative social information. *Journal of Personality and Social Psychology, 61*, 380–391.

Price, J., & Gardner, R. (1999). Sociophysiology of depression. In T. E. Joiner Jr. & J. C. Coyne (Eds.), *The interactional nature of depression* (pp. 247–268). Washington, DC: American Psychological Association.

Price, J., Sloman, L., Gardner, R., Jr., Gilbert, P., & Rohde, P. (1994). The social competition hypothesis of depression. *British Journal of Psychiatry, 164*, 309–315.

Prien, R. F., & Kocsis, J. H. (1995). Long-term treatment of mood disorders. In F. E. Bloom & D. J. Kupfer (Eds.), *Psychopharmacology: The fourth generation of progress* (pp. 1067–1079). New York: Raven Press.

Prien, R. F., & Kupfer, D. J. (1986). Continuation drug therapy for major depressive episodes: How long should it be maintained? *American Journal of Psychiatry, 143*, 18–23.

Prien, R. F., Kupfer, D. J., Mansky, P. A., Small, J. G., Tuason, V. B., Voss, C. B., & Johnson, W. E. (1984). Drug therapy in the prevention of recurrences in unipolar and bipolar affective disorders. *Archives of General Psychiatry, 41*, 1096–1104.

Pyszczynski, T., & Greenberg, J. (1987). Self-regulatory perseveration and the depressive self-focusing style: A self-awareness theory of reactive depression. *Psychological Bulletin, 102*, 122–138.

Radke-Yarrow, M., Nottelmann, E., Belmont, B., & Welsh, J. D. (1993). Affective interactions of depressed and nondepressed mothers and their children. *Journal of Abnormal Child Psychology, 21*, 683–695.

Radloff, L. S. (1977). The CES–D Scale: A self-report depression scale for research in the general population. *Applied Psychological Measurement, 1*, 385–401.

Rapoport, J. (1990). *The boy who couldn't stop washing*. New York: Plume.

Regier, D. A., Rae, D. S., Narrow, W. E., Kaelber, C. T., & Schatzberg, A. F. (1998). Prevalence of anxiety disorders and their comorbidity with mood and addictive disorders. *British Journal of Psychiatry, 173*(Suppl. 34), 24–28.

Rehm, L. P. (1977). A self-control model of depression. *Behavior Therapy, 8*, 787–804.

Rehm, L. P., & O'Hara, M. W. (1985). Item characteristics of the Hamilton Rating Scale for Depression. *Journal of Psychiatric Research, 1*, 31–41.

Reinherz, H. Z., Giaconia, R. M., Pakiz, B., Silverman, A. B., Frost, A. K., & Lefkowitz, E. S. (1993). Psychosocial risks for major depression in late adolescence: A longitudinal community study. *Journal of the American Academy of Child & Adolescent Psychiatry, 32,* 1155–1163.

Reiss, S. (1980). Pavlovian conditioning and human fear: An expectancy model. *Behavior Therapy, 11,* 380–396.

Reynolds, C. F., III, Frank, E., Perel, J. M., Imber, S. D., Cornes, C., Miller, M. D., et al. (1999). Nortriptyline and interpersonal psychotherapy as maintenance therapies for recurrent major depression: A randomized controlled trial in patients older than 59 years. *Journal of the American Medical Association, 281*(1), 39–45.

Rhodewalt, F. (1990). Self-handicappers: Individual differences in the preference for anticipatory self-protective acts. In R. Higgins, C. R. Snyder, & S. Berglas (Eds.), *Self-handicapping: The paradox that isn't* (pp. 69–106). New York: Guilford Press.

Rhodewalt, F., Sanbonmatsu, D. M., Tschanz, B., Feick, D. L., & Waller, A. (1995). Self-handicapping and interpersonal trade-offs: The effects of claimed self-handicaps on observers' performance evaluations and feedback. *Personality and Social Psychology Bulletin, 21,* 1042–1050.

Ritts, V., & Stein, J. R. (1995). Verification and commitment in marital relationships: An exploration of self-verification theory in community college students. *Psychological Reports, 76,* 383–386.

Robbins, D., & Conroy, R. C. (1983). A cluster of adolescent suicide attempts: Is suicide contagious? *Journal of Adolescent Health Care, 3,* 253–255.

Roberts, R. E., Lewinsohn, P. M., & Seeley, J. R. (1991). Screening for adolescent depression: A comparison of depression scales. *Journal of the American Academy of Child & Adolescent Psychiatry, 30,* 58–66.

Roberts, R. E., Roberts, C. R., & Chen, Y. R. (1997). Ethnocultural differences in prevalence of adolescent depression. *American Journal of Community Psychology, 25,* 95–110.

Roberts, R. E., & Sobhan, M. (1992). Symptoms of depression in adolescence: A comparison of Anglo, African, and Hispanic Americans. *Journal of Youth and Adolescence, 21,* 639–651.

Rogers, C. (1951). *Client-centered therapy.* Boston: Houghton Mifflin.

Rohde, P., Lewinsohn, P. M., & Seeley, J. R. (1990). Are people changed by the experience of having an episode of depression? A further test of the scar hypothesis. *Journal of Abnormal Psychology, 99,* 264–271.

Roos, R. W., & Cohen, L. H. (1987). Sex roles and social support as moderators of life stress adjustment. *Journal of Personality and Social Psychology, 52,* 576–585.

Rosenfarb, I. S., & Aron, J. (1992). The self-protective function of depressive affect and cognition. *Journal of Social and Clinical Psychology, 11,* 323–335.

Rothbart, M., & Park, B. (1986). On the confirmability and disconfirmability of trait concepts. *Journal of Personality and Social Psychology, 50,* 131–142.

Rudd, M. D., Joiner, T. E., Jr., & Rajab, M. H. (1996). Relationships among suicidal ideators, attempters, and multiple attempters in a young adult sample. *Journal of Abnormal Psychology, 105,* 541–550.

Rudd, M. D., Joiner, T. E., Jr., & Rajab, M. H. (2000). *Treating suicidal behavior: An effective time-limited approach.* New York: Guilford.

Rudd, M. D., Rajab, M. H., Orman, D. T., Stulman, D. A., Joiner, Jr., T. E., & Dixon, W. (1996). Effectiveness of an outpatient problem-solving intervention targeting suicidal young adults: Preliminary results. *Journal of Consulting and Clinical Psychology, 64,* 179–190.

Ruscio, J., & Ruscio, A. M. (2000). Informing the continuity controversy: A taxometric analysis of depression. *Journal of Abnormal Psychology, 109,* 473–487.

Sacco, W. P. (1999). A social-cognitive model of interpersonal processes in depression. In T. E. Joiner Jr. & J. C. Coyne (Eds.), *The interactional nature of depression* (pp. 329–362). Washington, DC: American Psychological Association.

Sacco, W. P., Dumont, C. P., & Dow, M. G. (1993). Attributional, perceptual, and affective responses to depressed and nondepressed marital partners. *Journal of Consulting and Clinical Psychology, 61,* 1076–1082.

Sacco, W. P., & Dunn, V. K. (1990). Effect of actor depression on observer attributions: Existence and impact of negative attributions toward the depressed. *Journal of Personality and Social Psychology, 59,* 517–524.

Sacco, W. P., Milana, S., & Dunn, V. K. (1988). The effect of duration of depressive episode on the response of others. *Journal of Social and Clinical Psychology, 7,* 297–311.

Sanderson, W. C., DiNardo, R. A., Rapee, R. M., & Barlow, D. H. (1990). Syndrome comorbidity in patients diagnosed with a DSM–III–R anxiety disorder. *Journal of Abnormal Psychology, 99,* 308–312.

Santor, D., & Coyne, J. C. (2001). Evaluating the continuity of symptomatology between depressed and nondepressed individuals. *Journal of Abnormal Psychology, 110,* 216–225.

Schachter, S., & Singer, J. E. (1962). Cognitive, social, and physiological determinants of emotional state. *Psychological Review, 69,* 379–399.

Schafer, R. B., Wickrama, R. A. S., & Keith, P. M. (1996). Self-disconfirmation, psychological distress, and marital happiness. *Journal of Marriage and Family, 58,* 167–177.

Scott, J., Teasdale, J. D., Paykel, E. S., Johnson, A. L., Abbott, R., Hayhurst, H., et al. (2000). Effects of cognitive therapy on psychological symptoms and social functioning in residual depression. *British Journal of Psychiatry, 177,* 440–446.

Segal, Z. V., Williams, J. M., Teasdale, J. D., & Gemar, M. (1996). A cognitive science perspective on kindling and episode sensitization in recurrent affective disorder. *Psychological Medicine, 26,* 371–380.

Segrin, C. (2000). Social skills deficits associated with depression. *Clinical Psychology Review, 20,* 379–403.

Segrin, C. (2001). *Interpersonal processes in psychological problems.* New York: Guilford Press.

Segrin, C., & Dillard, J. P. (1992). The interactional theory of depression: A meta-analysis of the research literature. *Journal of Social and Clinical Psychology, 11,* 43–70.

Seligman, M. E. P. (1989). Research in clinical psychology: Why is there so much depression today? In I. Cohen (Ed.), *The G. Stanley Hall Lecture Series* (Vol. 9, pp. 79–96). Washington, DC: American Psychological Association.

Shapiro, R. W., & Keller, M. B. (1981). Initial 6-month follow-up of patients with major depressive disorder. *Journal of Affective Disorders, 3,* 205–220.

Shea, M. T., Elkin, I., Imber, S. D., Sotsky, S. M., Watkins, J. T., Collins, J. F., et al. (1992). Course of depressive symptoms over follow-up: Findings from the National Institute of Mental Health treatment of depression collaborative research program. *Archives of General Psychiatry, 49,* 782–787.

Shea, M. T., Leon, A. C., Mueller, T. I., & Solomon, D. A. (1996). Does major depression result in lasting personality change? *American Journal of Psychiatry, 153,* 1404–1410.

Sheehan, D. V., Lecrubier, Y., Harnett-Sheehan, K., Janavs, J., Weiller, E., Bonara, L. I., et al. (1997). Reliability and validity of the MINI International Neuropsychiatric Interview (M.I.N.I.): According to the SCID-P. *European Psychiatry, 12,* 232–241.

Shelton, R. C., Davidson, J., Yonkers, K. A., & Koran, L. (1997). The undertreatment of dysthymia. *Journal of Clinical Psychiatry, 58,* 59–65.

Sherbourne, C. D., Hays, R. D., & Wells, K. B. (1995). Personal and psychosocial risk factors for physical and mental health outcomes and course of depression among depressed patients. *Journal of Consulting and Clinical Psychology, 63,* 345–355.

Sherman, J. W., & Klein, S. B. (1994). Development and representation of personality impressions. *Journal of Personality and Social Psychology, 67,* 972–983.

Shively, C. A., Laber-Laird, K., & Anton, R. F. (1997). Behavior and physiology of social stress and depression in female cynomolgus monkeys. *Biological Psychiatry, 41,* 871–882.

Simon, G., Ormel, J., VonKorff, M., & Barlow, W. (1995). Health care costs associated with depressive and anxiety disorders. *American Journal of Psychiatry, 152,* 352–357.

Simons, A. D., Angell, K. L., Monroe, S. M., & Thase, M. E. (1993). Cognition and life stress in depression: Cognitive factors and the definition, rating, and generation of negative life events. *Journal of Abnormal Psychology, 102,* 584–591.

Simons, A. D., Murphy, G. E., Levine, J. L., & Wetzel, R. D. (1986). Cognitive therapy and pharmacotherapy for depression: Sustained improvement over one year. *Archives of General Psychiatry, 43,* 43–48.

Skodol, A. E., Gallagher, P. E., & Oldham, J. M. (1996). Excessive dependency and depression: Is the relationship specific? *Journal of Nervous and Mental Disease, 184*(3), 165–171.

Sloman, L. (2000). How the involuntary defeat strategy relates to depression. In L. Sloman & P. Gilbert (Eds.), *Subordination and defeat: An evolutionary approach to mood disorders and their therapy* (pp. 47–67). Mahwah, NJ: Erlbaum.

Solomon, D. A., Keller, M. B., Leon, A. C., Mueller, T. I., Lavori, P. W., Shea, M. T., et al. (2000). Multiple recurrences of major depressive disorder. *American Journal of Psychiatry, 157*, 229–233.

Song, F., Freemantle, N., Sheldon, T. A., House, A., Watson, P., Long, A., & Mason, J. (1993). Selective serotonin reuptake inhibitors: Meta-analysis of efficacy and acceptability. *British Medical Journal, 306*, 683–687.

Spanier, G. B. (1976). Measuring dyadic adjustment: New scales for assessing the quality of marriage and similar dyads. *Journal of Marriage and the Family, 38*, 15–28.

Spitzer, R. L., Williams, J. B., Gibbon, M., & First, M. B. (1992). The Structured Clinical Interview for DSM–III–(SCID): I. History, rationale, and description. *Archives of General Psychiatry, 49*, 624–629.

Stahl, S. M., Nierenberg, A. A., & Gorman, J. M. (2001). Evidence of early onset of antidepressant effect in randomized controlled trials. *Journal of Clinical Psychiatry, 62*(4), 17–23.

Steer, R. A., Ball, R., Ranieri, W. F., & Beck, A. T. (1997). Further evidence for the construct validity of the Beck Depression Inventory–II with psychiatric outpatients. *Psychological Reports, 80*, 443–446.

Steer, R. A., Ball, R., Ranieri, W. F., & Beck, A. T. (1999). Dimensions of the Beck Depression Inventory—II in clinically depressed outpatients. *Journal of Clinical Psychology, 55*, 117–128.

Steer, R. A., Clark, D. A., Beck, A. T., & Ranieri, W. F. (1995). Common and specific dimensions of self-reported anxiety and depression: A replication. *Journal of Abnormal Psychology, 104*, 542–545.

Steer, R. A., Kumar, G., Ranieri, W. F., & Beck, A. T. (1995). Use of the Beck Anxiety Inventory with adolescent psychiatric outpatients. *Psychological Reports, 76*, 459–465.

Steer, R. A., Kumar, G., Ranieri, W. F., & Beck, A. T. (1998). Use of the Beck Depression Inventory—II with adolescent psychiatric outpatients. *Journal of Psychopathology and Behavioral Assessment, 20*, 127–137.

Steer, R. A., Rissmiller, D. J., & Beck, A. T. (2000). Use of Beck Depression Inventory—II with depressed geriatric inpatients. *Behaviour Research and Therapy, 38*, 311–318.

Steiger, H., Gauvin, L., Jabalpurwala, S., Seguin, J. R., & Stotland, S. (1999). Hypersensitivity to social interactions in bulimic syndromes: Relationship to binge eating. *Journal of Consulting and Clinical Psychology, 67*, 765–775.

Steiger, H., Leung, F., & Thibaudeau, J. (1993). Prognostic value of pretreatment social adaptation in bulimia nervosa. *International Journal of Eating Disorders, 14*, 269–276.

Stewart, A., Greenfield, S., Hays, R. D., Wells, K. B., Rogers, W. H., Berry, S. D., et al. (1989). The functioning and well-being of depressed patients: Results from the medical outcomes study. *Journal of the American Medical Association, 262*, 907–913.

Swann, W. B., Jr. (1990). To be known or to be adored: The interplay of self-enhancement and self-verification. In E. T. Higgins & R. M. Sorrentino (Eds.), *Handbook of motivation and cognition* (Vol. 2, pp. 408–448). New York: Guilford Press.

Swann, W. B., Jr. (1996). *Self-traps.* New York: Freeman.

Swann, W. B., Jr., De La Ronde, C., & Hixon, G. (1994). Authenticity and positivity strivings in marriage and courtship. *Journal of Personality and Social Psychology, 66,* 857–869.

Swann, W. B., Jr., Griffin, J. J., Predmore, S., & Gaines, B. (1987). The cognitive-affective crossfire: When self-consistency confronts self-enhancement. *Journal of Personality and Social Psychology, 52,* 881–889.

Swann, W. B., Jr., Pelham, B. W., & Chidester, T. R. (1988). Change through paradox: Using self-verification to alter beliefs. *Journal of Personality and Social Psychology, 54,* 268–273.

Swann, W. B., Jr., & Read, S. J. (1981a). Acquiring self-knowledge: The search for feedback that fits. *Journal of Personality and Social Psychology, 41,* 1119–1128.

Swann, W. B., Jr., & Read, S. J. (1981b). Self-verification processes: How we sustain our self-concepts. *Journal of Experimental Social Psychology, 17,* 351–372.

Swann, W. B., Jr., Stein-Seroussi, A., & Giesler, R. B. (1992). Why people self-verify. *Journal of Personality and Social Psychology, 62,* 392–401.

Swann, W. B., Jr., Wenzlaff, R. M., Krull, D. S., & Pelham, B. W. (1992). Allure of negative feedback: Self-verification strivings among depressed persons. *Journal of Abnormal Psychology, 101,* 293–305.

Swann, W. B., Jr., Wenzlaff, R. M., & Tafarodi, R. W. (1992). Depression and the search for negative evaluations: More evidence of the role of self-verification strivings. *Journal of Abnormal Psychology, 101,* 314–317.

Swanson, J. W., Linskey, A. O., Quintero-Salinas, R., & Pumariega, A. J. (1992). A binational school survey of depressive symptoms, drug use, and suicidal ideation. *Journal of the American Academy of Child & Adolescent Psychiatry, 31,* 669–678.

Sweeney, P. D., Anderson, K., & Bailey, S. (1986). Attributional style in depression: A meta-analytic review. *Journal of Personality and Social Psychology, 50,* 974–991.

Taschev, T. (1974). The course and prognosis of depression on the bases of 652 patients deceased. In J. Angst (Ed.), *Classification and prediction of outcome of depression* (pp. 152–172). Stuttgart, West Germany: Schattauer Verlag.

Taylor, S. E., & Brown, J. D. (1988). Illusion and well-being: A social psychological perspective on mental health. *Psychological Bulletin, 103,* 193–210.

Thase, M. E. (1990). Relapse and recurrence in unipolar major depression: Short-term and long-term approaches. *Journal of Clinical Psychiatry, 51*(Suppl. 6), 51–57.

Thase, M. E. (1993). Maintenance treatments of recurrent affective disorders. *Current Opinion in Psychiatry, 6,* 16–21.

Thase, M. E. (1999). Redefining antidepressant efficacy toward long-term recovery. *Journal of Clinical Psychiatry, 60*(Suppl. 6), 15–19.

Thase, M. E., & Kupfer, D. J. (1996). Recent developments in the pharmacotherapy of mood disorders. *Journal of Consulting and Clinical Psychology, 64,* 646–659.

Thase, M. E., & Sullivan, L. R. (1995). Relapse and recurrence of depression: A practical approach for prevention. *CNS Drugs, 4,* 261–277.

Thelen, M. K., Farmer, J., Mann, L. M., & Pruitt, J. (1990). Bulimia and interpersonal relationships: A longitudinal study. *Journal of Abnormal Psychology, 37,* 85–90.

Tkachuk, G. A., & Martin, G. L. (1999). Exercise therapy for patients with psychiatric disorders: Research and clinical implications. *Professional Psychology: Research and Practice, 30,* 275–282.

Tsuang, D., & Coryell, W. (1993). An 8-year follow-up of patients with DSM–III–R psychotic depression, schizoaffective disorder, and schizophrenia. *American Journal of Psychiatry, 150,* 1182–1188.

Turner, J. E., Jr., & Cole, D. A. (1994). Developmental differences in cognitive diatheses for child depression. *Journal of Abnormal Child Psychology, 22,* 15–32.

Uehara, T., Sato, T., Sakado, K., & Kameda, K. (1997). Discriminant validity of the Inventory to Diagnose Depression between patients with major depression and pure anxiety disorders. *Psychiatry Research, 71,* 57–61.

Uehara, T., Yokoyama, T., Goto, M., & Ihda, S. (1996). Expressed emotion and short-term treatment outcome of outpatients with major depression. *Comprehensive Psychiatry, 37,* 299–304.

U.S. Bureau of the Census. (1993). *Statistical abstract of the United States: 1993* (113th ed.). Washington, DC: U. S. Government Printing Office.

van Furth, E. F., van Strien, D. C., Martina, L. M. L., van Son, M. J. M., Hendrickx, J. J. P., & van Engeland, H. (1996). Expressed emotion and the prediction of outcome in adolescent eating disorders. *International Journal of Eating Disorders, 20,* 19–31.

VanValkenberg, C., Winokur, G., Lowry, M., Behar, D., & VanValkenberg, D. (1983). Depression occurring in chronically anxious patients. *Comprehensive Psychiatry, 24,* 285–289.

Vinokur, A. D., & Van Ryn, M. (1993). Social support and undermining in close relationships: Their independent effects on the mental health of unemployed persons. *Journal of Personality and Social Psychology, 65,* 350–359.

Voelz, Z. R., Walker, R. L., Pettit, J. W., Joiner, T. E., Jr., & Wagner, K. D. (2003). Depressogenic attributional style: Evidence of trait-like nature in youth psychiatric inpatients. *Personality and Individual Differences, 34,* 1129–1140.

Vohs, K. D., Voelz, Z. R., Pettit, J. W., Bardone, A. M., Katz, J., Abramson, L. Y., et al. (2001). Perfectionism, body dissatisfaction, and self-esteem: an interactive model of bulimic symptom development. *Journal of Social and Clinical Psychology, 20,* 476–497.

Volsan, O., & Berzewski, H. (1985). Baseline plasma cortisol and dexamethasone test in unselected psychiatric inpatients. *Psychopathology, 18,* 186–197.

Vredenburg, K., Flett, G. L., & Krames, L. (1993). Analogue versus clinical depression: A critical reappraisal. *Psychological Bulletin, 113*, 327–344.

Wachtel, H. (1990). The second messenger dysbalance hypothesis of affective disorders. *Pharmacopsychiatry, 23*, 27–32.

Wagner, K. D., Berenson, A., Harding, O., & Joiner, T. E., Jr. (1998). Attributional style and depression in pregnant teenagers. *American Journal of Psychiatry, 155*, 1227–1233.

Wallace, S. T., & Alden, L. E. (1997). Social phobia and positive social events: The price of success. *Journal of Abnormal Psychology, 106*, 416–424.

Waller, N. G., & Meehl, P. E. (1998). *Multivariate taxometric procedures.* Thousand Oaks, CA: Sage.

Ward, A. H., Lyubomirsky, S., Sousa, L., & Nolen-Hoeksema, S. (2003). Can't quite commit: Rumination and uncertainty. *Personality and Social Psychology Bulletin, 29*, 96–107.

Warner, V., Mufson, L., & Weissman, M. M. (1995). Offspring at high and low risk for depression and anxiety: Mechanisms of psychiatric disorder. *Journal of the American Academy of Child & Adolescent Psychiatry, 34*, 786–797.

Watson, D., Clark, L. A., & Tellegen, A. (1988). Development and validation of brief measures of positive and negative affect: The PANAS Scales. *Journal of Personality and Social Psychology, 54*, 1063–1070.

Watson, D., Clark, L. A., Weber, K., Assenheimer, J. S., Strauss, M. E., & McCormick, R. A. (1995). Testing a tripartite model: II. Exploring the symptom structure of anxiety and depression in student, adult, and patient samples. *Journal of Abnormal Psychology, 104*, 15–25.

Watson, D., Weber, K., Assenheimer, J. S., Clark, L. A., Strauss, M. E., & McCormick, R. A. (1995). Testing a tripartite model: I. Evaluating the convergent and discriminant validity of anxiety and depression symptom scales. *Journal of Abnormal Psychology, 104*, 3–14.

Weary, G., & Williams, J. P. (1990). Depressive self-presentation: Beyond self-handicapping. *Journal of Personality and Social Psychology, 58*, 892–898.

Weissman, M. M., Bland, R., Joyce, P. R., Newman, S., Wells, J. E., & Witchen, H. U. (1993). Sex differences in rates of depression: Cross-national perspectives. *Journal of Affective Disorders, 29*, 77–84.

Weissman, M. M., & Klerman, G. L. (1977). Sex differences in the epidemiology of depression. *Archives of General Psychiatry, 34*, 98–111.

Weissman, M. M., & Klerman, G. L. (1985). Gender and depression. *Trends in Neuroscience, 8*, 416–420.

Weissman, M. M., Klerman, G. L., Paykel, E. S., Prusoff, B. A., & Hanson, B. (1974). Treatment effects on the social adjustment of depressed patients. *Archives of General Psychiatry, 30*, 771–778.

Weissman, M. M., Klerman, G. L., Prusoff, B. A., Sholomskas, D., & Padian, N. (1981). Depressed outpatients: Results one year after treatment with drugs and/or interpersonal psychotherapy. *Archives of General Psychiatry, 38*, 52–55.

Weissman, M. M., Leaf, P. J., Tischler, G. L., Blazer, D. G., Karno, M., Bruce, M. L., & Florio, L. P. (1988). Affective disorder in five United States communities. *Psychological Medicine*, *18*, 141–153.

Weissman, M. M., & Paykel, E. S. (1974). *The depressed woman*. Chicago: University of Chicago Press.

Wells, K. B. (1991). Caring and depression in America: Lessons learned from early findings of the medical outcomes study. *Psychiatric Medicine*, *9*, 512.

Wells, K. B., Burnam, A., Rogers, W., Hays, R., & Camp, P. (1992). The course of depression in adult outpatients: Results from the Medical Outcomes Study. *Archives of General Psychiatry*, *49*, 788–794.

Wells, K. B., Rogers, W., Burnam, A., & Greenfield, S. (1991). How the medical comorbidity of depressed patients differs across health care settings: Results from the Medical Outcomes Study. *American Journal of Psychiatry*, *148*, 1688–1696.

Whisman, M., & Pinto, A. (1997). Hopelessness depression in depressed inpatient adolescents. *Cognitive Therapy and Research*, *21*, 345–358.

Whitman, W. (1892). *Leaves of grass*. New York: Penguin.

Williams, G. J., Chamove, A. S., & Miller, H. R. (1990). Eating disorders, perceived control, assertiveness and hostility. *British Journal of Clinical Psychology*, *29*, 327–335.

World Health Organization. (2002). *The World Health Report 2002: Reducing risks, promoting healthy life*. Geneva, Switzerland: World Health Organization.

Xenophon. (2004). *The Memorabilia* (H. G. Dakyns, Trans.). Whitefish, MT: Kessinger Publishing.

Ybarra, O., & Stephan, W. G. (1996). Misanthropic person memory. *Journal of Personality and Social Psychology*, *70*, 691–700.

Youngren, M. A., & Lewinsohn, P. M. (1980). The functional relation between depression and problematic interpersonal behavior. *Journal of Abnormal Psychology*, *89*, 333–341.

Zaider, T. I., Johnson, J. G., & Cockell, S. J. (2002). Psychiatric disorders associated with the onset and persistence of bulimia nervosa and binge eating disorder during adolescence. *Journal of Youth and Adolescence*, *31*, 319–329.

Zeiss, A. M., & Lewinsohn, P. M. (1988). Enduring deficits after remissions of depression: A test of the scar hypothesis. *Behaviour Research and Therapy*, *26*, 151–158.

Zeiss, A. M., Lewinsohn, P. M., & Munoz, R. F. (1979). Nonspecific improvement effects in depression using interpersonal skill training, pleasant activities schedules, or cognitive training. *Journal of Consulting and Clinical Psychology*, *74*, 427–439.

Zimbardo, P. G. (1977). *Shyness: What it is, what to do about it*. Reading, MA: Addison Wesley.

Zimmerman, M., & Coryell, W. (1987). The Inventory to Diagnose Depression (IDD): A self-report scale to diagnose major depressive disorder. *Journal of Consulting and Clinical Psychology*, *55*, 55–59.

INDEX

interaction of stable vulnerabilities with, 106
negative feedback-seeking and, 52, 112
self-esteem and, 52
self-focused attention and, 111
Negative self-concept, 43
Negative self-verification
in depression, 51–52
in dormitory roommate study, 46
in dysfunctional mate selection, 45–46
in suicide clustering, 46–47
Neurobiological sensitization, 8
Nonspuriousness
diagnostic specificity form of, 67
meaning of, 67
studies of, 67–68
Nosology, 13–16

Obsessive–compulsive disorder (OCD)
comorbid, assessment for, 141–142

Paradoxical questioning technique
in cognitive behavioral therapy, 135
Parents
influence on depressogenic cognitive style, 108
recurrent depression effect on daughters, 21
Paykel, E. S., 60
Personality
erosion of in youth, 7
Personality disorder(s)
avoidant personality disorder, 75–76, 116–117
borderline personality disorder, 116–117
defined, 116
depressive *versus* major depressive disorder, 116
positive distortions in, 43–44
self-enhancement and, 43–44
Pessimism
and depression in Mexican Americans, 23
as scar, 6
Point clustering, 46, 47
in high school, 48
Positive and Negative Affect Scale (PANAS)
in assessment of depressive and anxious symptoms, 142
Positive emotion

in enhancement of outcome, 162–163
in problem-solving treatment for suicidal persons, 163
Positive life events
increase in self-esteem and decrease in negative feedback-seeking, 53
remission and, 38
Postpartum depression, hopelessness and, 108–109
Prevalence, increasing, 18–19
Prevention of relapse and recurrence. *See also* Relapse and recurrence
combination therapy in, 169
continuation of cognitive therapy and cognitive–behavioral therapy for, 168–169
interpersonal psychotherapy for, 168
maintenance pharmacotherapy for, 166–167
Problem solving, family dysfunction and, 31
Psychosocial treatment(s)
cognitive–behavioral analysis system of psychotherapy, 156
cognitive–behavioral therapy, 155
efficacy of, 154–155
indirect effect on self-propagating behaviors, 158
interpersonal psychotherapy, 155–156
in prevention of relapse and recurrence, 168–169
Psychotherapy
decrease in usage rate for, 151
versus pharmacotherapy, 157
Psychotic depression, relapse in, 25
Pyszczynski, T., 110–111

Racamier, P. C., 60
Reassurance-seeking. *See also* Exccesive reassurance-seeking (ERS)
acceptance of reassurance and, 71–72
adaptive vs. repeated, persistent, 70
psychoeducational model for, 159–160
stability of, 113–114
Reassurance-Seeking Scale, 149
Relapse and recurrence. *See also* Prevention of relapse and recurrence
antidepressant medications and, 153
definitions of, 5
excessive reassurance-seeking as risk factor for, 71
experiences of loss and, 82
negative feedback-seeking in, 51–52

ABOUT THE AUTHORS

Jeremy W. Pettit, PhD, is an assistant professor of clinical psychology at the University of Houston. He received his PhD in clinical psychology at Florida State University in Tallahassee. Dr. Pettit's primary area of interest centers on etiological and maintaining factors in depression spectrum disorders. Secondary interests include treatment of depression and biopsychosocial approaches to understanding and preventing suicide. He has published over 35 scientific journal articles and edited book chapters on these topics.

Thomas E. Joiner, PhD, went to college at Princeton and received his PhD in clinical psychology in 1993 from the University of Texas at Austin. He is the Bright-Burton Professor and Director, University Psychology Clinic, in the Department of Psychology at Florida State University in Tallahassee. Dr. Joiner's work is on the psychology, neurobiology, and treatment of depression, suicidal behavior, anxiety, and eating disorders. Author of over 250 peer-reviewed publications, Dr. Joiner was recently awarded the Guggenheim Fellowship. He was elected fellow of the American Psychological Association (APA) and received the Young Investigator Award from the National Alliance for Research on Schizophrenia and Depression, the Shakow Award for Early Career Achievement from APA's Division 12 (Society of Clinical Psychology), the Shneidman Award for excellence in suicide research from the American Association of Suicidology, and the Award for Distinguished Scientific Early Career Contributions from the APA, as well as research grants from the National Institute of Mental Health and various foundations.